地域文化系列

邢雯芝 ◎ 编著

钟 意 ◎ 主审

实用苏州话
Practical Suzhou Dialect

【中英文对照版】

北京大学出版社
PEKING UNIVERSITY PRESS

内 容 简 介

本书主要供非苏州的国人、外国人和一些苏州话说得不标准的苏州孩子学习苏州话使用。全书共 10 个单元，每个单元均由"情景引入"、"场景对话"、"词语贴士"、"特色词汇"、"注释说明"、"巩固练习"、"参考答案"组成，涉及日常生活的方方面面。学完本书后，可以掌握苏州话的常用词语，并初步运用苏州话进行日常的会话交流，还可以了解一些苏州的风土民情和风景名胜。

图书在版编目(CIP)数据

实用苏州话(中英文对照版)/邢雯芝编著. —北京：北京大学出版社，2011.9
（地域文化系列）
ISBN 978-7-301-18998-6

Ⅰ.①实… Ⅱ.①邢… Ⅲ.①吴语－口语－苏州 Ⅳ.①H173

中国版本图书馆 CIP 数据核字(2011)第 111209 号

书　　　名：实用苏州话(中英文对照版)
著作责任者：邢雯芝 编著
策 划 编 辑：桂　春
责 任 编 辑：桂　春
标 准 书 号：ISBN 978-7-301-18998-6/H · 2857
出 版 发 行：北京大学出版社
地　　　址：北京市海淀区成府路 205 号　100871
网　　　址：http://www.pup.cn　新浪官方微博：@北京大学出版社
电 子 信 箱：zyjy@pup.cn
电　　　话：邮购部 62752015　发行部 62750672　编辑部 62765126　出版部 62754962
印　　刷　者：北京宏伟双华印刷有限公司
经　　销　者：新华书店

　　　　　　720 毫米×1020 毫米　16 开本　15.25 印张　400 千字
　　　　　　2011 年 9 月第 1 版　2018 年 2 月第 3 次印刷

定　　　价：43.00 元

未经许可，不得以任何方式复制或抄袭本书之部分或全部内容。
版权所有，侵权必究
举报电话：010-62752024　电子信箱：fd@pup.pku.edu.cn

前　　言

以苏州话为传统代表的吴语使用人口约七千万,总数上仅次于北方话,位居南方六大方言之首。它具有普通话所不能替代的文化功能和文化价值。苏州人澹泊平和的处世方式、细腻精致的生活习性、素雅相融的人文特色,也得益于"糯软"的苏州话的长期"润泽"。水能溶物,柔善克刚。在苏州话基础上发展起来的昆曲和苏州评弹艺术,一直以来为文人雅士所欣赏和推崇。时至现代文化蓬勃发展的今日,昆曲艺术更被联合国教科文组织列为首批"人类口述和非物质遗产代表作",其剧本、声腔、表演、音乐、舞台美术等方面的成就,为众多戏曲及其他艺术门类提供了可供借鉴和承继的范本。苏州评弹则以其生动的说表、优雅的弹唱及传神的舞台呈现,被誉为"中国最美的声音"并被列入国家级非物质文化遗产名录。而遗产艺术如何在当代青年学生中形成更大的文化认同,如何更为恒远地传承下去,已成为一项十分重要且有意义的工程。它们和苏州话之间的关系是鱼与水、毛与皮之间的伴生关系。水之将涸,鱼欲何往;皮之不存,毛将焉附? 讲不好苏州话、听不懂苏州话,却去奢谈弘扬传统艺术,无异于隔靴搔痒。从这个层面上来说,学好苏州话,对于深入感悟苏州文化美感大有裨益。编者有感于此,故诚以伏案得出此书。

本书内容丰富、结构清晰,具有较强的可操作性和实用性。主要供非苏州的国人、外国人和一些苏州话说得不标准的苏州孩子学习苏州话使用。本书具有较为突出的特色,有别于以往的苏州话学习资料:语义上,其一,所有对话、词语均用苏州话、普通话、英语一一对照列出以方便读者理解,对话中某些苏州话与普通话相对应的词语或短语还用波浪线加以突出;其二,当页注释说明,便于读者边学习边消化,有利于读者更清楚地弄懂并掌握特色词语。语音上,通过给每个词语、句子注音,且配以录音,解决了使初学者说一口标准苏州话的难题,填补了同类教材的空白。

本书共十个单元,每个单元均由"情景引入"、"场景对话"、"词语贴士"、"特色词汇"、"注释说明"、"巩固练习"、"参考答案"七个部分组成,涉及日常生活的方方面面。学完本书后,可以掌握苏州话的常用词语,并可初步运用苏州话进行日常的会话交流,还可以了解一些苏州的风土民情和风景名胜,初步感悟柔性、水性的苏州文化。

本书在创作过程中得到了吴语协会的大力支持,尤其是郭晔旻、王鑫康、张斐然、吴昊等先生对本书的拼音方案和方言正字提出了大量建设性的意见。

本书由苏州工业职业技术学院的高丰老师、韩婧老师担任英语翻译工作,由杨永怀女士、王伟先生担任英语校对工作。其中高丰老师翻译第一~七单元,韩婧老师翻译第八~十单元。本书由苏州工业职业技术学院的黄小梅老师全程负责编排。

本书由王鑫康、邢雯芝、钟意、陈拙共同完成配音工作,全书由钟意先生主审。

限于编著者水平,本书难免会有不妥之处,敬请读者批评指正。

邢雯芝
2011 年 8 月

目　录

绪论　吴语苏州话音系以及拼音方案 ·· 1

第一单元　称谓与时间 ·· 9

第二单元　学校与教育 ·· 32

第三单元　文化与名人 ·· 56

第四单元　体育与艺术 ·· 83

第五单元　饮食与服务 ·· 107

第六单元　交通与旅游 ·· 131

第七单元　气象与节气 ·· 155

第八单元　邻里与家常 ·· 175

第九单元　升学与就业 ·· 195

第十单元　交友与聚会 ·· 214

参考文献 ·· 237

绪 论
吴语苏州话音系以及拼音方案

第一节 声 母

1. 唇音 p ph b f v m

  p：国际音标[p]。类似于普通话拼音中的b。例字：帮 paon44

  ph：国际音标[pʰ]。类似于普通话拼音中的p。例字：扑 phoh43

  b：国际音标[b]。类似于英语音标中的[b]，是个浊音，比起普通话拼音中的b，在发音时会明显感觉到喉咙的震动。例字：旁 baon223

  f：国际音标[f]。类似于普通话拼音中的f。例字：方 faon44

  v：国际音标[v]。类似于英语音标中的[v]，"very"中的"v"，不能发成普通话的"威"。例字：房 vaon223

  m：国际音标[m]。类似于普通话拼音中的m。例字：网 maon231

2. 齿音 ts tsh s z

  ts：国际音标[ʦ]。类似于普通话拼音中的z。例字：增 tsen44

  tsh：国际音标[ʦʰ]。类似于普通话拼音中的c。例字：次 tshy523

  s：国际音标[s]。类似于普通话拼音中的s。例字：丝 sy44

  z：国际音标[z]。类似于英语音标中的[z]，"zero"中"z"，不能发成普通话的"贼"。例字：字 zy231

3. 舌头音 t th d l n

  t：国际音标[t]。类似于普通话拼音中的d。例字：担 te44

  th：国际音标[tʰ]。类似于普通话拼音中的t。例字：推 the44

  d：国际音标[d]。类似于英语音标中的[d]，是个浊音，比起普通话拼音中的d，在发音时会明显感觉到喉咙的震动。例字：抬 de223

  l：国际音标[l]。类似于普通话拼音中的l。例字：冷 lan231

n：国际音标[n]。类似于普通话拼音中的n。例字：南 noe223

4. 舌面音 c ch j sh ny

c：国际音标[tɕ]。类似于普通话拼音中的j。例字：织 cih43

ch：国际音标[tɕʰ]。类似于普通话拼音中的q。例字：吃 chih43

j：国际音标[dʑ]。类似于英语音标中的[dʒ]，是c的相应浊音，比起普通话拼音中的j，在发音时会明显感觉到喉咙的震动。例字：杰 jih23

sh：国际音标[ɕ]。类似于普通话拼音中的x。例字：喜 shi51

ny：国际音标[ɲ]。n是舌尖顶上腭，ny则是舌面顶上腭。例字：伲 nyi231

5. 牙音 k kh g ng

k：国际音标[k]。类似于普通话拼音中的g。例字：哥 kou44

kh：国际音标[kʰ]。类似于普通话拼音中的k。例字：枯 khou44

g：国际音标[g]。类似于英语音标中的[g]，是个浊音，比起普通话拼音中的g，在发音时会明显感觉到喉咙的震动。例字：环 gue223

ng：国际音标[ŋ]。相当于粤语"我"的声母，有点像把普通话拼音中的后鼻音韵尾ng当成声母来与韵母相拼。例字：硬 ngan231

6. 喉音 h gh

h：国际音标[h]。类似于英语音标中的[h]的发音。例字：好 hae51

gh（y w）：国际音标[ɦ]。类似于法语中的r（不颤动），可以用早上漱口时口中含水的感觉来发h。当gh和i开头的韵母相拼时简写为y；当与u开头的声母相拼时简写为w。例字：号 ghae23 闲 ghe223 盐 yie223 还 we223

第二节 韵　母

1. 基本元音 a e i o u y

a：国际音标[ɑ]。类似于英语"glass"中的这个"a"的发音。例字：摆 pa51

e：国际音标[E]。类似于英语"bed"中的这个"e"的发音。例字：班 pe44

i：国际音标[i]。比普通话拼音的i更扁，带摩擦腭。例字：衣 i44

o：国际音标[o]。有点像普通话拼音中u的发音，嘴唇收拢，开口较大。例字：沙 so44

u：国际音标[u]。在点像英语"food"中的这个"oo"的发音，唇形展开，比o要扁，不那么圆。例字：副 fu523

y：国际音标[ɿ]。类似于普通话"资"、"次"、"斯"的韵母。例字：斯 sy44

2. 组合元音

au[1]：国际音标[æ]。类似于英语"bag"中的这个"a"的发音。例字：好 hae51

eu：国际音标[øɤ]。有点像粤语"居"、"虽"的韵母，但开口较小，比普通话拼音ei的发音，嘴唇要圆。例字：州 tseu44

ie：国际音标[iɪ]。类似于普通话拼音中i的发音，比i要开。例字：烟 ie44

iu：国际音标[y]。比起普通话拼音中ü的发音，摩擦更强。例字：居 ciu44

oe：国际音标[ø]。比起普通话拼音e的发音，嘴唇要圆。例字：干 koe44

ou：国际音标[əu]。类似于普通话拼音ou的发音。但u的发音更突出，前面的ə是个滑音。例字：过 kou523

yu：国际音标[ɥ]，撅起嘴唇发y，就得到yu。类似y，这个韵母只能和ts、tsh、s、z相拼。例字：水 syu51

3. 鼻音

an：国际音标[ã]。介于普通话拼音中an和ang之间。例字：张 tsan44

aon：国际音标[ɑ̃]。有点像美式英语的on。例字：桩 tsaon44

en：国际音标[ən]。类似于普通话拼音中en的发音。例字：恩 en44

in：国际音标[in]。类似于普通话拼音中in[2]的发音。例字：英 in44

on：国际音标[oŋ]。类似于普通话拼音中ong的发音。例字：中 tson44

iuin：国际音标[yn][3]。类似于普通话拼音中yun的发音。例字：军 ciuin44

4. 入声

aeh：国际音标[aʔ]。类似于英式英语"bag"中的"a"，但更短促。例字：拔 baeh23

ah：国际音标[ɑʔ]。a的短音，接近于英式英语"car"中"ar"的发音，但更短促。例字：客 khah43

eh：国际音标[əʔ]。发音要短促，类似于英语"famous"中"ou"的发音。例字：没 meh23

ih：国际音标[iəʔ]。发音要短促，类似于英语"sit"中"i"的发音。例字：雪 sih43

---

[1] 为了方便记忆，在考虑到苏州城区中派无"来兰"的对立的情况下，原吴协拼音中体系的au在本书中均用ae代替。

[2] 苏州老派音，如评弹，实际发音是[iən]。

[3] 苏州老派音，如评弹，实际发音是[yən]。

oh：国际音标[oʔ]。发音要短促，类似于英语"book"中"oo"的发音。例字：薄 boh23

5. 自成音节韵母

r：国际音标[ɚ]。类似于普通话拼音中er的发音。例字：儿 r223
m：国际音标[m]。英语音标中[m]的发音。例字：亩 m231
n：国际音标[n]。英语音标中[n]的发音。例字：尔 n44
ng：国际音标[ŋ]。英语音标中[ŋ]的发音。例字：鱼 ng223

6. 介音

i：当i与a相拼就成了 ia，例字：呀 ia44。
u：当u与a相拼就成了ua，例字：洼 ua44。

第三节 声 调

1. 五度声调法

把一条竖线四等分，得到五个点，自下而上定为五度：1度是低音，2度是半低音，3度是中音，4度是半高音，5度是高音。一个人所能发出的最低音是1度，最高音是5度，中间的音分别是2度、3度和4度。

一个音如果又高又平，就是由5度到5度，简称为55，是个高平调；如果从最低升到最高，就是由1度到5度，简称为15，是个低升调；如果由最高降到最低，就是由5度降到1度，简称为51，是个全降调。

本书对于苏州话声调的标记方法就采用五度声调法。

2. 苏州的7个单字调

苏州方言（城区）一共有7个单字调。所谓单字调，也就是单独读这个字的声调，这个单字声调是固定的。

调类	调值	例字			
阴平	44	刚 kaon44	开 khe44	天 thie44	婚 huen44
阳平	223	穷 jion223	田 die223	寒 ghoe223	鹅 ngou223
上声	51	古 kou51	口 kheu51	草 tshae51	好 hae51
阴去	523	盖 ke523	靠 khae523	世 syu523	汉 hoe523
阳去	231	女 nyiu231	近 jin231	共 gon231	岸 ngoe231

阴入	43	吃 chih43	曲 chioh43	黑 heh43	各 koh43
阳入	23	局 jioh23	合 gheh23	木 moh23	额 ngah23

3. 连读变调简介①

苏州方言系统和普通话相比最大的特色就在于他的连读变调。也就是一个字，当它在一个词语的不同场合就有不同的声调。例：

子 tsy*51* ⟶ 狮子 sy*44*-tsy*31*

林 lin*223* ⟶ 狮子林 sy*44*-tsy*44*-lin*31*

路 lou*231* ⟶ 狮子林路 sy*44*-tsy*44*-lin*33*-lou*31*

注意看斜体数字，我们可以发现：

"子"，只念一个字的时候，它的声调为"51"，在"狮子"中，它的声调变为"31"，在"狮子林"中，它的声调变为"44"。

因此在苏州话中，同样一个字在一个词语的不同位置时表现出了不同的声调，这个现象就叫连读变调。

苏州方言中的连读变调看似复杂，但却有着它的一定的规律。

4. 二字组的连读变调的通行规律

① 阴平字起头的二字组连读变调的通行规律

以阴平字为起头的二字组在连读变调时整体呈平降的趋势。

例：

第2字声调	连调式	例词
阴平 44	44+31	新鲜 sin44+sie44 ⟶ sin44-sie31
阳平 223		灰尘 hue44+zen223 ⟶ hue44-zen31
阴上 51		开水 khe44+syu51 ⟶ khe44-syu31
阳去 231		医院 i44+yoe231 ⟶ i44-yoe31
阴去 523		空气 khon44+chi523 ⟶ khon44-chi31
阴入 43	44+3	心得 sin44+teh3 ⟶ sin44-teh3
阳入 23		中学 tson44+ghoh3 ⟶ tson44-ghoh3

② 阳平字起头的二字组连读变调的通行规律

以阳平字为起头的二字组在连读变调时常见的模式为平升模式。

例：

---

① 更多资料请参考苏州闲话网(http://www.suzhouhua.org/)

第2字声调	连调式	例词	
阴平 44	22+33	辰光 zen223+kuaon44	→ zen22-kuaon33
阳平 223		油条 yeu223+diae223	→ yeu22-diae33
阴上 51		团体 doe223+thi44	→ doe22-thi33
阳去 231		闲话 ghe223+gho231	→ ghe22-gho33
阴去 523		迷信 mi223+sin523	→ mi22-sin33
阴入 43	22+3	毛笔 mae223+pih43	→ mae22-pih3
阳入 23		红木 ghon223+moh23	→ ghon22-moh3

③ 阴上字起头的二字组连读变调的通行规律

以阴上字为起头的二字组在连读变调时常见的为降升模式。

例：

第2字声调	连调式	例词	
阴平 44	51+23	火车 hou51+tsho44	→ hou51-tsho23
阳平 223		本来 pen51+le223	→ pen51-le23
阴上 51		水果 syu51+kou51	→ syu51-kou23
阳去 231	51+31	漂亮 phiae51+lian231	→ phiae51-lian31
阴去 523		讨厌 thae51+ie523	→ thae51-ie31
阴入 43	51+3	美国 me51+kueh43	→ me51-kueh3
阳入 23		火着 hou51+zah23	→ hou51-zah3

④ 阳去字起头的二字组连读变调的通行规律

以阳去字为起头的二字组在连读变调时常见的同阳平连调，即平升模式。

例：

第2字声调	连调式	例词	
阴平 44	22+33	自家 zy231+ka44	→ zy22-ka33
阳平 223		老爷 lae231+ya223	→ lae22-ya33
阴上 51		校长 yae231+tsan51	→ yae22-tsan33
阳去 231		豆腐 deu231+vu231	→ deu22-vu33
阴去 523		忘记 maon231+ci523	→ maon22-ci33
阴入 43	22+3	料作 liae231+tsoh43	→ liae22-tsoh3
阳入 23		眼热 nge231+nyih23	→ nge22-nyih3

⑤ 阴去字起头的二字组连读变调的通行规律

以阴去字为起头的二字组在连读变调时常见的同阴平连调，即平降模式。

例：

第2字声调	连调式	例词
阴平 44	44+31	进深 tsin523+sen44 ⟶ tsin44-sen31
阳平 223		太阳 tha523+yan223 ⟶ tha44-yan31
阴上 51		要好 iae523+hae51 ⟶ iae44-hae31
阳去 231		吊桶 tiae523+don231 ⟶ tiae44-don31
阴去 523		告诉 kae523+sou523 ⟶ kae44-sou31
阴入 43	44+3	货色 hou523+seh43 ⟶ hou44-seh3
阳入 23		酱肉 tsian523+nyioh23 ⟶ tsian44-nyioh3

⑥ 阴入字起头的二字组连读变调的通行规律

以阴入字为起头的二字组在连读变调时基本不变调。

例：

第2字声调	连调式	例词
阴平 44	43+23	菊花 cioh43+ho44 ⟶ cioh43-ho23
阳平 223		色盲 seh43+maon223 ⟶ seh43-maon23
阴上 51	43+51	阿姐 aeh43+tsia51 ⟶ aeh43-tsia51
阳去 231	43+31	一部 ih43+bu231 ⟶ ih43-bu231
阴去 523	43+523	一夜 ih43+ia523 ⟶ ih43-ia523
阴入 43	43+43	八百 poh43+pah43 ⟶ poh43-pah43
阳入 23		吃力 chih43+lih23 ⟶ chih43-lih43

⑦ 阳入字起头的二字组连读变调的通行规律

以阳入字为起头的二字组在连读变调时基本呈升降的趋势。

例：

第2字声调	连调式	例词
阴平 44	23+31	学生 ghoh23+san44 ⟶ ghoh23-san31
阳平 223		肋条 leh23+diae223 ⟶ leh23-diae31
阴上 51		日本 zeh23+pen51 ⟶ zeh23-pen31
阳去 231		立夏 lih23+gho231 ⟶ lih23-gho31
阴去 523		绿化 loh23+ho523 ⟶ loh23-ho31
阴入 43	23+43	日脚 nyih23+ciah43 ⟶ nyih23-ciah43
阳入 23	23+3	学习 ghoh23+zih23 ⟶ ghoh23-zih3

⑧ 特殊的二字组连读变调的特殊现象

在苏州话的二字组连读变调，除了上述的通行规律之外，还有很多特殊的变调模式。如"儿童"，"儿（r223）"+"童（don223）"，实际连调为"r44-don31"；"啥个"，"啥（sa523）"+"个（keh43）"，实际连调为"sa523-keh3"；"一定"，"一（ih43）"+"定（din231）"，实际连调为"ih43+din313"；"林冲"，"林（lin223）"+"冲（tshon44）"，实际连调为"lin231+tshon31"。

5. 三字组及四字以上字组的连读变调的通行规律

三字组及四字以上字组，在连读变调时，第一字同二字组的首字变化，最后一个字通常呈降调，中间的字阴调类的则成平调。

例：

观前街 kuoe44 + zie223 + ka44 ⟶ kuoe44 - zie33- ka31

富郎中巷 fu523+laon223+tson44+ghaon231 ⟶ fu44-laon33-tson44-ghaon31

第一单元

称谓与时间

一 情景引入

甲：普通话 奶奶，我 今 天 运 气 真 好！
　　吴语音 ae44-bu31 ngou231 cin44-tsae31 ngah23-kueh43-deu31 ban22-zah3 thie44--ho44-pe31 tse44
　　吴语文 嫿婆，我 今 朝 额 骨 头 碰 着 天 花 板①哉！

---

① 在吴语区，方言里有一种正话反说、反话正说的现象。最经典的是"额骨头碰着天花板"，这句话本有嘲讽性质，其中"天花板"原指"棺材板"，后来，流传开来，慢慢演变成"运气极好"之意。

乙：普通话　　鬼 丫 头，什 么 事 情 这 么 开 心？连
　　吴语音　　siae51-ciu33-o44-deu31　sa523-keh3 zy22-thi33 zeh23-kan23 kha44 -weh3 lie22-tae33
　　吴语文　　小 鬼 丫 头，啥个 事 体 实 梗 快 活？连 到

　　　　　　　嘴 巴 都 合 不 上 了？
　　　　　　　tsyu51-po33 gha223 gheh23-feh23-lon31 tse0
　　　　　　　嘴 巴 也 合 弗 拢 哉？

甲：普通话　　傍 晚，　　我 去 超 市 买 一 部 新 款 手 机
　　吴语音　　ze22-ia44-khua31 ngou231 chi523 tshae44-zy31 ma231 ih43-tsah43 sin44- khuoe31 seu51-ci23
　　吴语文　　垂 夜 快，我 去 超 市 买 一 只 新 款 手 机

　　　　　　　和 一 堆 零 食，排 队 结 账　　时，　两 位
　　　　　　　taeh43 ih43-te23 lin22-zeh3 ba22-de33 cih43--tsan523 keh43 zen22-kuaon33 lian231-we31
　　　　　　　搭 一 堆 零 食，排 队 结 账 个① 辰 光，两 位

　　　　　　　爷 爷 希 望 我 让 他 们 先 结 账，因 为 他 们
　　　　　　　aeh43-tia23 shi44-vaon31 ngou231 nyian231 n44-toh3　sie44 cih43-tsan523 in44-we31 li44-toh3
　　　　　　　阿 爹 希 望 我 让 尔 笃 先 结 账，因 为 俚 笃

　　　　　　　要 赶 着 去 赴 宴。
　　　　　　　iae523 koe51-tsy33 chi523 fu523 ve22-jioh3
　　　　　　　要 赶 仔 去 赴 饭 局。

乙：普通话　　我 知 道 的，你 心 里 是 不 大 愿 意 的。你
　　吴语音　　ngou231 shiae51-teh43-keh3 ne231 sin44-li31 zy231 feh43-da313 nyioe231- i31- keh0 ne231
　　吴语文　　我 晓 得 个，倷 心 里 是 弗② 大 愿 意 个。倷

---

① "个"、"嗄"、"啘"、"则"、"末"与"哉"一样，也是比较常用的句末语气助词。其中"个"在句中用的也很多，在意思与语法作用上相当于普通话中的助词"的"。

② 苏州话常用语中至今还留有浓浓的古意和一种书卷气。如苏州人说"不"为"弗"，句子结尾的语气词不用"了"而用"哉"。另外，"勿"字在苏州话中无论读音还是语法意义，都与"弗"字相似。

一 向 不 肯 吃 亏 的。
ih43-shian523 feh43-khen51 chih43-chiu44-keh43-ue0
一 向 弗 肯 吃 亏 个 哇。

甲：普通话 一 开 始 我 是 想 拒 绝 的，但 是 话
　　吴语音 deu22-chi44-deu31 ngou231 zy231 sian51 we22-deu33-keh3 pih43-kou523 ghe22-gho33
　　吴语文 头 起 头 我 是 想 回 头① 个，不 过 闲 话

　　　　　到 口 边 留 半 句。
　　　　　tae51-tsy23 tsyu51-po44-pie44-laon31 koh43-tih43-toh43 yih23 ie51-tsy44-tsoe44-chi31
　　　　　到 仔 嘴 巴 边 浪 角 跌 笃 亦 咽 仔 转 去。

乙：普通话 你 怎 么 突 然 肯 让 人 了？
　　吴语音 ne231 naeh23-han31 zah23-san44-deu31 khen51 nyian231 nyin223 tseh43 cia44
　　吴语文 倷 哪 哼 着 生 头 肯 让 人 则 嘎？

甲：普通话 你 不 是 一 直 讲 "吃 亏 就 是 便 宜 吗"？
　　吴语音 ne231 feh43-zy231 ih43-zeh43 kaon51 chih43-chiu44 zeu22-zy33 bie22--nyih23 ma0
　　吴语文 倷 弗 是 一 直 讲 "吃 亏 就 是 便 宜② 吗"？

　　　　　真 的 有 道 理。我 让 他 们 先 结 账，哪 里
　　　　　zeh23-deu31 yeu231 miae22-deu33 ngou231 nyian231 li44-toh3 sie44 cih43-tsan523 lo22-taeh3
　　　　　实 头 有 苗 头③。我 让 俚 笃 先 结 账， 哪 搭

---

① "回头"在吴方言中可谓一词多义。a.拒绝，回言打发。此义同"情景引入"中"头起头我想回头个"。b.回复，答复。"倷倒是拿句闲话出来，我也好畀俚个回头。"（你倒是拿句话出来，我也好给他个答复。）c.告诉，报告。"小鬼，到学堂去，也弗搭阿爹回头一声。"（小鬼，到学校去，也不告诉爷爷一声。）d.辞退，解雇。"箇个老板黑心个，试用期一满，就拿伲回头哉。"（这个老板黑心噢，试用期一满，就把我们辞退了。）e.告辞，告别。"倷该趟到外地去读大学，走个前头，要到老师屋里去回头一埭个啊。"（你这次到外地去读大学，走之前，要到老师家里去告辞一下。）

② 这里"便宜"的"宜"读入声"nyih23"属于一种特殊音变。

③ "苗头"有四层意思。a.端绪，预兆，因由。"俚一钆苗头弗对，豪惨溜脱。"（他一看预兆不好，赶紧溜走。）b.门路，办法。"哀桩事体本来三弗803三末，要看倷自家阿有苗头哉。"（这桩事情成不成，得看你自己有没有办法了。）c.本领，道理。此义同"情景引入"中"实头有苗头"。d.来头，气派。"小赤佬，切理一番子倒苗头十足呢。"（小鬼头，打扮一下后倒气派十足呀。）

知 道, 轮 到 我　　　时,　　超 市 喇 叭 中 突 然
shiae51-teh3 a44-zah3 ngou31-keh3 zen22-kuaon44 tshae44-zy31 la22-pa44-li31 zah23-san44-
晓 得, 挨 着 我 个① 辰 光,　　超 市 喇 叭 里 着 生

　　　说, 现 在 轮 到 结 账 的 顾 客 一 律 免 费,
deu31 kaon51 yie22-ze33 len22-zah3 cih43-tsan523 keh0 kou523-khah3 ih43-lih43 mie231-fi31
　　　头 讲, 现 在 轮 着 结 账 个 顾 客 一 律 免 费,

　　这 是　　超 市 的 促 销 活 动。
e44-keh3 zy231　tshae44-zy44-keh3 tshoh43-siae23-weh3- don31
　　哀 个 是　超 市 个 促 销 活 动。

乙: 普通话 所 以 呀, 做 人 平 时 吃 亏 一 些　没 什 么
　　吴语音 sou51-i23 ia44 tsou523 nyin223 bin231-zyu31 chih43-chiu23 ih43-tie44- tie31 m22-peh3-sa44- keh3
　　吴语文 所 以 呀, 做 人 平 时 吃 亏 一 点 点 呒 不 啥 个

　　　大 不 了 的, 你 看 最 后 的 结 局　　多 好。
dou22-feh3-liae33-keh3 ne231 khoe523 tse51-gheu33-keh3 loh23-zan33-deu33-syu31 ci51-ho23 hae51
　　　大 弗 了 个, 俚 看 最 后 个 落 场 头 势 几 许 好。

• •

甲: Grandma, I'm lucky today.

乙: Little girl, why are you so happy? You are grinning from ear to ear.

甲: I went to the supermarket to buy a new cell phone and a variety of snacks in the evening. At the checkout counter, two old men lined up behind us asked whether they could check out first as they were hurrying for a dinner.

乙: I know you really don't want to. You are always alive to your own interests.

甲: I was going to refuse at first, But an ill tongue may do much.

---

① 苏州话中,涉及"……的人"和"……的物"的习惯性用法是不一致的。拿来修饰人的,即便定语是单数,也习惯用人称代词的复数表示"……的",省略"个"字。例如,"我的妈妈"不说"我个姆妈"而表达为"伲姆妈","你的爷爷"不说"倷个阿爹"而表达为"尔笃阿爹","他的哥哥"不说"俚个哥哥"而表达为"俚笃哥哥"。拿来修饰物的,则定语是单数就用单数表达,定语是复数就用复数表达。比如"我的杯子"读作"我个杯子","她的手表"读作"俚个手表","你们的书"读作"尔笃个书"。在"……的物"中表示"的"的"个"字不能省略。

乙：What made you concede everything to people?

甲：Don't you always say, "Sometimes the best gain is to lose". It does make sense. I let them check out first. Who could have thought that when it was my turn I was told over the loudspeaker that the customers who are checking out now could take their purchases for free, Which was the sales promotion of the supermarket.

乙：So sometimes the best gain is to lose. It turned out everything is all right.

场景对话

1. 甲：普通话 伯父， 您 好！ 我 是 您 的 朋 友 张 贤
   吴语音 lae22-pah43-pah43 ne231 hae51 ngou231-zy31 ne231-keh3 ban22-yeu33 tsan44-yie44-
   吴语文 老 伯 伯， 倷 好！ 我 是 倷 个 朋 友 张 贤

   的 女 儿。
   keh3 noe22-ng33
   个 囡 儿①。

   乙：普通话 哦， 真 是 女 大 十 八 变， 好 久
   吴语音 oh43 tsen44-keh43-zy31 waon22-mae33-o44-deu31 zeh23-poh43-pie31 zan22-yoe33-
   吴语文 喔， 真 个 是 黄 毛 丫 头 十 八 变， 长 远

   不 见， 小 姑 娘 变 成 漂 亮 的 大 姑 娘 了。
   feh43-cie31 siae51-nyian44-ng31 pie51-tsy33-keh3 piae44--tsyu31 dou22-kou44-nyian33-tse0
   弗 见， 小 娘 儿 变 仔 个 标 致 大 姑 娘 哉。

甲：Nice to meet you, Uncle. I am your friend Zhang Xian's daughter.

乙：Oh, you change fast and become more and more beaetiful. Long time no see. The little girl is a fine well-grown young lady.

---

① 囡儿，即"女儿"的合音脱落鼻化演变而来niu+ng→noen→noe，"儿"作儿尾时读作ng。

2. 甲：普通话 奶奶，我 肚子 饿 了，可不可以 吃 午 饭 了？
　　　 吴语音 ae44-bu31 ngou231 dou22-bi33 ngou231-tse0 aeh43　khou51-i23 chih43 tson44-ve33-leh0
　　　 吴语文 媼婆，我 肚皮 饿 哉，阿① 可以 吃 中 饭 勒？

　 乙：普通话 小 东 西，你 是 天 吃 星 下 凡 呀！早 饭
　　　 吴语音 siae51-tsheh43-lae31 ne231-zy31 thie44-chih43-sin31 gho22-ve33 gha223 tsae51-ve23
　　　 吴语文 小 赤 佬，倷 是 天 吃 星 下 凡 也！早 饭

　　　　　　才 　　吃没多久，难 道 又 肚子 饿 了？不
　　　　　　kaon44-chiae31 chih43-kou523 ne22-feh23-zen31 yih23 dou22-bi33 ngou231-tse0 feh43
　　　　　　刚 巧 吃 过，难 弗 成 亦 肚 皮 饿 哉？弗

　　　　　　行， 到 时 候 再 吃。
　　　　　　le22-se33　a51-mo33-yan31 tse44 chih43
　　　　　　来 三②，挨 模 样③ 再 吃。

　 甲：Grandma, I am hungry. Can I have lunch?
　 乙：My little thing, you are a real greedy guts. I've had breakfast not long before. Are you hungry again? No. You should eat at lunch time.

3. 甲：普通话 大 家 下 午 　　好，下 面 　　我 来 谈 谈 我
　　　 吴语音 da22-ka33 gho22-me33-tseu31 hae51 gho22-ti44-deu31 ngou231 le223 de22-de33 ngou23-
　　　 吴语文 大 家 下 晚 昼 好，下 底 头 我 来 谈 谈 我

---

① "阿"字在问句中频繁出现，与动词搭配，作用等同于英文中两动词间加一个否定副词"不"的搭配。

② "来三"，"半二弗来三"有两层意思。a. 可以，行。此义同"场景对话"例句2。b. 能干。"覅看他年纪弗大，来三得弗得了。"（别看他年纪不大，能干得不得了。）

③ "挨模样"相当于英文中的"到时候"，其中的"挨"字发音等同于吴方言中的"矮"。"下晚昼"相当于英文中的"下午"，其中的"晚"字发音等同于吴方言中的"迈"。

```
                     的   观   点。
                     keh3 kuoe44-tie3
                     个   观   点。
```

乙：普通话 你 讲 得 非 常 好，我们 真 是 受 益 匪 浅。
　　吴语音 ne231 kaon51-teh3 ciae44-kue44-hae31 nyi231 tsen44-keh43-zy31 zeu22-ih3-fi44-tshie31
　　吴语文 倷 讲 得 交 关① 好，伲 真 个 是 受 益 匪 浅。

甲：Good afternoon, everyone. Then I will talk about my opinions.
乙：Very well said. We have benift a lot from your presentation.

4. 甲：普通话 王 静，你 怎 么 这 么 晚 才 回 来，你 妈 妈
　　　 吴语音 waon22-zin33 ne231 naeh23-han31 e44-zaon31 e523 tse44 tsoe51-le23 n22-toh3 m44-ma31
　　　 吴语文 王 静，倷 哪 哼 哀 状 晏 再 转 来，尔 笃 姆 妈

```
                  一 个 人 在    宿 舍 等 了 你 有 一 会 儿 了。
                  ih43-ka44-deu31 leh23-laon31 soh43-seu51 ten51-tsy33-ne31 me44-hae31 ih43-shih43-tse0
                  一 家 头  勒 浪  宿 舍 等 仔 倷 蛮 好 一 歇 哉。
```

乙：普通话 小 静，不 要 紧 的，妈妈 等 了 没 多 久 呢。
　　吴语音 siae51-zin23 feh43-iae44-cin44-keh3 m44-ma31 ten51-tsy33 ih43- shih43-shih43-leh0
　　吴语文 小 静，弗 要 紧 个，姆 妈 等 仔 一 歇 歇 勒。

甲：Wang Jing, Why do you come back so late? Your mum has been waiting at the dormitory for a long time.
乙：Xiao Jing, It's all right. Mum I haven't been here long.

---

① "交关"在苏州话中有三层意思。a. 很，非常，十分。"黄天源个糕团是苏州一绝，交关好吃。"（黄天源的糕团是苏州一绝，非常好吃。）b. 很多。此义同"场景对话"例句3。c. 紧要，关系重大。"哀个事体真是性命交关，马虎不得。"（这个事情可是性命攸关，马虎不得。）

5. 甲：普通话 我 真 搞 不 明 白，是 我 的 电脑 坏 了，
   吴语音 ngou231 tsen44-keh3 lon44-feh43-ton44-tse31 zy231 ngou31-keh3 die22- nae33 wa22-theh3
   吴语文 我 真 个 弄 弗 懂 哉，是 我 个 电脑 坏 脱，

   他 干 嘛 一 直 哭 丧 着 脸 哟。
   n44-ne31 tsoh43-sa523 ih43-zeh43 khoh43-tsheh43-ou44-la44-keh3-cia31
   尔 傽 作 喨 一 直 哭 出 乌 拉 个 嘎。

乙：普通话 他 准 备 今 晚 用 你 的 电脑 过 一
   吴语音 li44 ti51-kaon33 cin44-tsae31 ia44-li31 yon231 ne231-keh3 die22- nae33 kou523-ih43-
   吴语文 俚 抵 杠 今 朝 夜 里 用 㑚 个 电脑 过 一

   下 游 戏 瘾 的，现 在 玩 不 成 了，心 里
   kou31 yeu22-shi33-in44-keh0 yie22-ze33 beh23- sian523 feh43-zen223 tse44 sin44-li31
   过 游 戏 瘾 个，现 在 孛 相 弗 成 哉，心 里

   可 郁 闷 呢。
   jion231 ae44-tsae44-keh3
   穷① 奥 糟 个。

甲：I really confused. It is my computer that has broken. Why is he always pulling a long face?

乙：He is going to use your computer to have some fun tonight. But his fat is all in the fire now. He is then depressed and in despair.

6. 甲：普通话 你 不 要 再 闹 个 不 停 了，你 闹 了 多 久
   吴语音 ne231 feh43-iae523 tse44 tsoh43-thie44-tsoh43-di33-tse0 ne231 tsoh43-tsy51 ci51-ho23
   吴语文 㑚 弗 要 再 作 天 作 地 哉，㑚 作 仔 几 许

---

① "穷"是苏州话中使用频率很高的副词，相当于普通话中的"很"、"非常"、"十分"。

　　　　　　　了，　　　　　我　喊　你　大爷　总　　　可以了吧。
　　　　　zen22-kuaon44 tse44 ngou231 he51 ne231 ya22- soh3 tson51-kue23 khou51-i23 tseh43 ba0
　　　　　辰　光　哉，我　喊　侬　爷叔　总　归　可　以　则吧。

乙：普通话 如果　　　你　不　答　应，我　还　要　大　闹　　呢！
　　吴语音 cia51-sy33-dae31 ne231 feh43-tah43-in31 ngou231 we22-iae33 jion22--pin44-pan31 le0
　　吴语文 假　使　道　侬　弗　答　应，　我　还　要　穷　冰　浜来！

甲：Don't come the bully with me! How long is this going to go on? I say uncle, OK?
乙：If you don't promise, I will make more trouble.

7. 甲：普通话 老　婆，　　　你　不要　羡　慕　了，已经　半　夜　了，这
　　　　吴语音 ka44-tsyu44-bu31 ne231 fiae523 nge22-nyih3 tse44 i44-cin31 poe44-ia44-po31 tse0 ke44-
　　　　吴语文 家　主　婆，侬　覅　眼　热　哉，已经　半　夜　把哉，该

　　　　　　　种　大　人　物　不　可　能　睬　你　的。
　　　　　　tson31 dou22-hae44-lae31 feh43 khou51- nen23 tshe51 ne231 keh0
　　　　　　种　大　好　佬　弗　可　能　睬　侬　个。

　　乙：普通话 不　见　得，我　一　定要试　一　试。
　　　　吴语音 feh43-cie44-teh3 ngou231 pe51-iae23　syu51-syu33-khoe31
　　　　吴语文 弗　见　得，我　板　要　　试　试　看。

甲：Honey, Don't be jealous. It's past midnight. There's no way the big shot is talking to you.
乙：Not necessary. I've got to try it.

8. 甲：普通话 好　　　一　个　孝　顺　的　媳　妇，吃　过　晚饭
　　　　吴语音 tsen44-keh43-zy31 ih43-keh43 shiae44-zen33-keh31 sin44-vu31 chih43 kou523 ia44-ve31
　　　　吴语文 真　个　是　一　个　孝　顺　个　媳　妇，吃　过　夜　饭

又 带 你 婆婆 出 来 散步 了。
yih23 ta523 n22-toh3 ae44-bu31 tsheh43-le223 se51- bu33 tse44
亦 带 尔笃 媪婆 出 来 散 步 哉。

乙：普通话 伯 父， 您 过 奖 了。
吴语音 lae22-pah3-pah3 ne231 kou51-tsian31 tse44
吴语文 老 伯伯， 倷 过 奖 哉。

甲：What a filial daughter-in-law! You take your mother-in-law out for walks after supper again.
乙：Oh, Uncle, it's nothing! You are flattering me.

9. 甲：普通话 你们 不要 唱 了， 都 唱 了几个 小 时 了，
吴语音 n22-toh3 fiae523 tshaon523 tse44 ze223 tshaon51-tsy23 ci51-keh3 tson44-deu31 tseh43
吴语文 尔笃 覅 唱 哉， 侪① 唱 仔 几个 钟 头 则

是不是 准备 一下子 把 会唱 的 歌 全部
ia0 aeh43-zy231 tsen51-be31 ih43-ci44- deu33 no223 ue44-tshaon44-keh3 kou44 ze223
呀， 阿是 准备 一记头 拿 会 唱 个 歌 侪

唱 完？
tshaon523 kuaon44 aeh0
唱 光 啊？

乙：普通话 再 唱 三首， 这样 好不好？
吴语音 tse44 tshaon523 se44-seu31 zeh23-kan23 yian44-tsy31 aeh43 hae51
吴语文 再 唱 三首， 实梗样子 阿 好？

甲：You don't sing, Have sung for several hours Isn't ready The singers to sing at the end.
乙：To sing again, like stems of 3, ok?

---

① "侪"是苏州话中使用频率很高的副词，相当于普通话中的"都"。

三 词语贴士

（一）人称代词

序号	英文	苏州话
1.	I 我	ngou231,jion22- kaeh23-li31 我，　　　穷夹里
2.	you 你	ne231 倷
3.	he, she 他，她	li44,li44- ne31,n44-ne31 俚，俚倷，　尔倷
4.	we 我们	nyi231,ngou231-nyi31 伲　　　　我伲
5.	you 你们	n22-toh3 尔笃
6.	they 他们（她们）	li44-toh3,n44-toh3 俚笃，　尔笃

（二）家庭成员

序号	英文	苏州话
1.	father 爸爸	tia44-tia31 爹爹
2.	mother 妈妈	m44-ma31 姆妈
3.	grandfather 爷爷，外公	aeh43-tia23 阿爹
4.	grandmother 奶奶（外婆）	ae44-bu31 媼婆
5.	son 儿子	nyi22-tsy33 儿子
6.	daughter 女儿	noe22-n33 囡儿
7.	elder brother 哥哥	aeh43-kou23,kou44-kou31 阿哥，　　哥哥
8.	younger brother 弟弟	di22-di33 弟弟
9.	elder sister 姐姐	aeh43-tsia51,tsia51-tsia23 阿姐，　　姐姐

续表

序号	英文	苏州话
10.	younger sister	me22-tsy33
	妹妹	妹子
11.	husband	nyi231 noe22-nyin33,, nyi231 oh43-li231
	丈夫	伲男人, 伲屋里
12.	wife	ka44-tsyu44-bu31,nyi231 oh43-li31,ka44-siae31
	妻子	家主婆, 伲屋里, 家小

（三）直系亲属

序号	英文	苏州话
1.	uncle	lae22-pah43-pah3
	伯伯，伯父	老伯伯
2.	aunt	m22-me33,dou22-m44-ma31
	伯母	姆媒, 大姆妈
3.	uncle	soh43-soh43
	叔叔	叔叔
4.	aunt	sen51-sen23
	婶婶	婶婶
5.	uncle	jieu22-jieu33
	舅舅	舅舅
6.	aunt	jieu22-m33
	舅妈	舅姆
7.	father-in-law	aeh43-kon23
	公公	阿公
8.	mother-in-law	aeh43-bu23
	婆婆	阿婆
9.	father-in-law	zan22-nyin33,zan22-nyin33-aeh43-pah3
	岳父	丈人, 丈人阿伯
10.	mother-in-law	zan22-m33,zan22-m33-nyian31
	岳母	丈姆, 丈姆娘
11.	son-in-law	nyiu231-si31
	女婿	女婿
12.	daughter-in-law	sin44-vu31
	媳妇	媳妇
13.	all but son in law	mae22-ciah3,mae22-ciah3-nyiu44-si31
	准女婿	毛脚, 毛脚女婿

续表

序号	英文	苏州话
14.	all but daughter in law 准媳妇	mae22-ciah3- sin44-vu31 毛脚媳妇
15.	relative 亲戚	tshin44-cioe31 亲眷

（四）社会关系

序号	英文	苏州话
1.	friend 朋友	ban22-yeu33 朋友
2.	classmate 同学	don22-ghoh3 同学
3.	colleague 同事	don231-zy31 同事
4.	deskmate 同桌	don22-tsoh3 同桌
5.	side-kick 铁哥们	tsheh43-khou44-di33-shion31 出裤弟兄
6.	enemy 敌人	te44-deu31,si51-te44-deu31 对头，死对头
7.	enemy 仇人	ioe44-ka31 冤家
8.	lovers 情侣	zin22-nyin33 情人
9.	affair 不正当男女	phin44-deu31 姘头

（五）大众称呼

序号	英文	苏州话
1.	baby 婴儿	siae51-mae33-deu31 小毛头
2.	kid 小孩（昵称）	noe44-noe31 囡囡
3.	child 小孩	siae51-kuoe23,siae51-noe23 小倌，小囡

续表

序号	英文	苏州话
4.	boy	noe22-siae44-kuoe31
	男孩	男小倌
5.	girl	siae51-nyian23-ng31,siae51-ciu44-o44-deu31,waon22-mae33-o44-deu31
	女孩	小娘儿，小鬼丫头，黄毛丫头
6.	little thing	tshin44-deu33-ciu31,siae51-tsheh43-lae31,siae51-ciu23
	小伙子（不踏实的）	青头鬼，小赤佬，小鬼
7.	crazy girl	fon44-o44-deu31,tshyu44-siae44-nyian33-ng31
	女孩（不稳重的）	疯丫头，痴小娘鱼
8.	young man	siae51-hou44-tsy31
	小伙子	小伙子
9.	yound lady	dou22-siae44-tsia31
	姑娘	大小姐
10.	youth	ya22-soh3
	男青年（令人厌恶的）	爷叔
11.	troublemaker	siae51-ya33-soh3
	男孩（令人厌恶的）	小爷叔
12.	son of the boss	siae51-khe23
	老板儿子	小开
13.	maid	dou22-tsia33
	年轻女佣（未婚的）	大姐
14.	elder brother	dou22-lae33-kuoe31
	老大	大老倌
15.	youngest brother	lae22-meh23-thou31
	老幺	老末拖
16.	big shot	dou22-hae44-lae31
	大人物，杰出人才	大好佬
17.	nobody	siae51-paeh43-laeh43-tsy31
	小人物	小八卒子
18.	wretched-looking tramp who lives by begging or stealing	pih43-se23
	生存状态不好的人	瘪三
19.	beggar	kae44-ho44-tsy31
	乞丐	叫化子
20.	thief	zeh23-kueh43-deu31,se44-tsah43-seu31
	贼	贼骨头，三只手

(六) 年月日

序号	英文	苏州话
1.	time	zen22-kuaon33
	时间(时候,时代,朝代)	辰光
2.	this year	cin44-nyie31
	今年	今年
3.	next year	min22-nyie33
	明年	明年
4.	the year after next	gheu22-nyie33
	后年	后年
5.	last year	jieu22-nyie33
	去年	旧年
6.	this month	e44-keh3-ghae22-deu33
	本月	哀个号头
7.	last month	zaon22-keh3-ghae22-deu33
	上月	上个号头
8.	next month	gho31-keh3-ghae22-deu33
	下月	下个号头
9.	today	cin44-tsae31
	今天	今朝
10.	tomorrow	men22-tsae33
	明天	明朝
11.	the day after tomorrow	gheu231-nyih31
	后天	后日
12.	yesterday	zoh23-nyih3
	昨天	昨日
13.	week	li231-pa33
	周	礼拜
14.	day and night	ih43-tseu44-zyu31
	一天一夜	一昼时
15.	one day	ih43-nyih43
	一天	一日
16.	every day	me44-nyih31,nyih23-zoh3
	每天	每日, 日逐
17.	one night	ih43-ia523
	一夜	一夜

(七)跨度长的时间

序号	英文	苏州话
1.	lifetime 一辈子（一世）	ih43-pe44-tsy31,ih43-san44-ih43-syu31 一辈子， 一生一世
2.	half one's life 半辈子，半世	poe44-pe44-tsy31,poe44-yu31 半辈子，半世
3.	a long period 很长一段日子	me44-hae44-ih43-tshian31 蛮好一饮
4.	a period of time 一阶段	ih43-tshian31 一饮
5.	usually 平时	bin231-zyu31 平时
6.	always 一直	ih43-zeh43 一直
7.	always 一向	ih43-shian523 一向
8.	for a long time 好久	zan231-yoe31 长远
9.	at present 现在	yie22-ze33 现在
10.	in the past 过去	kou44-chi31 过去
11.	in the future 将来	tsian44-le31 将来
12.	recently 最近	tse51-jin31，geh23-tshian23 最近， 箇饮

(八)一天之内的时间

序号	英文	苏州话
1.	time 时间	zen22-khuaon33 辰光
2.	early morning 一大早	dou22-tshin44-lae33-tsae31 大清老早
3.	morning 早晨	tsae44-laon33-shian31 早浪向
4.	morning 上午	zaon22-me33-tseu31,zaon22-tseu33 上晚昼， 上昼

续表

序号	英文	苏州话
5.	noon 中午	tson44-laon33-shian31 中浪向
6.	afternoon 下午	gho22-me33-tseu31, gho22-tseu33 下晚昼, 　　　　下昼
7.	evening 黄昏	waon22-huen33 黄昏
8.	evening 傍晚	ze22-ia44-khua31, ia44-khua44-tie31 垂夜快, 　　　　夜快点
9.	night 晚上	ia44-li31 夜里
10.	midnight 半夜	poe44-ia44-po31, poe44-ia44-se44-kan31 半夜把, 　　　　半夜三更
11.	all day 一天到晚	ih43-nyih43-tae44-ia31 一日到夜
12.	for a relatively long time 较久	poe44-poe44-nyih43-nyih3 半半日日
13.	hour 小时	tson44-deu31 钟头

（九）较短的时间

序号	英文	苏州话
1.	for a moment 一刹那	ih43-keh43 nge22-soe33, ih43-keh43 nge22-saeh43 一个眼闪, 　　　　一个眼霎
2.	for a short while 片刻	ih43-shih43-shih3 一歇歇
3.	for a while 一会儿	ih43-shih43 一歇
4.	for a relatively long time 相对较久	hae51-ih23-shih3, ih43-dou33-shih3 好一歇, 　　　　一大歇
5.	at a stroke 速度快	soh43-phih43 速劈
6.	from the beginning 一开始	deu22-chi44-deu31, deu22-laon33-shian31 头起头, 　　　　头浪向
7.	afterwards 后来	gheu22-seu33-le31, gheu22-me33-le31 后首来, 　　　　后慢来

续表

序号	英文	苏州话
8.	interlude	taon44-tson44-wan44-li31
	当中	当中横里
9.	suddenly	zah23-san44-deu31
	突然	着生头

（十）交往中的时间

序号	英文	苏州话
1.	last time	zaon231-tsoe33, zaon22-thaon33
	上次	上转，　　　上趟
2.	next time	gho231-tsoe33, gho22-thaon33
	下次	下转，　　　下趟
3.	this time	ke44-thaon31, ke44-tsoe31
	这次	该趟，　　　该转
4.	that time	ue44-thaon31, ue44-tsoe31
	那次	弯趟，　　　弯转
5.	on time	tsen51-zyu23
	准时	准时
6.	in advance	di22-zie33
	提前	提前
7.	be late	zyu22-tae33
	迟到	迟到
8.	late	ia523
	晚	夜
9.	find out the timing	khaeh43-tsen51
	掐准	掐准
10.	then	a51-mo44-yan31, tae51-zen33-kuaon31
	到时候	挨模样，　　　到辰光

四　对话中的特色词汇

序号	英文	苏州话
1.	lucky	ngah23-kueh43-deu31 ban22-zah3 thie44-ho44-pe31
	运气好	额骨头碰着天花板
2.	happy	kha44-weh3
	开心，快乐	快活

续表

序号	英文	苏州话
3.	matter 事情	zy22-thi33 事体
4.	thus 这样，这么	zeh23-kan23, e44-zan31, geh23-meh3 实梗，　　　哀场，　　　简末
5.	dinner 宴会（聚餐）	ve22-jioh3 饭局
6.	refuse 拒绝	we22-deu33 回头
7.	but 但是（可是）	pih43-kou523, de22-bih23-kou31 不过，　　　　但必过
8.	An ill tongue may do much. 话到口边留半句	ghe22-gho33 tae51-tsy23 tsyu51-po33 pie44-laon33-koh43-tih43-toh3 yih23 ie51-tsy23 tsoe51-chi23 闲话到仔嘴巴边浪角跌笃亦咽仔转去
9.	how 怎么	naeh23-han31 哪哼
10.	suddenly 突然	zah23-san44-deu31 着生头
11.	make sense 有办法（有道理）	yeu231 miae22-deu33 有苗头
12.	where 哪里	lo23-taeh3 哪搭
13.	suffer losses 吃亏	chih43-chiu23 吃亏
14.	ending 结局	seu44-zan33-cih43-kou31 收场结果
15.	how 多么，多少	ci51-ho23 几许
16.	A girl change fast and become more and more beaetiful. 女大十八变	waon22-mae33-o44-deu31 zeh23-poh43-pie31 黄毛丫头十八变
17.	pretty 漂亮（美丽）	piae44-tsyu31 标致
18.	Could it be that...? 难道	ne22-feh23-zen31, ne22-sin33-dae31 难弗成，　　　　难信道
19.	just now 刚才，刚刚	kaon44-tsen31 刚正

续表

序号	英文	苏州话
20.	bad 不行，不好	feh43 le22-se33, feh43-hae51 弗来三，　　弗好
21.	next 下面	gho22-ti44-deu31 下底头
22.	very 非常	ciae44-kue31 交关
23.	alone 一个人	ih43-koe44-tsy31, ih43-ka44-deu31 一干仔，　　　一家头
24.	at 在	leh23-laon31, leh23-he31 勒浪，　　勒嗨
25.	pull a long face 哭丧着脸	khoh43-tsheh43-ou44-la31 哭出乌拉
26.	be going to 准备	ti51-kaon23, ti51-phe23 抵杠，　　抵配
27.	play 玩	beh23-sian523 孛（白）相
28.	fairly 很（非常，十分）	me44 蛮
29.	depressed 郁闷	ae44-tsae31, oh43-seh43 懊糟，　　殟塞
30.	come the bully with 无理取闹且闹个不停	tsoh43-thie44-tsoh43-di31 作天作地
31.	make trouble 大闹	jion22-pin44-pan31 穷冰浜
31.	be jealous 羡慕	nge22-yih3 眼热
32.	insist on 一定	pe51-iae23 板要

五 巩固练习

1 甲：本周六，我这个准女婿被邀请去未来的岳父家吃晚饭。

乙：这顿晚饭可不好吃呀。

甲：还有两天呢，现在心里已经很紧张了。万一审核不过，老婆就要飞走了。

乙：早晚都要见面的，再说人人都这样过来的，没什么大不了的。
甲：听你这么一说，我一下子安心多了。谢谢。

2 甲：很长一段日子没见到你，最近你到哪儿去了？
乙：去年生了一场病，在医院里呆了半年。出院后又到外地的女儿那儿修养了半年。
甲：怪不得老是见不到你。那你现在身体如何？
乙：托你的福，现在倒蛮健康的。

六、参考答案

1

甲：普通话 本　　周六，　　我　这个准　　女婿被邀
　　吴语音 e44-keh3 li22-pa33 loh23 ngou231 ke44-keh3 mae22-ciah43-nyiu44- si31 peh43 iae44-
　　吴语文 哀个礼拜六，我　该个毛　脚女婿畀邀

　　　　　　请　去未来的岳父　　家　吃晚饭。
　　　　　　tshin31 chi523 vi22-le33-keh3 lae22-zan33-nyin31 oh43-li31 chih43 ia44-ve31
　　　　　　请　去未来个老丈人　屋里　吃夜饭。

乙：普通话 这顿 晚饭 可 不 好 吃 呀。
　　吴语音 e44-ten31 ia44-ve31 feh43-da313 hae51 chih43 keh43 a0
　　吴语文 哀顿夜饭弗大好吃个啊。

甲：普通话　就　是 呀！还 有　两　天　呢，现 在 心里　　已经
　　吴语音 zeu22-zy33 ia44　we22-yeu33 lian31-nyih1 neh0　yie22-ze33 sin44-li33-shian31 i44-cin31
　　吴语文　就　是 呀！还 有　两　日　呢，现 在 心 里 向 已经

　　　　　　紧张了。万一 审 核 不 过，老婆　　就要
　　　　　　cin51-tsan33 tse0　ve22-ih3 sen51-ngeh3 feh43 kou523 ka44-tsyu44-bu31 zeu22-iae33
　　　　　　紧　张　哉。万一 审 核 弗 过，家主婆　就要

飞 走 了。
fi44-theh43-tse0
飞 脱 哉。

乙：普通话 早 晚 都 要 见 面 的，再 说 人 人 都 这 样
　　吴语音 tsae51-e23 ze22-iae33 cie51-mie23 keh0 tse44 kaon51 nyin22-nyin33 ze223 zeh23-kan22
　　吴语文 早 晏 侪 要 见 面 个，再 讲 人 人 侪 实 梗

过 来 的，没 什 么 大 不 了 的。
kou44-le31 keh0 m22-peh3 sa523-keh3 dou22- feh43-liae31 keh0
过 来 个，呒 不 啥 个 大 弗 了 个。

甲：普通话 听 你 这 么 一 说， 我 一 下 子 安 心 多
　　吴语音 thin44 ne231 e44-zaon31 ih43 kaon51-meh3 ngou231 ih43-ci44-deu31 oe44- sin31 tou44
　　吴语文 听 倷 哀 状 一 讲 末，我 一 记 头 安 心 多

了。谢 谢。
tse44 zia22-zia33-oh0
哉。谢 谢 喔。

甲：This saturday, I, the all but son-in-law, was invited to visit my future father-in-law's home for dinner.

乙：There's no doubt that it's going to be difficult.

甲：That's what I thought! That's two nights from now. I am getting nervous every day. If they are not pleased with me. My wife will fly away.

乙：Even if you avoid this death, another will find you. Moreover, everyone will have. It's all right.

甲：I'm glad to hear you saying that. I feel that there's a certain weight that lifts. Thank you.

2

甲：普通话 很 长 一 段 日 子 没 见 到 你， 最 近 你 到
　　吴语音 me44-hae31 ih43-tshian23　　fen44 khoe44-cie44-ne44-tse31 tse51-jin23 ne231 tae523
　　吴语文 蛮 好 一 饯　　 勿 看 见 倷 哉，最 近 倷 到

哪儿 去 了?
lo22-taeh3 chi523 tse44
哪搭 去 哉?

乙：普通话 去 年 生 了 一 场 病， 在 医 院 里 呆 了
　　吴语音 jieu22-nyie33 san44-tsy31 ih43-zan231 mae22-bin33 leh23-he31 i44-yoe33-li31 ten44-tsy31
　　吴语文 旧 年 生 仔 一 场 毛病， 勒嗨① 医院 里 蹲 仔

半 年。 出 院 后 又 到 外 地 的 女 儿
poe523-nyie23 tsheh43 yoe231 tsy0 i51-gheu23 yih23 tae523 nga22-di33-keh3 noe22-ng33
半 年。 出 院仔 以 后 亦 到 外 地 个 囡儿

那 儿 修 养 了 半 年。
ue44-mie31 yan231-tsy31 poe523-nyie23
弯 面 养 仔 半 年。

甲：普通话 怪 不 得 总 是 见 不 到 你。 那 么 你 现
　　吴语音 kua44-feh44-teh31 lae231-zy31 khoe44-feh43-zah43-ne33-tse0 geh23-meh3 ne231 yie22-
　　吴语文 怪 弗 得 老 是 看 弗 着 侬 哉。 箇 末 侬 现

在 身 体 如 何?
ze33 sen44-thi31 naeh23-han44 cia0
在 身 体 哪 哼 嘎?

乙：普通话 托 你 的 福， 现 在 倒 蛮 健 康 的。
　　吴语音 thoh43 ne231-keh3 foh43 yie22-ze33 tae523 me44 jie22-khaon44-keh3
　　吴语文 托 侬 个 福， 现 在 倒 蛮 健 康 个。

甲：Long time no see. Where did you go these days?
乙：I took a serious illness last year, and was in hospital for half a year. After I was discharged from the hospital, I recuperated at my daughter's for another half.
甲：No wonder I haven't seen you for a long time. How are you now?
乙：I'm very well. Thank you.

---

① "勒嗨"、"勒浪"、"勒"在意思与语法作用上相当于英文中的介词"在"。

第二单元

学校与教育

一 情景引入

甲：普通话　张　明，你　知不知道，奥　数　竞　赛　的　结　果
　　吴语音　tsan44-min31 ne231 aeh43　shiae51-teh3　ae51--sou31 jin22 - se33 keh0 cih43-kou51
　　吴语文　张　明，侬　阿　晓　得，奥　数　竞　赛　个　结　果

　　　　　　出　来　了。
　　　　　tsheh43-le223 tse44
　　　　　出　来　哉。

第二单元　学校与教育

乙：普通话　真的？　我　考得好不好？
　　吴语音　tsen44-keh3 a0 ngou231 khae51-teh3 aeh43 lin223
　　吴语文　真个啊？　我　考得阿灵①？

甲：普通话　你做好思想准备，作为同桌，我说
　　吴语音　ne231 tsou44-hae31 sy44-sian31 tsen51-be31 tsoh43--we231 don22-tsoh3 ngou231 kaon51-
　　吴语文　俫做好思想准备，作为同桌我讲

　　　　　　出来生怕你身体一时　　吃不消？
　　　　　　tsheh3-le31 tsan44--pho31 ne231 sen44-thi31 ih43-zyu33-deu33-laon31 ghaon22-feh3-zyu31 ia0
　　　　　　出来张怕俫身体一时头浪行弗住呀？

乙：普通话　你不要故弄玄虚　了呀快点告诉我吧。
　　吴语音　ne231 fiae523 ma231 kue44-tsy44-tseh43- -ia0 ghae22-sae33 kae44-sou44-ngou33-ba0
　　吴语文　俫覅卖关子哉呀，豪慅告诉我吧。

甲：普通话　那么你凝神　听好了，陈老师说
　　吴语音　geh23-meh3 ne231 tsoh43-tsen44-zen31 thin44-hae44-tsy31-a0 zen22-lae33-sy31 kaon51
　　吴语文　笛末俫作正神听好仔啊，陈老师讲

　　　　　　你这次考得是好极了，全省第一名！
　　　　　　ne231 e44-thaon31 khae51-teh3 kuaeh43-kuaeh43-ciae523 zie22-san33 deu22-ih3-min31 oh0
　　　　　　俫哀趟考得刮刮叫，全省头一名喔！

乙：普通话　你这人　好不应该，我额头
　　吴语音　ne231-keh3 tsheh43-lae231 feh43-tsoh43-shin44-keh3-a0 ngou231 ngah23-kueh43-deu33-
　　吴语文　俫个赤佬弗作兴②个啊，我额骨头

---

①　吴方言里，"灵"的意思特别丰富。a. 好。此义同"情景引入"中"我考得阿灵？"b. 有效果。"哀个退烧药一吃就灵。"（这个退烧药一吃就有效果。）c. 聪明。"个小囡只脑子灵个啊。"（这个小孩的脑子聪明的。）d. 应验。"陆瞎子老早讲，土根一家以后要发个，现在是发煞啦里，真个灵个。"（陆瞎子以前说，土根一家以后要发，现在是发得很，真的应验了。）e. 机敏。"我个搭档灵个，我一豁翎子，俚马上就接。"（我的搭档真机敏，我稍一暗示，他马上就明白了。）

②　"作兴"与"弗作兴"在意思上并不完全是相反的。在"应该，可以"与"时兴，流行"这两个意义上，他们构成一组反义词。但"作兴"还有"可能，也许"的意思。

上 冷 汗 也 渗 出 来 了。
laon31 lan231-ghoe31 ghaeh23 in523-tseh43-le33-tse31
浪 冷 汗 也① 瀴 出 来 哉。

甲：普通话 开 个 玩 笑 哼。祝 贺 你！
吴语音 zin22-zin33 khe44-sin44-ioh0 tsoh43-ghou33-ne31
吴语文 寻 寻 开 心 哼。祝 贺 倷！

乙：普通话 我 无 论 如 何 没 想 到 得 全 省 第
吴语音 ngou231 ze22-bie33 naeh23-han31 feh43-khoh43-tsan31 no223 zie22-san33 deu22-ih44-
吴语文 我 无 论 哪 哼 弗 壳 张 拿 全 省 头 一

一 名，我 觉 得 隔 壁 班 级 的 王 亮 比 我
min33-keh3 ngou231 koh43-zah3 kaeh43-pih43 pe44-cih43-keh3 waon22--lian33 pi51 ngou231
名 个，我 觉 着 隔 壁 班 级 个 王 亮 比 我

厉 害。你 不 要 让 我 空 欢 喜 一 场，
cih43-kuen51 ne231 fiae523 peh43 ngou231 chih43-tsah43 khon44-sin44-thaon44-doe31-
结 棍。倷 麫 畀 我 吃 只 空 心 汤 团

有 没 有 这 回 事？
oh0 aeh43 yeu231 ka51-zy31
喔，阿 有 介 事？

乙：普通话 你 这 个 书 呆 子！这 个 是 你 平 时 苦 读 的
吴语音 ne231-tsah3 doh23-deu31 ke44-keh43-meh3 zy231 ne231 bin22-zan3 khou51-doh23-keh3
吴语文 倷 只 毒 头！该 个 末 是 倷 平 常 苦 读 个

结 果 呀。
cih43-kou51-ue0
结 果 啘。

---

① 也：读gha223，但视语气情况，会促化成ghaeh23。

甲：Zhang Ming, do you know that the results of International Mathematical Olympiad (IMO) have been announced.

乙：Really? Did I do well or not?

甲：You ought to be prepared for some unpleasantness. I am afraid you can't take it.

乙：Come on. Don't be so mysterious. Please hurry, tell me!

甲：OK. Listen carefully. Mr. Chen said that you had performed...excellent this time! You ranked first in the entire province.

乙：You are kidding me. The cold sweat ran from my forehead，I was horrified.

甲：I was merely joking. Congratulations!

乙：I never thought of it. I think Wang Liang from next class is stronger than me. Don't let my happiness vanish. Is that true?

乙：You bookworm! Your efforts finally paid off.

一　场景对话

1. 甲：普通话　大家　　下　午　好，我　是　新　来　的　同学，
   吴语音　da22-ka33 gho22-me33-tseu31 hae51 ngou231-zy31 sin44-le33-keh4 don22-ghoh3
   吴语文　大　家　下　晚　昼　好，我　是　新　来　个　同　学，

   　　　　我　　叫　李　明。
   　　　　ngou231 ciae523 li22--min33
   　　　　我　　叫　李　明。

   乙：普通话　我　是　班　长　王　亮，我们　全　班　欢　迎　你。
   吴语音　ngou231-zy31 pe44-tsan31 waon22-lian33 nyi231 zie22-pe33 huoe44-nyin33-ne31
   吴语文　我　是　班　长　王　亮，倷　全　班　欢　迎　㑚。

   甲：Good afternoon. I am a new student here. My name is Li Ming.
   乙：Welcome! I am the monitor of the class. My name is Wang Liang.

2. 甲：普通话 请问，电脑培训班<u>什么时候</u>开班？
   吴语音 tsin51-men31 die22-nae33 be22-shiuin44-pe31 sa523- keh3 zen22-kuaon33 khe44-pe44 cia0
   吴语文 请问，电脑培训班 啥个① 辰光 开班嘎？

   乙：普通话 啊呀，最近的一期也 排<u>在</u>下个月
   吴语音 oh43-ioh43 tse51-jin33-keh3 ih43-ji223 yih23 ba22-leh3-laon31 gho31-keh43-ngeh23-
   吴语文 喔唷，最近个一期亦排 <u>勒浪</u> 下个月

   的 2 0 号呢！
   keh43 er22-seh3- ghae31 teh43-le0
   个 2 0 日 得唻！

   甲：Excuse me. When does the computer training class begin?
   乙：I am sorry. The latest one is scheduled for the 20th of next month.

3. 甲：普通话 <u>今天</u>的化学课<u>在</u> 实验室上，同
   吴语音 cin44-tsae44-keh3 ho523-yoh23-khou31 leh23-he31 zeh2-nyie33-seh3 zaon231 don22-
   吴语文 <u>今朝</u>个化学课 勒嗨 实验室上，同

   学们不要<u>忘记</u>带实验报告。
   ghoh23-men31 fiae523 maon22-ci44-theh3 ta523 zeh23-nyie31 pae51- kae23
   学们覅<u>忘记脱</u>② 带实验报告。

   乙：普通话 太棒了！今天<u>下午</u> 上课<u>不</u>会打
   吴语音 theh43-hae51-tse44 cin44-tsae31 gho22-me33-tseu31 zaon231-khou31 feh43-ue523 tan51-
   吴语文 忒好哉！今朝<u>下晚昼</u>上课弗会打

---

① "啥个"、"啥"分别对应普通话中的"什么"和"怎么"。例1："倷讲啥个？"（你说什么？）
例2："我啥个迟到嘎？现在弗是还勮到两点钟么？"（我怎么迟到了？现在不是还没到两点钟吗？）

② "忘记脱"以及下一页中的"做不动主啦里"中的"脱"、"啦里"是苏州话中习惯性加上去的"话搭头"，相当于普通话中的句末助词。

　　　　　　瞌　睡　了。
　　　　　　keh43-tshon44-tse0
　　　　　　瞌　眈　哉。

甲：Today's chemistry class will be held in the laboratory. Dear students, don't forget to bring your lab reports.

乙：Great! I will not doze off in class this afternoon.

4. 甲：普通话　张　强，拜　托　你　晚上　　　　睡　觉　呼　噜　声
　　　吴语音　tsan44-jian31　pa51-thoh43-ne31　ia44-li4-shian31　khuen44-kae31　huen44-dou33-sen44-
　　　吴语文　张　强，拜　托　侬　夜里　向　　瞓　觉　昏　图　声

　　　　　　低　点，可以吗?
　　　　　　in31　chin44-tie31　aeh43-le22-se33
　　　　　　音　轻　点，阿　来　三?

乙：普通话　我　最　好　不　打　呢，倒　是　自己　做　不　了　主
　　吴语音　ngou231　tse51-hae23　feh43-tan51-ne0　tae44-zy31　zy22-ka33　tsou44-feh43-don31　tsyu51-
　　吴语文　我　最　好　弗　打　呢，倒　是　自家　做　弗　动　主啦

　　　　　　唻。影　响　一　个　宿　舍　同　学　睡　觉，真　的
　　　　　　laeh-li0　in51-shian23　ih43-keh43　soh43-seu523　don22-ghoh3　khuen44-kae31　tsen44-keh3
　　　　　　里。影　响　一　个　宿　舍　同　学　瞓　觉，真　个

　　　　　　非常　不　好　意思。
　　　　　　me44　feh43-hae51　i44-sy31　keh0
　　　　　　蛮　弗　好　意思个。

甲：Zhang Qiang, please keep your snoring down at night, will you?

乙：I never hope to do so, but I can not stop it. I am sorry to disturb you guys of the same dorm while you are sleeping.

5. 甲：普通话 臭 小 子，不 及 格 科 目 五 门 一 来，你 算
   吴语音 siae51-tsheh3-lae31 feh43-jih3-kah3 khou44-moh3 ih43-ho23 ih43-le223 ne231 soe523
   吴语文 小 赤 佬，弗 及 格 科 目 一 花①一 来，倷 算

   　　　　在　　　学　　校　里　　读　书　吗，简 直 在
   leh23-laon31 ghoh23-daon31 li22-shian33 doh23-syu44-keh3-a0 cie51-zeh3 leh23-laon31
   勒 浪　学　堂　里　向　读　书　个 阿，简 直 勒 浪

   做 无 用 功！
   o44-khon31
   㧅 空②！

   乙：普通话 爸 爸，我 不 是 最　　差　的，还 有 同 学
   吴语音 tia44-tia31 ngou231 feh43-zy231 tse523-tse31 bih23-ciah3 ke h0 we22-yeu33 doh22-ghoh3
   吴语文 爹 爹，我 弗 是 最 最 蹩脚③个，还 有 同 学

   比 我 更 差。
   ka44-nyi31 the44-pe31 le0
   加 二④ 推 板⑤ 来。

   甲：普通话 哼，你 不 是 最 后 还 光 荣 得 很 呐。
   吴语音 hen0 ne231 feh43-zy231 aeh43-meh43 we223 kuaon44-yon44-saeh43-leh3-ue0
   吴语文 哼，倷 弗 是 阿 末 还 光 荣 煞 勒 啘。

---

① "一花"来代表数词"五"，"一折"代表数词"十二"。
② "㧅空"也可以说为"㧅死空"，带有比较强烈的贬义色彩，是指做落空的事情。
③ "蹩脚"与"推板"在"差劲"的意义上一致，但它们还另有意义。"蹩脚"还作"落魄"解，"推板"还作"相距、将就"解。例1："我就要着破衣裳，让俚当仔我蹩脚哉。"（我就要穿破衣服，让她以为我落魄了。）例2："吃力煞脱哉，离开目的地还推板几许路？"（累死了，离目的地还相距多少路？）例3："倷勿臭讲究哉，就推板点吧。"（你不要臭讲究了，就将就点吧。）
④ "加二"指程度上深。
⑤ 见注释③。

乙：普通话 我 再 怎 么 迟 钝， 也 听 得 出 你
吴语音 ngou231 tse44 naeh23-han31 nge22-moh3-moh3 meh0 gha223 thin44-teh3-tsheh3 ne231
吴语文 我 再 哪 哼 呆 木 木 末， 也 听 得 出 倷

在 讽刺 我。
leh23-he31 den31-ngou31 ue0
勒 嗨 钝 我 啘。

甲：You brat! You failed in five subjects all at once. How on earth did you study at school? You are just wasting time!

乙：Dad, I am not at the bottom of the class. There are still some students who are worse than me.

甲：Well, you are proud, instead of being ashamed of it.

乙：Even the most insensitive person can understand you are digging at me.

6. 甲：普通话 古 话 说 寒 窗 十 年, 现 在 哪 里
吴语音 lae231-gho33-deu31 kaon51 ghoe22-tshaon33 zeh23-nyie31 yie22-ze33 naeh23-han31
吴语文 老 话 头 讲 寒 窗 十 年, 现 在 哪 哼

止 十 年 唷。
tsyu51 zeh23-nyie31 ioh43
止 十 年 唷。

乙：普通话 掐 指 一 算, 倒 真 是 的, 本 科 毕 业 都
吴语音 khaeh43-tsyu51 ih43-soe523 tae44 tsen44-zy31 keh0 pen51-khou23 pih43-nyih43 gha223
吴语文 掐 指 一 算, 倒 真 是 个, 本 科 毕 业 也

要 读 16 年 书, 如果 读 个 博
ia523 doh23 zeh23-loh23 nyie223 syu44 keh43 le0 cia51-sy44-dae31 doh23-keh43 poh43-
要 读 16 年 书 个 来, 假使道 读 个 博

士 起 码 要 20 年。
zy231 chi51-mo31 iae523 er22-seh3 nyie223
士 起 码 要 20 年。

甲：As the old saying goes, after ten years' hard study noticed by none, his fame fills the land once honors are won. Now it seems it will take more than ten years.

乙：That's true. It takes 16 years to get a bachelor degree. For a PhD, you will spend at least 20 years.

7. 甲：普通话 喂，李明，老师已经 走了，你不要 装模作
   吴语音 we231 li231-min31 lae44-sy31 i44-cin31 tseu51 tse44 ne231 fiae523 zian22-saeh3 yeu22-
   吴语文 喂，李明，老师已经 走哉，倷 朆 像 煞 有

   样 假装 看书了。
   ka44-zy31 ka51-lae33-shi51 khoe523 syu44 tse44
   介 事 假 老 戏 看 书 哉。

乙：普通话 张石，你 不可以 胡说八道， 难
   吴语音 tsan44-zah3 ne231 feh43-tsoh43-shin31 tshih43-tsyu51 poh43-taeh43 keh43-a0 ne22-
   吴语文 张石，倷 弗 作兴 七 嘴 八 搭 个 啊，难

   道 我 就 不能 认真 读书！
   sin44-dae31 ngou231 zeu231 feh43--khou44-i31 nyin22-tsen33 doh23 syu44
   信 道 我 就 弗可以认真 读书！

甲：普通话 想不到李明也 变成 读书郎了，
   吴语音 feh43-khoh43-tsan31 li22-min33 gha223 pie51-tsy31 keh43 doh23-syu44-laon31 tse44
   吴语文 弗 壳 张 李明也 变仔个 读书郎哉，

   真是 蹊跷。
   tsen44-keh3-zy31 ih43-toh43-syu51 ti51-leh3 yeu22-bin33-lin31
   真个是 一 笃 水 渧 勒 油 瓶 里。

乙：普通话 你不要 瞧不起人， 说不定我 能
   吴语音 ne231 fiae523 khoe44-feh43-chi31 nyin223 tse0 tshoh43- shin44-dae31 ngou231 khou51-
   吴语文 倷 朆 看弗起人哉，作 兴 道 我 可

靠读书飞黄腾达 呢。
i23 syu44-pae31 fe44--sen31 nae0
以 书 包 翻 身 喏。

甲：Hey, Li Ming, the teacher has left. Do try not to pretend to study.

乙：Zhang Shi, you must do me justice. Can't I study diligently?

甲：I'm surprised that Li Ming had become a studio boy. It is weird.

乙：Don't despise me. Perhaps I will ,get to the top of the tree by study.

8. 甲：普通话 哎 呦，你 干 嘛 突 然 大 叫 一 声, 这 样 子
  吴语音 oh43-ioh43 ne231 tsoh43-sa523 zah23-san44-deu31 da22-chi44-bae33-deu31 ke44-zaon31
  吴语文 喔 唷，俚 作 啥 着 生 头 大 起 爆 头，该 状①

  很 吓 人。
  me44 hah43-nyin33-tae44-kua31 keh0
  蛮 吓 人 倒 怪 个。

乙：普通话 对 不 起，打 扰 了。可 我 太 高 兴,
  吴语音 te44-feh43-chi31 tan51-zae31 tse44 de22-pih3- kou31 ngou231 theh43 khe44-sin31 tse0
  吴语文 对 弗 起，打 扰 哉。但 不 过 我 忒② 开 心 哉，

  不 擅 长 的 物 理 考 了 100 分，真 是
  feh43 zoe22-zan33 keh43 veh23-li31 khae51-tsy23 ih43-pah43-fen31 tsen44-keh3-zy31
  弗 擅 长 个 物 理 考 仔 100 分，真 个 是

  幸 运 极 了。
  ngah23-kueh3-deu31- ban22-zah3 thie44-ho44-pe31
  额 骨 头 碰 着 天 花 板。

---

① "该（哀）状"、"箇状"在苏州话中是使用频率较高的代词，意思为"这样"、"那样"。
② "忒"字在意思与语法作用上都相当于普通话中的副词"太"。

甲：Oh, why do you scream suddenly? It is too horrid.

乙：Sorry to disturb you, but I am so glad that I have got full marks for physics. You know, I am not good at it. I am so lucky.

9. 甲：普通话 我们 新来 的 班 主 任 非但 年 轻 漂 亮，而
   吴语音 nyi231 sin44-le44-keh3 pe44-tsyu44-zen31 fi44-de31 nyie22-chin33 phiae51-lian31 we22-
   吴语文 伲 新来 个 班 主 任 非但 年 轻 漂 亮，还

   且 为 人 爽 快 干 脆，大家 都 很 喜 欢 她。
   kaon33 tsou523 nyin223 zeh23-sy44-zeh23-loh3 da22-ka33 ze223 me44 huoe44-shi44-li44-keh3
   讲 做 人 直丝直络，大家 侪 蛮 欢 喜① 俚个。

   乙：普通话 你们 多么 幸 福啊！我们 可 惨 了，来了一
   吴语音 n22-toh3 ci51-ho23 yin22-foh3 a0 nyi231 zeu231 ze231-kou31 tse44 le22-tsy33 ih43-
   吴语文 尔笃 几许 幸 福啊！伲 就 罪 过哉，来仔一

   个 老 姑 娘， 脾 气 怪怪 的。 那 天
   keh3 lae22-dou33-siae44-tsia31 bi22-chi33 oh43-laeh43- feh43-tsheh3 ue44-nyih3-tsy44-
   个 老大 小姐②，脾 气 齷 齪 弗 出③。弯日仔

   生 气 还 摔 了 一 个 黑 板 擦。
   taeh3 faeh43-hou51 we223 toh43-theh43-ty31 ih43-tsah43 kha44-fen44- pe31
   搭 发 火 还 挓 脱仔 一 只 揩 粉板。

甲：Our new head teacher is as petty as straight. Everybody likes her.

乙：You are so lucky. We are unfortunate enough to have an peculiar old maid. She threw a blackboard eraser down that day when she got angry.

---

① 苏州人习惯把"喜欢"倒过来说成"欢喜"。

② "大小姐"在苏州话中有两层不同的意思：一为家中排行第一的女儿，二为年龄较大但尚未出嫁的姑娘。

③ "齷齪弗出"意思是"说不清，道不明，怪怪的，让人不舒服"。

三、词语贴士

(一) 坊间俗语

序号	英文	苏州话
1.	school 学校	ghoh23-daon31 学堂
2.	go to school 上学	tae44-ghoh3-daon31 到学堂
3.	leave school 放学	faon51-ia44-ghoh3 放夜学
4.	stay in after school 放学后留下来	kue44-ia44-ghoh3 关夜学
5.	study 学习	doh23-syu44 读书
6.	apply oneself to study 认真	yon22-kon33 用功
7.	win the first prize 第一名	baeh23-deu33-2eu31 拔头筹
8.	come last 最后	aeh43-meh43 阿末
9.	secrets 奥妙之处	ho44-deu31 花头
10.	be suitable in every way 样样都好	ho44-hae31 dae22-hae33 花好稻好
11.	to be criticized 挨批评	chih43 ba22-deu33 吃排头
12.	to stand in the corner as punishment 罚站	lih23-pih43-koh3 立壁角
13.	an air 状态，样子	then44-deu33-syu31 吞头势
14.	be struck dumb 一时愣住	deh23-deu33-nge31 突头呆
15.	slow response 反应迟钝	nge22-moh3-moh3 呆木木
16.	a dull 反应迟钝者	nge22-moh3-deu31 呆木头

续表

序号	英文	苏州话
17.	a shrewd man 极精明的人	nyin22-tsin33 人精
18.	efficiently 速度快	soh43-phih43 速劈
19.	have a good relationship with 关系好	nyih23-loh3 热络

（二）学校布局与设施

序号	英文	苏州话
1.	campus 校园	yae22-yoe33 校园
2.	office block 办公区	be22-kon44-chiu31 办公区
3.	academic area 教学区	ciae523-yoh3-chiu31 教学区
4.	living area 生活区	sen44-weh3-chiu31 生活区
5.	classroom 教室	khou44-daon31 课堂
6.	laboratory 实验室	zeh23-nyie33-seh3 实验室
7.	gymnasium 体育馆	thi51-yoh3-kuoe31 体育馆
8.	playground 运动场	tshae44-zan31 操场
9.	dormitory 宿舍	soh43-seu523 宿舍
10.	labrary 图书馆	dou22-syu44-kuoe31 图书馆
11.	electronic reading-room 电子阅览室	die22-tsy33 yueh23-le33-seh3 电子阅览室
12.	multimedia network 多媒体网络	tou44-me33-thi31 maon22-loh3 多媒体网络
13.	multifunctional lecture hall 多功能报告厅	tou44-kon44-nen31 pae523-kae44-thin31 多功能报告厅

（三）学历教育与学位

序号	英文	苏州话
1.	primary school 小学	siae51-ghoh3 小学
2.	middle school 初中	tshou44-tson31 初中
3.	high school 高中	kae44-tson31 高中
4.	college 大专	da22-tsoe33 大专
5.	undergraduate 本科	pen51-khou23 本科
6.	postgraduate 研究生	nyie44-cieu44-san31 研究生
7.	bachelor degree 学士	yoh23-zy31 学士
8.	master degree 硕士	zah23-zy31 硕士
9.	doctor degree 博士	poh43-zy231 博士
10.	post doctorate 博士后	poh43-zy33-gheu31 博士后

（四）学制和学期

序号	英文	苏州话
1.	full-time 全日制	zie22-zeh3-tsyu31 全日制
2.	correspondence course 函授	ghoe22-zeu33 函授
3.	spare-time program 业余	nyih23-yiu31 业余
4.	work-study program 半工半读	poe44-kon44-poe44-doh3 半工半读
5.	short course 短训	toe51-shiuin31 短训
6.	academic year 学年	yoh23-nyie31 学年

续表

序号	英文	苏州话
7.	term	yoh23-ji31
	学期	学期
8.	summer holiday	syu44-ka31
	暑假	暑假
9.	winter holiday	ghoe22-ka33
	寒假	寒假

（五）教育与教学方法

序号	英文	苏州话
1.	praise	piae51-yan23
	表扬	表扬
2.	encourage	kou51-li31
	鼓励	鼓励
3.	admire	tse523-saon23
	赞赏	赞赏
4.	reason	phi44-bin31
	批评	批评
5.	present	seh43-li231
	说理	说理
6.	implant	kuoe44-syu31
	灌输	灌输
7.	inspire	chi51-faeh3
	启发	启发
8.	induce	kue44-naeh3
	归纳	归纳
9.	deduce	ie51-yih3
	演绎	演绎
10.	reson	the44-li31
	推理	推理
11.	analyse	fen44-sih3
	分析	分析
12.	summarize	tson51-cih3
	总结	总结
13.	give lessons	zeu231 khou523
	授课	授课

续表

序号	英文	苏州话
14.	lecture 讲座	kaon51-zou31 讲座
15.	examination 考试	khae51-syu31 考试

（六）教师系列

序号	英文	苏州话
1.	headmaster 校长	yae22-tsan33 校长
2.	dean of students 教导主任	ciae51-dae31 tsyu51-zen31 教导主任
3.	department chairman 系主任	yi22-tsyu44-zen31 系主任
4.	tutor 导师	dae22-sy33 导师
5.	professor 教授	ciae51-zeu31 教授
6.	associate professor 副教授	fu44-ciae44-zeu31 副教授
7.	lecture 讲师	kaon51-sy23 讲师
8.	assistant 助教	zou22-ciae33 助教
9.	head teacher 班主任	pe44-tsyu44-zen31 班主任
10.	counsellor 辅导员	fu51-dae33-yoe31 辅导员
11.	full-time teacher 专职教师	tsoe44-tseh3-ciae44-sy31 专职教师
12.	part-time teacher 兼职教师	cie44-tseh3-ciae44-sy31 兼职教师

（七）学生系列

序号	英文	苏州话
1.	student at school 在校生	ze22-yae33-san31 在校生
2.	graduate 毕业生	pih43-nyih3-san31 毕业生
3.	holdover 留级生	leu22-cih3-san31 留级生
4.	overseas student 留学生	leu22-ghoh3-san31 留学生
5.	auditor 旁听生	baon22-thin44-san31 旁听生
6.	day student 走读生	tseu51-doh3-san31 走读生
7.	residential student 寄宿生	ci44-soh3-san31 寄宿生
8.	government-supported student 公费生	kon44-fi44-san31 公费生
9.	self-supported student 自费生	zy22-fi44-san31 自费生
10.	classmate 同学	don22-ghoh3 同学
11.	deskmate 同桌	don22-tsoh3 同桌
12.	senior 学长	ghoh23-tsan31 学长
13.	former student 校友	yae22-yeu33 校友

（八）课程和活动

序号	英文	苏州话
1.	main course 主修课	tsyu51-seu44-khou31 主修课
2.	sideline course 辅修课	fu51-seu44-khou31 辅修课
3.	specialized course 专业课	tsoe44-nyih3-khou31 专业课

续表

序号	英文	苏州话
4.	basic course 基础课	ci44-tshou44-khou31 基础课
5.	compulsory course 必修课	pih43-seu44-khou31 必修课
6.	elective course 选修课	sie51-seu44-khou31 选修课
7.	social involvement 社会实践	zo22-we33-zeh3-zie31 社会实践
8.	academic activity 学术活动	yoh23-zeh3 weh23-don313 学术活动
9.	entertainment 娱乐活动	nyiu22-loh3 weh23-don313 娱乐活动
10.	sports 体育活动	thi51-yoh3 weh23-don313 体育活动

（九）学习方法和奖励

序号	英文	苏州话
1.	attend the lecture 听课	thin44-khou523 听课
2.	preview 预习	yu22-zih3 预习
3.	review 复习	foh43-zih3 复习
4.	study on one's own 自学	zy22-ghoh3 自学
5.	think 思考	sy44-khae31 思考
6.	scholarship 奖学金	tsian51-yoh3-cin31 奖学金
7.	excellent leader 优秀干部	ieu44-seu44 koe51-bu31 优秀干部
8.	top student 三好生	se44-hae44-san31 三好生

（十）教育功能和效用

序号	英文	苏州话
1.	develop capacity 培养能力	be22-yan33 nen22-lih3 培养能力
2.	build character 塑造性格	sou51-zae31 sin523-kah3 塑造性格
3.	impart knowledge 传授知识	zoe22-zeu33 tsyu44-seh3 传授知识
4.	developing one's individual personalities 发展个性	faeh43-tsoe51 kou44-sin31 发展个性
5.	talent 人才	nyin22-ze33 人才
6.	elite 精英	tsin44-in31 精英
7.	scholar 学者	yoh23-tse31 学者
8.	knowledge 学问	ghoh23-ven31 学问
9.	learned 博学	poh43-yoh43 博学
10.	master ancient and modern learning 博古通今	poh43-khou51 thon44-cin31 博古通今
11.	have a thorough knowledge of both western and Chinese learning 学贯中西	yoh23 khuoe31-tson44- si44 学贯中西

四 对话中的特色词汇

序号	英文	苏州话
1.	work 好，有效果	lin223 灵
2.	fear 生怕	tsan44-pho31 张怕
3.	temporary 一时	ih43-zyu33-deu33-laon31 一时头浪
4.	can not take it 吃不消	ghaon22-feh3-zyu31 行弗住

续表

序号	英文	苏州话
5.	do not 不要	fiae523 覅
6.	be mysterious 故弄玄虚	ma231 kue44-tsy31 卖关子
7.	hurry 赶快	ghae22-sae33 豪悛
8.	carefully 凝神	tsoh43-tsen44-2en31 作正神
9.	excellent 好极了	kuaeh43-kuaeh43-ciae523 刮刮叫
10.	cannot 不应该，不可以	feh43-tsoh3-shin31,feh43 le22-se33 弗作兴，弗来三
11.	forehead 额头	ngah23-kueh3-deu31 额骨头
12.	exude 渗	in523 瀴
13.	never thought of 没料到，想不到	feh43-khoh43-tsan31 弗壳张
14.	strong 厉害	cih43-kuen51 结棍
15.	a windy joy 不能兑现的诺言	khon44-sin44-thaon44-doe31 空心汤团
16.	case 这回事	ka51-zy31 介事
17.	bookworm 书呆子	syu44-doh3-deu31 书毒头
18.	usually 平时	bin231-zan31 平常
19.	what 什么	sa523-keh3 啥个
20.	doze off 瞌睡	kheh43-tshon523 瞌冲
21.	snore 呼噜	huen44-dou31 昏图
22.	sleep 睡觉	khun44-kae31 睏觉

续表

序号	英文	苏州话
23.	five	ih23-ho23
	五	一花
24.	waste time	o44-khon31
	做无用功	挜空
25.	bad	bih23-ciah3, the44-pe31
	差	蹩脚，推板
26.	dig at sb	den231
	讽刺	钝
27.	if	ka51-sy44-dae31
	如果，假使	假使道
28.	put on airs	zian22-saeh3 yeu22-ka44-zy31
	装模作样	像煞有介事
29.	pretend	ka51-lae33-shi31
	假装	假老戏
30.	talk nonsense	tshih43-tsyu44-poh43-teah3, tshih43-feh43-taeh43-poh43, tshih43-taeh43-poh43-taeh43
	胡说八道,胡言乱语	七嘴八搭，七弗搭八，七搭八搭
31.	weird	ih43-toh43 syu51 ti51-leh3 yeu22-bin33-li31
	碰巧，蹊跷	一笃水滴勒油瓶里
32.	get to the top of the tree by study	syu44-pae31 fe44 sen44
	通过读书改换门庭	书包翻身
33.	why	tsoh43-sa523
	干嘛，干什么	作啥
34.	scream suddenly	chi51-bae33-deu31
	突然发出的较响的声音	起爆头
35.	may	tsoh43-shin33
	可能	作兴
36.	straight	zeh23-sy44-zeh23-loh3
	爽快干脆	直丝直络
37.	old maid	lae22-dou33-siae44-tsia31
	老处女	老大小姐
38.	peculiar	oh43-laeh43-feh43-tseh43
	奇怪,说不清道不明	龌龊弗出
39.	throw down	toh43
	摔	丢
40.	blackboard eraser	kha44-fen44-pe31
	黑板擦	揩粉板

五 巩固练习

1 甲：老王，你儿子这次考得好吗？
乙：不好，连平均分数都不到。
甲：他还小呢，一时还不懂学习的窍门，大了就会好的。
乙：看目前这种状态是难呐。
甲：你放心，你那小孩极其精明，没问题的。
乙：如果像你这样说的就好了。

2 甲：小张，你知道吗，黄教授今天下午的讲座取消了。
乙：大家都说黄教授的讲座好极了，我盼望了好久。真是的，害我空欢喜一场。
甲：我也没料到会取消讲座。朋友约我去看电影，我还拒绝了。
乙：那我们索性去看电影吧。

六 参考答案

1

甲：普通话 老 王，你 儿 子 这 次 考得 好 吗？
吴语音 lae22-waon33 ne231 nyi22-tsy33 ke44-thaon31 khae51- teh3 aeh43- lin223- cia0
吴语文 老 王，倷 儿 子 该 趟 考得 阿 灵 嗄？

乙：普通话 不 好，连 平 均 分 数 都 不 到。
吴语音 feh43 lin223 lin223 bin22-ciuin44-fen31 gha223 fen44-tae523
吴语文 弗 灵，连 平 均 分 也 朆 到。

甲：普通话 他 还 小 呢，一 时 不 懂 学 习 的 窍
吴语音 li44 we223 siae51 le0 ih43-zyu33-deu33- laon31 feh43-ton51 doh23-syu44-keh3 chiae44-
吴语文 俚 还 小 咪，一 时 头浪 弗 懂 读 书 个 窍

门，大 了 就 会 好 的。
khe31 dou31-tsy31 zeu22-we33 hae51-keh3
坎，大 仔 就 会 好 个。

乙：普通话 看 目 前 这 种 状 态 是 难 呐。
　　吴语音 khoe523 nge22-men33-zie31 e44-tson31 then44-deu33- syu31 zy231 ne223 leh23-he31
　　吴语文 看 眼 门 前 哀 种 吞 头 势 是 难 勒 嗨。

甲：普通话 你 放心， 你 那 小 孩 极其 精 明， 没
　　吴语音 ne231 faon44-sin31 n44-toh3 keh43 siae51-noe33 zy22-keh3 nyin22-tsin33 m22-peh3
　　吴语文 倷 放 心， 尔 笃 个 小 囡 是个 人 精， 呒 不

　　　　问 题 的。
　　　　ven22-di33- keh3
　　　　问 题 个。

乙：普通话 如 果 像 你 这 样 说 的 就 好 了。
　　吴语音 ka51-sy44-dae31 zian231 ne231 e44-zaon31 kaon51-keh3 zeu231 hae51 tse44
　　吴语文 假 使 道 像 倷 哀 状 讲 个 就 好 哉。

甲：Lao Wang, did your son do well in the exam?
乙：No, below average.
甲：He is still too young to get the hang of study. He will get it as he grows up.
乙：It is difficult for him at present.
甲：Do not worry. No problem. Your boy is exceedingly smart.
乙：I hope so.

2

甲：普通话 小 张， 你 知 道 吗， 黄 教 授 今 天 下 午
　　吴语音 siae51-tsan23 ne231 aeh43 shiae51-teh3 waon22-ciae44- zeu31 cin44-tsae31 gho22-me33-
　　吴语文 小 张， 倷 阿 晓 得， 黄 教 授 今 朝 下 晚

　　　　的 讲 座 取 消 了。
　　　　tseu44-keh3 kaon51- zou31 tshi51-siae23 tse44
　　　　昼 个 讲 座 取 消 哉。

乙：普通话　大家都　说　黄教授　的　讲座　好极
　　吴语音　da22-ka33 ze22-kaon33 waon22-ciae44-zeu33-keh3 kaon51-zou31 kuaeh43-kuaeh43-
　　吴语文　大家侪　讲　黄教授　个　讲座　刮刮

　　　　　了，我　盼望　了　好久。　真是的，害
　　　　　ciae523 ngou231 po44-maon33- tsy31 zan31-yoe31 tse44 tsen44-cia44-hou31 ghe231
　　　　　叫，我　巴望　仔　长远　哉。真家伙，害

　　　　　我　空欢喜一场。
　　　　　ngou231 chih43-tsah3 khon44-sin44-taon44-doe31
　　　　　我　吃只　空心汤团。

甲：普通话　我　也　没料到　会　取消讲座。
　　吴语音　ngou231 gha223 feh43-khoh43-tsan31 ue523-teh3 tshi51- siae23 kaon51-zou31-keh0
　　吴语文　我　也　弗壳张　会得　取消　讲座　个。

　　　　　朋友　约　我　去　看　电影，我　还　拒绝
　　　　　ban22-yeu33 iah43 ngou231 chi523 khoe523 die22-in33 ngou231 we223 we22-deu33-
　　　　　朋友　约　我　去　看　电影，我　还　回头

　　　　　了。
　　　　　theh43-li44-leh43
　　　　　脱俚勒。

乙：普通话　那　我们　索性　去　看　电影　吧。
　　吴语音　geh23 nyi231 soh43-ciah43 chi523 khoe523 die22- in33 ba0
　　吴语文　箇　伲　索脚　去　看　电影　吧。

甲：Xiao Zhang, do you know that this afternoon's lecture of Prof. Wang's is cancelled.

乙：Prof. Wang's lecture is said to be excellent. I've been looking forward to it for a long time. Now a windy joy.

甲：It didn't occur to me that the lecture would be cancelled. My friend asked me to go to the cinema a moment ago. I turned him down.

乙：Let's go to the cinema instead.

第三单元

文化与名人

 情景引入

甲：普通话 泰伯是我们苏州人的始祖。
  吴语音 tha44-pah3 zy231 nyi231 sou44-tseu44-nyin33 keh3 syu51-tsou23
  吴语文 泰伯是倪苏州人个始祖。

乙：普通话 据我所知，泰伯是周太王的长子，
  吴语音 tsae51 ngou231 liae231-cia31 tha44-pah3 zy231 tseu44--tha44-waon33-keh3 dou22-nyi33-
  吴语文 照我了解，泰伯是周太王个大儿

什么 原因 使 他 成 了 吴 国 的 开
tsy31 sa523-keh3 lou22-dae33 pie523-zen33-kon44-tsy31 ghou22-kueh43-keh43 khe44
子, 啥 个 路 道① 变 成 功 仔 吴 国 个 开

创 者?
tshaon44-tse31 tseh43-nae0
创 者 则 呢?

甲: 普通话 因 为 太 王 幼 子 季 历 有 才 干, 这么一来
吴语音 in44-we31 tha44-waon31 siae51-nyi33-tsy31 ci44--lih3 pen51-zy31 dou231 nan22-meh3
吴语文 因 为 太 王 小 儿 子 季 历 本 事 大, 难 末

太 王 想 传 位 给 季 历。泰 伯 知 道 后,
tha44-waon31 sian51 zoe22-we33 peh43 ci44-lih3 tha44-pah3 shiae51-teh43-tsy31 khou51-
太 王 想 传 位 畀 季 历。泰 伯 晓 得 仔 过

就 顺 从 他 父亲的 意思, 让 出 王
gheu31 meh0 zeu231 zen231-tsy31 li44-toh3 ya22-keh3 i44-sy31 nyian231-tsheh3 waon22-
后 末, 就 顺 仔 俚 笃 爷 个 意思, 让 出 王

位, 跑 到 了 南 方。
we33 bae22-tae44-tsy31 noe22-faon33
位, 跑 到 仔 南 方。

乙: 普通话 噢, 泰 伯 倒 真 不 容 易! 王 位 呀, 哪 个
吴语音 oh0 tha44-pah3 tae523 tsen44-keh3 feh43-yon33- yi31 aeh0 waon22-we33 ia0 sa523-nyin31
吴语文 喔, 泰 伯 倒 真 个 弗 容 易 啊! 王 位 呀, 啥 人

---

① "路道"有四层意思。a. 原因, 道理。此义同"情景引入"中"啥个路道变成功仔吴国个开创者?" b. 门路, 途径。"我想买只笔记本电脑, 倷阿有路道?"(我想买个笔记本电脑, 你有没有门路?) c. 本事, 办法。"小张是倷办公室路道最粗个人。"(小张是我们办公室本领最大的人。) d. 行径, 品性。"箇只饭碗头宁可壳脱, 路道弗正, 要俚作啥?"(这份工作宁可丢掉, 行径不正, 要它干嘛?)

　　　　　肯　让？　　生了耳朵　也　没怎么　听　说　过。
　　　　　khen51 nyian231 cia0 san44-tsy31 nyi22-tou33 gha223 fen44-nan31 thin44-seh43-kou31 ue0
　　　　　肯　让　嗄？生仔耳朵　也　覅僧　听说过啘。

　　　　是不是　这样，　人家　才　称　他　为　"让　王"？造
　　　　aeh43-zy31 zeh23-kan44--leh3 nyin22-ka33 tse44 tshen44 li44 we223 nyian22-waon33 zae231-
　　　　阿　是　实　梗　勒　人家　再　称　俚　为　"让　王"，造

　　了　泰　伯　庙　纪　念　他。
　　tsy31 tha44-pah4-miae31 ci51-nyie31 li44 keh43-aeh0
　　仔　泰　伯　庙　纪　念　俚　个　啊。

甲：普通话　是呀，现在　有　些　小辈　跟　泰伯　比　都　不
　　吴语音　ghe22-ia33 yie22-ze33 yeu231-tson31 siae51-pe31 taeh43 tha44-pah43 pi51 gha223 feh43-
　　吴语文　诶呀，现在　有　种　小辈　撘　泰伯　比　也　弗

　　　　能　比，　为了　　　父母　很　小　的　　房子　也
　　　　hae44-pi31 ue0 we22-tsy33 ya22-nyian33-tie31 ciu44-mi44- deu31 vaon22-tsy33 gha223
　　　　好　比　啘，为仔　爷娘　点　鬼咪头　　房子　也

　　　　狠　命　地　争　夺，　　　　甚　至　　连　　头
　　　　tsan44-teh43-leh3 ih43- thie44-syu44-ka31 zen22-tshae44-tsyu44-yu31 lie22- teh3 khou44-
　　　　争　得　勒　一　天　世界，甚　超　至　于　连　得　颗

　　　　　　都　打　破。
　　　　laon33-deu31 gha223 khoh43-khe44 teh43 le0
　　　　浪　头　也　壳　开　得　来。

乙：普通话　这　样　吧，叫　他们　经常　到　泰伯庙里去，是
　　吴语音　ke44-zan33-ba31 ciae523 li44-toh3 cin44-zan31 tae523 tha44-pah3-miae33-li31 chi523 aeh43-
　　吴语文　该　场　吧，叫　俚笃　经常　到　泰伯　庙里去，阿

　　　　　否　能把泰伯的　谦　让　精神　学　点　过来。
　　　　yeu31 sa523 no223 tha44-pah43-keh3 chie44-nyian31 tsin44-zen31 ghoh23-tie31 kou44-le31
　　　　有　啥　拿　泰　伯　个　谦　让　精神　学　点　过来。

甲：Tai Bo is the legendary ancestor of the local people in Suzhou.

乙：As far as I know, Tai Bo was the eldest son of King Tai of the Zhou Dynasty. What caused him to be the inaugurator of Country Wu?

甲：Because King Tai's youngest son Ji Li was talented, King Tai had decided to pass the crown to him. Learning the news, Tai Bo renounced the throne in compliance with his father's desire, and emigrated to the south.

乙：Oh, that is indeed remarkable! Renounce the throne? I never heard of it before. That is the reason why he is called "Rang Wang". People built Tai Bo Temple in memory of him.

甲：There's no comparison between Tai Bo and some of the descendants. They struggled for their parents' little house, and even broke one another's heads.

乙：They should be required to visit Tai Bo Temple frequently to learn to be modest.

 场景对话

1. 甲：普通话 我们 都 是 炎 黄 子 孙 龙 的 传人，中 国 人
   吴音语 nyi231 ze22-zy33 yie22-waon33 tsy51-sen23 lon22-tih3 zoe22-zen33 tson44-kueh43-nyin31
   吴语文 伲 倷 是 炎 黄 子 孙 龙 的 传人，中 国 人

   讲 究 的 是 含 蓄 美。
   kaon51-cieu44-keh3 zy231 ghoe22-shioh43-me51
   讲 究 个 是 含 蓄 美。

乙：普通话 是 的， 青 年 男 女 谈 恋 爱，不 应 该 在
   吴语音 zy31-keh3, tshin44-nyie31 noe22-nyiu33 gaeh23 ban22-yeu33 feh43-tsoh43-shin31 leh23-
   吴语文 是 个， 青 年 男 女 钆 朋 友，不 作 兴 勒

   大 庭 广 众 之 下 抱 在 一 起 的。
   laon31 da22-din33-kuaon44-tson31 zan22-ho33 geh23-leh23 ih43-dae31-keh0
   浪 大 庭 广 众 场 化 孵 勒 一 淘 个。

甲: We Chinese are descendants of the dragon. We put great emphasis on the connotation of beauty.

乙: Yes, the couples who are in love should not hold each other in pubic.

2. 甲: 普通话　跟　你　说　这本《唐 诗 三 百 首》刚　　买
　　　　吴语音 taeh43-ne231-kaon51 ke44-pen31 daon22-syu33 se44- pah43-seu31 kaon44-chiae31 ma231-
　　　　吴语文 搭　倷　讲　该本《唐 诗 三 百 首》 刚 巧　买

　　　　来，　　全　　　新的，看　的　时　候　爱　惜些。
　　　　teh43-le31 tshaeh43- kuaeh43-laeh3 sin44 le0 khoe523-keh3 zen22-kuaon44 e523-sih43-tie31
　　　　得来，擦　刮　拉新哎，看　个　辰　光　爱　惜点

　　　　怎么 又 折页　　了？不要　说　正好　又　有
　　　　oh0 naeh23-han31 yih23 iae51-chi33-le31 tse0　fiae523 kaon51 yih23-zy31 kaeh43-maon33
　　　　喔。哪哼　亦　天　起　来　哉？朆　讲　亦是　夹　忙

　　　　要　紧　事　情。
　　　　deu33-li31 phaon51-chie44-cin31
　　　　头　里　胖　牵　筋①。

乙: 普通话　知　道　了，老 妈。您 已 经　　说过　　好　多
　　　　吴语音 shiae51-teh43 tse44　m44-ma31 ne231 i44-cin31 kaon51-kou23 feh43-tsyu51 ci51-ho23
　　　　吴语文 晓　得　哉，姆　妈。倷 已 经　 讲过　 弗止 几 许

　　　　遍　了，年 纪 不 大，怎　么
　　　　pie44-sou31 tse44 nyie22-ci33 feh23-dou231 naeh23-han31 zeh23-kueh43-loe33-boe31
　　　　遍　数　哉，年 纪 弗 大，哪 哼 实 骨 乱 盘②

---

① "夹忙头里瘖牵筋"，原意是说，某人正忙碌之中，突然大腿抽筋了，或者叫脚抽筋了，来比喻越忙越乱。后来比喻紧要关头，突然发生意外。苏州还有一句话，意思与此类似，叫做"夹忙头里炒螺蛳"。

② "实骨乱盘"意为"絮絮叨叨嘀咕不停"。

没完没了了?
m22-peh3 ti51 tse44 nau0
呒不底哉呢?

甲: I have bought the book "The Three Hundred Tang Poems" just now. Look, it is a brand-new copy. Take care of it while reading. Why did you fold up the pages again? Don not say there is just something important to do.

乙: I've got it, Mum. You have repeated it many times. You can't be so garrulous at your age.

3. 甲: 普通话 老张,你早。你一向 忙得 很,
   吴语音 lae22-tsan33 ne231 tsae51 ne231 ih43-shian523 maon22- teh43-leh3 feh43-teh43 liae231
   吴语文 老张, 侬早。侬一向 忙得了弗得了

   今天 怎么 有 空 到 公 园 里 来
   teh43 le0 cin44-tsae31 naeh23-han31 yeu31 khon523 tae523 kon44--yoe33-li31 le223
   得来,今朝 哪哼 有 空 到 公 园里来

   走 走?
   daon231- daon31 tseh43 neh
   趟 趟 则呢?

乙: 普通话 喔,原来是老李,我 上 周 退休了。
   吴语音 oh43 nyioe22-le33-zy31 lae22-li33 ngou231 zaon22- keh3-li22-pa33 the51-shieu23 tse44
   吴语文 喔,原来是老李,我 上 个礼拜退休哉。

甲: 普通话 你突然 空 下来, 适应吗?
   吴语音 ne231 zah23-san44-deu31 khon523-gho33-le31 tseh43 meh0 aeh43 seh43-in44 cia44
   吴语文 侬眷生头 空 下来则末,阿适应嘎?

乙: 普通话 没 问题。我 早晨 到 公园
   吴语音 m22-peh3 ven22-di23 keh0 ngou231-meh3 tsae44-laon33-shian31-tae523 kon44-yoe33-
   吴语文 呒不 问题个。我 末早浪向 到 公园

里 打 打 太 极 拳，谈 谈 山 海 经， 中 午
li31 tan51-tan31 tha44- jih23-jioe31 de22-de33 se44-he44-cin31 tson44-laon33-shian31
里 打 打 太 极 拳， 谈 谈 山 海 经， 中 浪 向

吃 过　　　　　 饭　 睡　　　 一 觉，晚上 喝 一
chih43-kou44- tsy31 tson44-ve31 meh0 khuen51 theh43-ih43 hueh43 ia44-li31 mi44-tie31
吃 过 仔 中 饭 末 　睏 脱 一 吻， 夜里 咪 点

点 酒， 日 子 过 得 蛮 舒 坦。
lae22-tseu33 nyih23- ciah43 kou523-teh3 le22-teh43-keh43 loh23-we31
老 酒， 日 脚 过 得 来 得 个 乐 胃。

甲：Good Morning, Lao Zhang. You are always busy. Why are you so free today to come to the park?
乙：Hi, Li. Long time no see! I was retired last week.
甲：Can you adapt yourself to your leisure time?
乙：Sure. Every morning I come to the park to chat and play Taiji, and take a nap after lunch. In the evening I usually have a little wine . What a wonderful day.

4. 甲：普通话 不 好 意 思， 又 迟 到 了。 近来 交了 霎
吴语音 feh43-hae51 i44-sy31 yih23 zyu22-tae33 tse44 ke44-tshian31 kae44-tsy31 mo22-khou44-
吴语文 弗 好 意思，亦 迟 到 哉。 该馀 交仔 暮 库

运，　　　 今 天 不 知　　　　 怎 么 回
yiuin31 laeh23- li31 cin44-tsae31 feh43 shiae51-teh3 yih23-zy31 naeh23-han31 ih43-tsaon23
运 啦里，今 朝 弗 晓 得 亦 是 哪 哼 一 桩

事，　　 经 过 西 园 时　　　　 挤 得 不 得 了，
zy22-thi33 cin44-kou31 si44-yoe33-keh3 zen22-kuaon33 gaeh23-teh43 feh43-teh43 liae231
事 体，经 过 西 园 个 辰 光 轧 得 弗 得 了，

加上为了抢道,还有人　　　吵架,
ka44-zaon31 we231-tsy31 tshian51-dae31 we22-yeu33 nyin223 leh23-laon31 sian44-mo31
加上为仔抢道,还有人勒浪相骂,

甚至　　打架
zen22- tsyu44-yu31 sian44-tan31
甚至于相打。

乙：普通话 今天是二月十九,观音娘娘生日,
吴语音 cin44-tsae44-zy31 nyi22-ngeh3 zeh23-cieu31 kuoe44- in44-nyian33-nyian31 san44-nyih3
吴语文 今朝是二月十九,观音娘娘生日

大家都去庙里烧香,　西园那儿
ia0 da22-ka33 ze223 chi523 miae231-li31 sae44 shian44 tseh43 ue0 si44-yoe31 geh23- mie31
呀,大家侪去庙里烧香则哦,西园箇面

肯定挤的。但是你迟到　肯定
khen51-din31 gaeh23-keh3 de22-pih43-kou31 ne231 zyu22-tae33 meh0 khen51-din31
肯定轧个。但不过侬迟到末肯定

连累我们一起倒霉。
ta44-le31 shian44- lin31 ih43-dae231 chih43 mah23-tsoh43 tse0
带累乡邻一淘吃麦粥哉。

甲：Sorry, I am late again. It was really bad luck on me recently. When I passed Xiyuan Temple today, the road was awfully crowded. Besides, some people were quarrelling and fighting for carving up the rest of the traffic on the way.

乙：Today is February 19th, Guanyin's birthday. Everyone will go to Xiyuan Temple to burn incense and pray. There must be crowded. But you'll do us fellow members all in because of your lateness.

5. 甲：普通话 小李演的 唐伯虎 做起事来 莽撞
　　吴语音 siae51-li31 ie51-keh3 daon22-pah43-hou31 tsou523- chi31 zy22-thi33-le31 deu22-ng33-
　　吴语文 小李演个 唐伯虎 做起事体来 投五

　　　　　　冒失， 说起话来 语无伦次， 哪里
　　　　　　deu33-loh23 kaon51-chi31 ghe22-gho33-le31 tshih43-jiae33-poh43 lih23 lo31-taeh3
　　　　　　投六①，讲起闲话来 七翘八裂②，哪搭

　　　　　　有才子的样子喔。
　　　　　　yeu231 ze22-tsy33 keh43 yian22-tsy33 cia0
　　　　　　有才子个样子嘎。

乙：普通话 是的， 低级趣味， 疯疯癫癫， 简
　　吴语音 zy231-keh3 nyoh23-mo31 taon44 yeu231-tshi31 zeh23- se44-tie44-shi44-shi31 cie51-
　　吴语文 是个， 肉麻当有趣③， 十三点兮兮④，简

　　　　　　直 糟透了， 真 受不了。他好
　　　　　　zeh23-zy31 ih43- thaeh43-ghou33-dou31-ue0 tsen44-keh3 chih43-feh43-siae31 li44 hae51-
　　　　　　直是一塌糊涂碗，真个吃弗消。俚好

　　　　　　歹 也 是 个 有身价的人，这么 做， 算 怎么 一回事！
　　　　　　wa31 ghaeh23-zy33-keh3 mo22-tsy33 geh23-zaon31 tsou523 soe523 sa523 ih43-tsheh43 nau0
　　　　　　坏 也 是 个 模子⑤，箇状 做，算 啥 一 出 呢！

---

① "投五投六"与下页的"七翘八裂"、"肉麻当有趣"、"十三点兮兮"、"一塌糊涂"均是贬义词，意为言行举止不上台面。
②③④ 同上。
⑤ "模子"一词在苏州话中的意思比较有趣，同一个词语，却集褒贬于一体。它共有四层意思：a.身坯。"哀个人是个大模子。"（这个人身坯很大。）b.有勇气、胆量、魄力的人。"该个警察是个模子，一倌仔赤手空拳对付三个拿刀个坏人。"（这个警察胆色过人，一人赤手空拳对付三个持刀歹徒。）c.有实力的人，多指经济实力雄厚。"俚穷有钞票个，是个模子。"（他很有钱，是个大老板。）d.在公共场所进行倒卖等非法活动的人。"看，市场门口个个人，是专门倒卖外币个模子。"（看，市场门口那个，是专门倒卖外币的人。）

第三单元　文化与名人

甲：Xiao Li appeared reckless and incoherent in the role of Tang Bohu. A wit should not be like that.

乙：Yes, his acting impressed me as being cheapjack and crazy. It was a total wreck! I am really fed up with it! He is a celebrity after all. Why did he do so?

6. 甲：普通话　我　最近　要　到　美国　去　做　访问　学者，
　　　吴语音　ngou231 tse51-jin31 iae523 tae523 me51-kueh3 chi523 tsou523 faon51-ven31 yoh23-tse31
　　　吴语文　我　最近　要　到　美国　去　做　访问　学者

　　　　　　送　什么　<u>给</u>　外国人　比较　好？
　　　　　　tseh0 son523 sa51-meh23-zy31 peh43 nga22-kueh43-nyin31 pi51-ciae33 hae51
　　　　　　则，送　<u>啥</u>　物事　畀　外国人　比较　好？

乙：普通话　你　好　<u>傻</u>　　　喔，当然　是　刺绣　作品
　　　吴语音　ne231-tsah3 aeh43-moh43-lin31 aeh0 taon44-zoe33- zy31 tshy523-seu31 tsoh43-phin51
　　　吴语文　侬　只　<u>阿木林</u>①啊，当然　是　刺绣　作品

　　　　　　罗。苏绣　那么　有名，沈寿　开创　的"仿
　　　　　　ue0 sou44-seu31 zeh23-kan23 yeu231 min223 sen51-zeu31 khe44-tshaon44- keh3 faon51-
　　　　　　睕。苏绣　<u>实梗</u>　有名，沈寿　开创　个"仿

　　　　　　真绣"已经　让　人　<u>惊叹不已</u>　了，现在　的
　　　　　　tsen44-seu31 i44-cin31 nyian231 nyin223 de22-nge33-loh3-tsin31 tse44 yie22-ze33-keh3
　　　　　　真绣"已经　让　人　<u>弹眼落睛</u>②哉，现在　个

　　　　　　"乱绣针""双面绣"更　　　神奇，外国人
　　　　　　loe22-tsen44-seu31 saon44-mie33-seu31 ka44-nyi31 shi44-ji31 nga22-kueh3-nyin31
　　　　　　"乱绣针""双面绣"<u>加二</u>　稀奇，外国人

---

① "阿木林"有"笨蛋"、"傻瓜"的意思，但不含贬义，往往是对熟悉的、关系友好的对象说的。
② "弹眼落睛"形容看到的事物特别突出，特别吸引人的眼球，让人不由自主惊叹不已。

一 定 喜 欢。
khen51-din31 huoe44-shi31 keh0
肯 定 欢 喜 个。

甲: I am going to study in the United States as a visiting scholar. What present shall I send to foreigners?

乙: How stupid can you get! Embroidery, of course. The simulated embroidery created by Shen Shou is so famous that it won people's great admiration. Random stitch embroidery and double-sided embroidery are very rare in foreign countries, they will like it.

7. 甲: 普通话 雨 前 碧 螺 春 毕 竟 不 一 样, 香 得 很,
   吴语音 yiu22-zie33 pih43-lou33-tshen31 tae44-ti31 feh43- ih43-yian31 shian44-teh3-leh3 feh43-
   吴语文 雨 前 碧 螺 春 到 底 弗 一 样, 香 得 勒 弗

   不 愧 为 又 名 "吓 煞 人 香"。而
   teh43-liae231 feh43- gue231 we231 yeu231 min223 hah43-saeh43 nyin223 shian44 we22-
   得 了, 弗 愧 为 又 名 "吓 煞 人 香"。还

   且 喝 进 嘴 里 苦 中 带 甜, 苦 滋 滋, 甜
   ka44 chih43-tae523 tsyu51-li31 khou51-tson33 ta523 die223 khou51-tsi44-tsi31 die22-
   加 吃 到 嘴 里 苦 中 带 甜, 苦 济 济, 甜

   津 津, 感 觉 特 别 舒 服。
   tsin44-tsin31 koe51-cioh3 deh23-bih3 seh43-i523
   津 津, 感 觉 特 别 适意。

乙: 普通话 我 也 要 去 买 一 斤 尝 尝, 这 个 月
   吴语音 ngou231 gha22-iae33 chi523 ma231-ih3-cin31 zaon22-zaon33-khoe31 e44-keh3 ghae22-
   吴语文 我 也 要 去 买 一 斤 尝 尝 看, 哀个 号

奖　金　当　作　没有　拿　到。
deu33 tsian51-cin23 phi44- zyu31 fen44 no22-zah3
头　奖　金　譬如①　齆　拿　着。

甲：Biluochun Tea, picked before the Grain Rain, is unusual. It smells sweet and is locally known as "Fearful Incense". What's more, it tastes good, in a kind of bittersweet way. You will feel nice because of the bitter and sweet aftertaste left in your mouth.

乙：I will try some. Just forget about the bonus this month.

8. 甲：普通话　王　阿姨，你　手　里　拿 的 <u>什么　东西</u>，<u>那　么　当　心</u>！
吴语音 waon22-a44-yi31 ne231 seu51-li31 no22-keh3 sa523 meh23-zy31 cia0 geh23-zan31 taon44-sin31
吴语文　王　阿姨，倷　手　里　拿　个　<u>啥　物　事　嗄</u>？<u>箇　场　当　心</u>！

乙：普通话　这　　是　苏　州　有　名　的　桃　花　坞　木　刻。
吴语音 ke44-keh3-zy31 sou44-tseu31 yeu231 min223 keh43 dae22-ho44-ou31 moh23-kheh3
吴语文　该　个　是　苏　州　有　名　个　桃　花　坞　木　刻。

因　为　快　过　年　了，买　<u>回　来</u>　<u>给</u>　家　里
in44-we31 iae523 kou523 nyie223 tse44 ma231 tsoe44-le31 peh43 oh43- li33-shian31
因　为　要　过　年　哉，买　<u>转　来</u>　<u>畀</u>　屋　里　向

增　添　些　喜气。
tsen44-ka44-tie31 shi51-chi33
增　加　点　喜气。

甲：Ms Wang, what is that in your hand? It seems very precious.

乙：I've got some Taohuawu Woodcutting New Year Pictures which are famous in Suzhou. It'll soon be New Year. I bought them to make some festival atmosphere in my house.

---

① "譬如"一词的意义与普通话中"比如"的意思差别很大，在苏州话中，"譬如"为"当它是"之意，例：补发的钱被小偷偷了，当它没加到工资。（补发格铜钿畀贼骨头偷脱哉，譬如齆加着工资。）

9. 甲：普通话 我们 家乡 城 门 一般 以 东 南 西 北 来命
    吴语音 nyi231 cia44-shian31 zen22-men33 ih43-pe23 no223 ton44-noe33-si44-poh43 le223 min231
    吴语文 伲 家乡 城 门 一般 拿 东 南 西 北 来 命

    名， 苏州 怎么 有"胥门"这样 的 城
    min223 keh0 sou44-tseu31 naeh23-han31 yeu23 si44-men31 geh23-zan33-keh3 zen22-
    名 个，苏州 哪嗥 有"胥门"箇 场 个 城

    门？
    men33 keh43 neh0
    门 个 呢？

乙：普通话 喔，那 是 为了 纪念 春 秋 时 从 楚
    吴语音 oh43 geh23-keh3-zy31 we231-tsy31 ci523-nyie31 tshen44-tsheu44-zyu31 zon223 tshou51-
    吴语文 喔，箇 个 是 为仔 纪念 春 秋 时 从 楚

    国 逃 过 来 帮 助 吴 国 的 伍 子 胥。
    kueh3 dae22-kou44- le31 paon44-zou31 ghou22-kueh3 keh43 ou44- tsy44-si31 keh0
    国 逃 过 来 帮 助 吴 国 个 伍 子 胥 个。

甲： The gates of our city are usually named after north, south, east, and west. What does "Xumen" refer to?

乙： To commemorate WuZixu, who escaped from Country Chu to help the King of Country Wu.

10. 甲：普通话 李 明， 围 棋 棋谱 带来了吗？
    吴语音 li22-min33 we22-ji33 ji22-pu33 an44 ta51-teh3-le31
    吴语文 李 明，围 棋 棋谱 覅 带 得 来？

乙：普通话 啊呀，我 又 忘 了。真的 是 太 健忘
    吴语音 aeh43-ia44 ngou231 yih23 maon22-ci33-theh3 tse44 tsen44-keh3-zy31 dou22-bi33-zaon31
    吴语文 啊呀，我 亦 忘 记 脱 哉！真 个 是 肚 皮 上

了。

tsan51 tshin44-cin44-tse31

长　青　筋　哉。

甲：Li Ming, have you brought the chess manual of Weiqi?
乙：Oh, dear! I forgot it again. Oh no, how forgetful of me.

三 词语贴士

（一）神话人物

序号	英文	苏州话
1.	Yellow Emperor 黄帝	waon22-ti33 黄帝
2.	Emperor Yan 炎帝	yie22-ti33 炎帝
3.	Shen Nong 神农	zen22-non33 神农
4.	Fu Hsi 伏羲	voh23-shi31 伏羲
5.	Emperor Yao, Emperor Shun and Emperor Yu 古圣王尧舜禹	kou51-sen44-waon31 yae22-sen44-yu31 古圣王尧舜禹
6.	Jade Emperor 玉皇大帝	nyioh23-waon33-da33-ti31 玉皇大帝
7.	Queen Mother of the West 皇母娘娘	waon22-m33-nyian33-nyian31 皇姆娘娘
8.	The three gods of fortune, prosperity and longevity 福禄寿三星	foh43-loh3-zeu31 se44-sin31 福禄寿三星
9.	Match-maker 月老	nyiuih23-yia3-lae33-zen31 月下老人

(二) 神话故事

序号	英文	苏州话
1.	Pan Gu created the heaven. 盘古开天	boe22-kou33 khe44 thie44 盘古开天
2.	Nv Wa mended the sky. 女娲补天	nyiu22-kua33 phu51 thie44 女娲补天
3.	Hou Yi shot the sun. 后羿射日	gheu22-yi33 zo223 zeh23 后羿射日
4.	Chang'e flied to the moon. 嫦娥奔月	zan22-ngou33 pen44 nyiueh23 嫦娥奔月
5.	Da Yu controlled the floods. 大禹治水	da22-yu33 zyu231 syu51 大禹治水
6.	The Eight Immortals crossed the sea. 八仙过海	poh43-sie23-kou51-he31 八仙过海
7.	Yu Gong removed mountains. 愚公移山	nyiu22-kon33 yi223 se44 愚公移山
8.	Niu Lang and Zhi Nv meet on a bridge of magpies across the Milky Way. 鹊桥相会	tshiah43-jiae223 sian44-we31 鹊桥相会

(三) 中国宗教

序号	英文	苏州话
1.	Buddhism 佛教	veh23-ciae31 佛教
2.	temple 佛寺	ghou22-zaon33-daon31 和尚堂
3.	karma 因果报应	in44-kou44-pae44-in31 因果报应
4.	Guanyin Bodhisatta 观音	kuoe44-in31 观音
5.	Buddhist monk 和尚	ghou22-zaon33 和尚
6.	Buddhist nun 尼姑	sy44-kou31 师姑
7.	Taoism 道教	dae22-ciae33 道教

续表

序号	英文	苏州话
8.	temple 道观	dae22-kuoe33 道观
9.	Taoist priest 道士	dae22-zy33 道士

（四）古代圣人

序号	英文	苏州话
1.	the greatest sage and teacher Confucius 至圣孔丘	tsyu44-sen31 khon51-chieu44 至圣孔丘
2.	the second sage Mencius 亚圣孟轲	ia44-sen31 man22-khou33 亚圣孟轲
3.	the historical records sage Sima Qian 史圣司马迁	sy51-sen31 sy44-mo231-tshie44 史圣司马迁
4.	the calligraphy sage Wang Xizhi 书圣王羲之	syu44-sen31 waon22-shi44-tsyu44 书圣王羲之
5.	the cursive style calligraphy sage Zhang Xu 草圣张旭	tshae51-sen31 tsan44-shioh43 草圣张旭
6.	the painting sage Wu Daozi 画圣吴道子	gho22-sen33 ng22-dae33-tsy31 画圣吴道子
7.	the chess sage Huang Longshi 棋圣黄龙士	ji22-sen33 waon22-lon33-zy31 棋圣黄龙士
8.	the music sage Li Guinian 乐圣李龟年	yoh23-sen31 li22-kue44-nyie231 乐圣李龟年
9.	the Tang poetry sage Du Fu 诗圣杜甫	syu44-sen31 dou22-fu33 诗圣杜甫
10.	the Song poetry sage Su Shi 词圣苏轼	zy22-sen33 sou44-seh3 词圣苏轼
11.	the opera sage Guan Hanqing 曲圣关汉卿	chioh43-sen31 kue44-hoe44-chin44 曲圣关汉卿
12.	the prose sage Ou Yangxiu 文圣欧阳修	ven22-sen33 eu44-yan223-seu44 文圣欧阳修
13.	the tea sage Lu Yu 茶圣陆羽	zo22-sen33 loh23-yu31 茶圣陆羽
14.	the wine sage Du Kang 酒圣杜康	tseu51-sen31 dou22-khaon33 酒圣杜康

续表

序号	英文	苏州话
15.	the medicine sage Zhang Zhongjing 医圣张仲景	i44-sen31 tsan44-zon231-cin51 医圣张仲景
16.	the Chinese pharmacology sage Li shizhen 药圣李时珍	yiah23-sen31 li22-zyu223-tsen44 药圣李时珍
17.	the science sage Zhang Heng 科圣张衡	khou44-sen31 tsan44-ghen223 科圣张衡
18.	the Chinese god of war Guan Yu 武圣关羽	vu22-sen33 kue44-yiu31 武圣关羽
19.	the military science sage Sun Wu 兵圣孙武	pin44-sen31 sen44-vu31 兵圣孙武
20.	the strategy sage Zhang Liang 谋圣张良	meu22-sen33 tsan44-lian223 谋圣张良

(五) 古代典籍

序号	英文	苏州话
1.	The Four Books and Five Classics 四书五经	sy44-syu44-ou44-cin44 四书五经
2.	Historical Records 史记	sy51-ci31 史记
3.	Comprehensive Mirror for Aid in Government 资治通鉴	tsy44-zyu33-thon44-cie31 资治通鉴
4.	Compendium of Materia Medical 本草纲目	pen51-tshae44-kaon44-moh3 本草纲目
5.	The Story of the Stone 红楼梦	ghon22-leu33-mon31 红楼梦
6.	Heroes of the Marshes 水浒	syu51-hou23 水浒
7.	Pilgrimage to the West 西游记	si44-yeu33-ci31 西游记
8.	The Romance of Three Kingdoms 三国演义	se44-kueh3 ie51-nyi31 三国演义
9.	Strange Tales of a Lonely Studio 聊斋志异	liae22-tsa33 tsyu51-yi31 聊斋志异
10.	The Scholars 儒林外史	zyu22-lin33-nga33-sy31 儒林外史

（六）文化艺术

序号	英文	苏州话
1.	pictograph 象形字	zian22-yin33-zy31 象形字
2.	Chinese zither 古琴	kou51-jin223 古琴
3.	Weiqi 围棋	we22-ji33 围棋
4.	calligraphy 书法	syu44-faeh3 书法
5.	Chinese painting 国画	kueh43-gho231 国画
6.	embroidery 刺绣	tshy51-seu523 刺绣
7.	papercuts 剪纸	tsie51 tsy51 剪纸
8.	seal cutting 篆刻	zoe22-kheh3 篆刻

（七）传统节日

序号	英文	苏州话
1.	New Year's Eve 除夕	zyu22-zih3, dou22-nyie33-ia31 除夕，大年夜
2.	Spring Festival 春节	tshen44-tsih3 春节
3.	Lantern Festival 元宵	nyioe22-siae33 元宵
4.	Tomb Sweeping Day 清明	tshin44-min31 清明
5.	Dragon Boat Festival 端午	toe44-ng31 端午
6.	Double Seventh Festival 七夕	tshih43-zih43 七夕
7.	Mid-Autumn Festival 中秋	tson44-tsheu31 中秋
8.	Double Ninth Festival 重阳	zon22-yan33 重阳

(八) 民俗活动

序号	英文	苏州话
1.	paste up Spring Festival couplets 贴春联	thih43 tshen44-lie31 贴春联
2.	visit the temple fair 逛庙会	teu44 miae22-we33 兜庙会
3.	guess the lantern riddles 猜灯谜	tshe44 ten44-me31 猜灯谜
4.	dragon dance 舞龙灯	diae22-lon33-ten31 调龙灯
5.	high-stilt walking 踩高跷	daeh23 kae44-chiae31 踏高跷
6.	offer sacrifice to the ancestors 祭祖先	sae51 tsou51-ven31 扫祖坟
7.	dragon boat race 赛龙舟	se523 lon22-zoe33 赛龙船
8.	gaze at the full moon on the Middle Autumn Festival 赏月亮	tseu51 ngeh23-lian31 走月亮

(九) 与苏州相关的名人

序号	英文	苏州话
1.	Tai Bo 泰伯	tha44-pah3 泰伯
2.	Wu Zixu 伍子胥	ou44-tsy44-si31 伍子胥
3.	Lu Ji 陆机	loh23-ci31 陆机
4.	Bai Juyi 白居易	bah23-ciu44-yi31 白居易
5.	Lu Guimeng 陆龟蒙	loh23-kue44-mon31 陆龟蒙
6.	Fan Zhongyan 范仲淹	ve22-zon33-ie31 范仲淹
7.	Fan Chengda 范成大	ve22-zen33-da31 范成大

续表

序号	英文	苏州话
8.	Tang Yin 唐寅	daon231-yin31 唐寅
9.	Zhu Yunming 祝允明	tsoh43-iuin44-min31 祝允明
10.	Wen Zhengming 文徵明	ven22-tsen44-min31 文徵明
11.	Feng Menglong 冯梦龙	von22-mon33-lon31 冯梦龙
12.	Jin Shengtan 金圣叹	cin44-sen523-the31 金圣叹
13.	Wang Zhoushi 王周士	waon22-tseu44-zy31 王周士
14.	Sun Yunqiu 孙云球	sen44-yiuin33-jieu223 孙云球
15.	Mao Zonggang 毛宗岗	mae33-tson44-kaon31 毛宗岗
16.	Shen Shou 沈寿	sen51-zeu31 沈寿
17.	Gu Jiegang 顾颉刚	kou44-cih3-kaon44 顾颉刚
18.	Ye Shengtao 叶圣陶	yih23-sen51-dae223 叶圣陶

（十）苏州风俗

序号	英文	苏州话
1.	On January 5th in the Chinese lunar calendar, the local people in Suzhou welcome the god of wealth. 正月初五接财神	tsen44-ngeh3 tshou44-ng31 tsih43 lou22-deu33 正月初五接路头①
2.	On February 2nd in the Chinese lunar calendar, local people in Suzhou eat Chengyao Gao (glutinous rice dumplings). 二月初二撑腰糕	lian22-ngeh3 tshou44 lian231 tshan44 iae44-kae44 两月初两撑腰糕

① "路头神"是吴地所信奉的财神。民间习俗正月初五是他的生日，要祭晒迎接，颇为壮观。

续表

序号	英文	苏州话
3.	On February 2nd in the Chinese lunar calendar, local people in Suzhou celebrate the birthday of Queen of All Flowers'.	lian22-ngeh3 zeh23-nyi31 hou51-chieu23 ho44-tsae31
	二月十二虎丘花神节	两月十二虎丘花朝
4.	Local people in Suzhou enjoy the sight of peonies three days after Grain Rain.	koh43-yu231 se44-tsae31 khoe523 mae22-te33
	谷雨三朝看牡丹	谷雨三朝看牡丹
5.	Local people in Suzhou go to the temple fair at Tomb Sweeping Day.	zaon22-nyioe33 se44-daon31 khoe44-we31
	清明山塘看会	上元山塘看会
6.	On April 14th in the Chinese lunar calendar Ya Shen Xian falls.	sy51-ngeh3 zeh23-sy523 gaeh23 zen33-sie31
	四月十四轧神仙	四月十四轧神仙
7.	On Dragon Boat Festival local people in Suzhou hold a memorial ceremony for Wu Zixu.	toe44-ng31 tsi44-ou44-tsy31 nyin223 syu51-sie23
	端午祭伍子迎水仙	端午祭伍子迎水仙①
8.	On June 6th in the Chinese lunar calendar local people in Suzhou air the Buddhist Scriptures.	loh23-ngeh3 tshou44 loh23 bae22-syu44 fe44 cin44
	六月初六曝书翻经	六月初六曝书翻经
9.	At the Beginning of Summer local people in Suzhou eat three kinds of delicacies and weigh themselves.	lih23-gho31 zaon223 se44-sie31 tshen44 thi51-zon31
	立夏尝三鲜称体重	立夏尝三鲜称体重
10.	On June 24th in the Chinese lunar calendar local people in Suzhou enjoy the sight of water lilies at the pond.	loh23-ngeh3 nyie22-sy33 ghou22-daon33 kuoe44 lie223
	六月廿四荷塘观莲	六月廿四荷塘观莲
11.	On June 24th in the Chinese lunar calendar local people in Suzhou have a vegetarian diet to worship the God of Thunder.	loh23-ngeh3 nyie22-sy33 chih43 le22-tsa44-sou31
	六月廿四吃雷斋素	六月廿四吃雷斋素②

① "端午祭伍子迎水仙"是因为伍子胥被夫差赐死,悬目于城门,尸首被装入牛皮袋,投入河中,这天正好是五月初五,端午。从此,"祭伍子,迎水仙"就成了吴地端午的重要内容。伍子胥死后的206年,也是端午节,楚地汨罗江畔的屈原抱石投江,人们也以相同的方式祭祀着这位伟大的诗人。

② "六月廿四吃雷斋素"是为了崇奉雷尊而吃素,据说可以消灾避疫保平安。

续表

序号	英文	苏州话
12.	On June 7th in the Chinese lunar calendar local people in Suzhou plead for skills.	tshih43-ngeh3 tshou44 tshih43 chi51-chiae31
	七月初七乞巧	七月初七乞巧
13.	On July 15th in the Chinese lunar calendar local people in Suzhou offer Sacrifices to Ghosts.	tshih43-ngeh3 soh43-ng31 tson44-nyioe31 miae22-we33
	七月十五中元庙会	七月十五中元庙会
14.	On July 13th in the Chinese lunar calendar local people in Suzhou burn incense under the shadow of the wall.	tshih43-ngeh3 se44-seh31 sae44 di22-deu33-shian31
	七月三十烧地头香	七月三十烧地头香
15.	During the Mid—Autumn Festival local people admire the Full Moon by Shihu Lake.	poh43-ngeh3 tson44-tsheu31 zah23-ghou31 tshoe523-nyiueh3
	八月中秋石湖串月	八月中秋石湖串月
16.	In September in the Chinese lunar calendar local people in Suzhou watch the sunrise on Yang Hill	cieu51-ngeh3 yan22-se33 kuoe44 zeh23-tsheh43
	九月阳山观日出	九月阳山观日出
17.	The Winter Solstice should be celebrated as grandly as the New Year.	ton44-tsyu31 da231-zyu231 nyie223
	冬至大如年	冬至大如年

四 对话中的特色词汇

序号	英文	苏州话
1.	why	sa523-keh3 lou22-dae33
	什么原因，什么道理	啥个路道
2.	get to know	shiae51-teh3
	知道	晓得
3.	the eldest son	dou22-nyi33-tsy31
	长子	大儿子

续表

序号	英文	苏州话
4.	the youngest son	siae51-nyi33-tsy31
	幼子	小儿子
5.	his father	li44-toh3 ya223
	他父亲	俚笃爷
6.	so	nan22-meh3
	这么一来	曩末
7.	no	fen44
	没，没有	朆
8.	yes	ghe22-ia33
	是呀	诶呀
9.	small	ciu51-mi44-deu31
	很小	鬼咪头
10.	bitter	ih43-thie44-syu44-ka31
	表示程度很深	一天世界
11.	even	zen22-tshae44-tsyu44-yu31
	甚至	甚超至于
12.	head	khou44-laon33-deu31
	头	颗浪头
13.	break	khoh43-khe23
	打开	壳开
14.	brand new	tshaeh43-kuaeh43-sin44
	全新	察刮新
15.	again	yih23
	又	亦
16.	fold	iae51-chi44-le31
	折起	夭起来
17.	something important to do	kaeh43-maon33-deu33-li31 phaon44-chie44-cin31
	紧要关头（突发意外）	夹忙头里膀牵筋
18.	garrulous	zeh23-kueh3-loe33-boe31
	叽里咕噜	实骨乱盘
19.	constant	m22-peh3 woe223 tse44
	没完没了	呒不完哉
20.	bad luck	mo22-khou44-yiuin31
	噩运	暮库运
21.	quarrel	sian44-mo31
	吵架	相骂

续表

序号	英文	苏州话
22.	fight 打架	sian44-tan31 相打
23.	do us all in 连累大家倒霉	ta44-le31 shian44-lin31 chih43 mah23-tsoh3 带累乡邻吃麦粥
24.	all 一起	ih43-dae223 一淘
25.	a man of condition 有身价的人	mo22-tsy33 模子
26.	reckless 没目标瞎撞	deu22-ng33-deu33-loh3 投五投六
27.	incoherent 语无伦次	tshih43-feh3-taeh3-poh3 七弗搭八
28.	cheapjack 低级趣味	nyoh23-mo31 taon44 yeu31-tshi31 肉麻当有趣
29.	give 给	peh43 畀
30.	fool 傻瓜	aeh43-moh3-lin31 阿木林
31.	won people's great admiration 出挑，引人注目	de22-nge33-loh3-tsin31 弹眼落睛
32.	bitter 苦滋滋	khou51-tsi44-tsi31 苦济济
33.	feel nice 舒服，称心	seh43-i523 适意
34.	thing 东西，事物	meh23-zy31 物事

五 巩固练习

1 甲：苏州人非常看重冬至节，民间有"冬至大如年"的说法。

乙：是的，那天喝冬酿酒、吃羊羔是少不了的。

甲：苏州人还希望冬至那天下雨。

乙：因为俗称"邋遢冬至干净年"。

2 甲：金圣叹是苏州的大师，他的主要成就在于文学批评，人称"百批大王"。
乙：他的评点很注重思想内容的阐发，往往借题发挥，议论政事。
甲：金圣叹文笔幽默，为人风趣，连砍头时也滑稽得很。
乙：在刑场上，他泰然自若，向监斩官索酒畅饮，饮罢大笑，说："割头，痛事也；饮酒，快事也；割头而先饮酒，痛快痛快！"

六 参考答案

1

甲：普通话 苏州人 非常 看重 冬至节，民间有
吴语音 sou44-tseu44-nyi31 ciae44-kue31 khoe44-zon31 ton44-tsyu44-tsih3 min22-cie33 yeu231
吴语文 苏州人 交关 看重 冬至节，民间有

"冬至大如年" 的 说法。
ton44-tsyu31 da22- zyu33 nyie233 keh43 kaon51-faeh3 keh0
"冬至大如年" 个 讲法个。

乙：普通话 是的，那天 喝 冬酿酒、吃羊羔 是少
吴语音 me44-tsen31 geh23-nyih3 chih43 ton44-nyian33-tseu31 chih43 yan22-kae33 zy231 sae51-
吴语文 蛮正，箇日 吃 冬酿酒、吃羊羔 是少

不了的。
feh3-theh3-keh3
弗脱个。

甲：普通话 苏州人 还希望 冬至那天下雨。
吴语音 sou44-tseu44-nyin31 we223 shi44-vaon31 ton44-tsyu31 geh23-nyih3 loh23 yiu231 le0
吴语文 苏州人 还希望 冬至 箇日 落雨来。

乙：普通话 因为俗称"邋遢冬至干净年"。
吴语音 in44-we31 zoh23-chen31 laeh43-thaeh43 ton44-tsyu31 koe44-zin31 nyie223
吴语文 因为俗称"邋遢冬至干净年"。

甲: Local people in Suzhou attach great importance to the Winter Solstice. The statement "The Winter Solstice should be celebrated as grandly as the New Year." is popular here.

乙: Yes. Dong Niang Jiu and mutton are essential to the festival.

甲: What's more, people in Suzhou hope it will rain that day.

乙: As the saying goes, a rainy Winter Solstice goes with a sunny Spring Festival.

2

甲: 普通话 金圣叹是苏州的<u>大师</u> <u>他的</u>主要
吴语音 cin44-sen44-the31 zy231 sou44-tseu44-keh3 dou22- hae44-lae31 li44-keh3 tsyu51-iae31
吴语文 金圣叹是苏州个 <u>大好佬，俚个</u>主要

成就<u>在于</u>文学批评，人称"百批大王"。
zen231-zeu31 leh23-laon31 ven22-yioh3 phi44-bin31 nyin22-tshen33 pah43-phi44 da22-waon33
成就<u>勒浪</u>文学批评，人称"百批大王"。

乙: 普通话 <u>他的</u>评点<u>很</u>注重思想内容的阐发，
吴语音 li44-keh3 bin22-tie33 me44 tsyu51-zon31 sy44- sian31 ne22-yon33 keh43 zoe22-faeh3
吴语文 <u>俚个</u>评点<u>蛮</u>注重思想内容个阐发，

往往借题发挥，议论政事。
uaon51-uaon31 tsia523 di223 faeh43-hue23 nyi231-len31 tsen51-zy31
往往借题发挥，议论政事。

甲: 普通话 金圣叹文笔幽默，为人风趣，<u>连</u> <u>砍</u>
吴语音 cin44-sen44-the31 ven22-pih3 ieu44-meh3 we22- zen33 fon44-tshi31 lie22-teh3 saeh43
吴语文 金圣叹文笔幽默，为人风趣，<u>连得杀</u>

<u>头</u> <u>时</u> 也滑稽得很。
khou44-laon44- deu33-keh3 zen22-kuaon33 gha223 waeh23-ci44-teh3 ih43-thie44-syu44-ka31
<u>颗浪头个辰光</u> 也滑稽得<u>一天世界</u>。

乙：普通话 在 刑 场 上，他 泰然自若，向 监 斩 官
吴语音 leh23 yin22-zan33-laon31 li44 toh43-toh43-din33-din31 men231 ke44-tse44-kuoe31
吴语文 勒 刑 场 浪，俚 笃 笃 定 定，问 监 斩 官

索 酒 畅饮，饮 罢 大 笑，说："割 头，
thae51 tseu51 chih43 chih43-woe223 da22-siae33 kaon51 keh43 khou44-laon44-deu31
讨 酒 吃，吃 完 大 笑，讲："割 颗 浪 头，

痛 事 也；饮 酒，快 事 也； 割
thon51-keh3 zy22-thi33 cheh43 tseu51 kha44-weh3-keh3 zy22-thi33 keh43 khou44-
痛 个 事 体；吃 酒，快活 个 事 体； 割 颗

头 而 先 饮 酒，痛 快 痛 快！"
laon33-deu31 zie22-deu33 sie44 chih43-tseu51 thon51-khua31 thon51-khua31
浪 头 前 头 先 吃 酒，痛 快 痛 快！"

甲：Jin Shengtan was a master who was born in Suzhou. He noted for his trenchant literary criticism, and known as "the king of literary criticism".

乙：He seized on a theme as a false pretext to express his political view.

甲：He was humorous both of his writing style and his behaviour. He even showed his sense of humour when he was beheaded.

乙：He remained serene and in control at the execution ground, and asked for wine to the officials in charge of the execution. He laughed after drinking and said, "Being beheaded is painful yet wine always cheers me up. Drinking before execution is cheerful".

第四单元

体育与艺术

一 情景引入

甲：普通话 老李，青春版昆剧《牡丹亭》好 看得很，
　　吴语音 lae22-li33 tshin44-tshen44-pe31 khuen44-jiah3 mae22- te44-din31 hae51-khoe44-teh3-le31
　　吴语文 老李，青春版昆剧《牡丹亭》好 看得来，

两个青年演员的嗓子响亮清脆,
lian231-keh3 tshin44-nyie31 ie51-yoe33-keh3 ghoh23-lon33 kuaeh43- laeh3-son44-tshe31
两个青年演员个喉咙刮拉松脆①,

好得没话说。你不看要后悔的。
hae51-teh3 iae523 min231 ne231 feh43-khoe523 meh0 zy22-iae33 ae44-lae33-keh3-a31
好得要命。倷弗看末,是要懊劳个啊。

乙:普通话 是 不 是 白 先 勇 改 编 的?
吴语音 aeh43-zy231 bah23-sie44-ion31 ke51-pie44-keh3- la0
吴语文 阿 是 白 先 勇 改 编 个 啦?

甲:普通话 是 的。
吴语音 zy231-keh3 ue44
吴语文 是 个 碗。

乙:普通话 台 湾 人 来 搞 昆 剧 行 吗?再 说
吴语音 de22-ue44-nyin31 le223 lon231 khuen44-jiah3 meh0 aeh43 le22-se33-keh3 cia0 tse44-kaon31
吴语文 台 湾 人 来 弄 昆 剧 末 阿 来 三 个 嘎?再 讲

大热天, 我 也 怕 出 门。
nyih23-thie31 nyih23-seh3 ngou231 gha22-pho33 tsheh43-men223 ia0
热 天 热 色,我 也 怕 出 门 呀。

甲:普通话 不 骗 你,真 的 好 的。路 上 热
吴语音 feh43-phie523 ne231 tsen44-keh3 lin22-kuaon44-keh0 ia0 lou22-laon33-shian31 nyih23
吴语文 弗 骗 倷,真 个 灵 光 个 呀。路 浪 向 热

一会 儿 碍 什么 呢。
shih43-shih3 meh0 nge231-tie44-keh3 sa523 cia0
歇 歇 末 碍 点 个 啥 嘎。

---

① "刮辣松脆"形容食物脆、做事爽、嗓子好。a."该爿店个绞劳棒刮辣松脆,味道着实赞。"(这家店的麻花很松脆,味道非常好。)b."伲阿哥做事体一向刮辣松脆。"(我哥哥做事情一向爽快利落。)c."该个小娘鱼个喉咙刮辣松脆。"(这个小姑娘的嗓子清脆响亮。)

乙：普通话 好 的， 我 也 确 定 去 看 了。
　　吴语音 hae51-keh3 ngou231 gha223 tsen51-din31 chi523 khoe523 tse44
　　吴语文 好 个， 我 也 准 定 去 看 哉。

甲：Li, the youth version of Peony Pavilion is very interesting. The performers' voice sounds clear and sweet. Excellent! I bet you will regret missing it.

乙：Was the one adapted by Bai Xianyong?

甲：Yes.

乙：Would a Taiwannese be able to do that? Besides, it is so hot today, I don't feel like going out.

甲：Really, no kidding. I do think it is very good. What is a hot day beside a brilliant performance.

乙：OK, I will go too.

二 场景对话

1. 甲：普通话 这 次 南 非 世 界 杯 西 班 牙 夺 冠，
　　吴语音 ke44-thaon31 noe22-fi33 syu44-ka44-pe31 si44- pe44-nga31 no223 kuoe51-ciuin23
　　吴语文 该 趟 南 非 世 界 杯 西 班 牙 拿 冠 军，

　　　　　　　　真 是　　大 爆 冷 门。
　　　　　　　tsen44-keh3- zy31 lan22-ghoh3-tsy31 pae523 tsheh43 nyih23-lih3- tsy31 ue0
　　　　　　　　真 个 是 冷 镬 子 爆 出 热 栗子① 哕。

乙：普通话 我 倒 觉 得 西 班 牙 夺 冠　　 靠 的 是
　　吴语音 ngou231 tae523 koh43-zah3 si44-pe44-nga31 no223 kuoe51-ciuin23 khae523 keh43-zy31
　　吴语文 我 倒 觉 着 西 班 牙 拿 冠 军 靠 个 是

---

① "冷镬子爆出热栗子"比喻突然、出人意料。

实　实　在　在、的　的　确　确　的　技术。
zah23-kueh3 thih43- ngan231 tih43-tih3-kuaeh3-kuaeh3 keh43 ji22-zeh3
石　骨　铁　硬①、的　的　刮　刮　个　技术。

乙：普通话　哎，中　国　男　足　什么　时　候　能　走　向
吴语音　ghe223 tson44-kueh3 noe22-tsoh3 sa523 keh3 zen22- kuaon33 khou51-i23 tseu51-shian31
吴语文　唉，中　国　男　足　啥个　辰　光　可以　走　向

世　界　哦。
syu44-ka31 oh0
世　界　喔。

甲：普通话　哼，你　指　望　那　帮　有名无实的人　　　，希望
吴语音　hen0 ne231 tsyu51-vaon31 geh23-paon31 khon44-sin44-dou22- lae33-kuoe31 a0
吴语文　哼，倷　指　望　箇　帮　空　心　大　佬　倌②啊，

肯　定　落　空。
pe51-din33-zy31 tshah43-kon523 lae22-zeu33-sin31 chih43-tsah43 khon44-sin44-
板　定　是　拆　供　老　寿　星③，吃　只　空　心

thaon44-doe31 ue0
汤　团④　喔。

甲：In the final of World Cup 2010, Spain won the game with the Netherlands to produce an unexpected winner.

乙：I think the result was deserved. They became world champion because of their unbelievable technical abilities.

---

① "石骨铁硬"也写作"石刮铁硬""石括铁硬""石括挺硬""实刮铁硬"，有四层意思：a. 形容非常坚强。"覅看俚瘦骨拉带，倒是个石骨铁硬个男人。"b. 形容非常坚硬。"个面包石骨铁硬，还好吃啦！"（那面包那么坚硬，还能吃吗！）c. 形容非常确定，不容置疑。"人赃俱获，石骨铁硬，倷强掰嘴点啥？"（人赃俱获，不容置疑，你强辩点啥？）d. 实实在在，十足。"该个真丝被头货真价实，石骨铁硬。"（这个真丝被子货真价实，实实在在。）

② "空心大老倌""拆供老寿星""吃空心汤团"带有调侃意味，指的是有名无实，让人希望落空。

③④　见上注释。

乙：Oh dear, when on earth is the Chinese man's team able to dash out of Asia and walk up to the world?

甲：Don't expect too much of those who are in name only, or you will be disappointed. those who are in name only, or you will be disappointed.

2. 甲：普通话　姚　明　的　身材　很　单薄，　看　他　在　Ｎ Ｂ
　　　吴语音　yae22-min33-keh3 sen44-phe31 me44 te44-liae31 keh0 khoe523 li44 leh23-he51 en44-bi33-
　　　吴语文　姚　明　个　身坏　蛮单料①　个，看　俚　勒　嗨　Ｎ Ｂ

　　　　　Ａ　那　么　激烈　的　赛场　上　比赛　好　　为　他
　　　　　e31 geh23-zan31 cih43-lih3-keh3 se51-zan33-laon31 pi51-se31 fiae523 theh43-taeh3 li44
　　　　　Ａ　箇场　激烈　个　赛场　浪　比赛　勥　忒　搭　俚

　　　　　担　心　呐！
　　　　　te44-sin31 oh0
　　　　　担　心　喔！

乙：普通话　就　　是。　那些　黑人　一个个　都　是　　凶
　　　吴语音　zeu22-zy33 kaon51 ia0 geh23-tie31 heh43-nyin23 ih43- keh3-keh3 ze22-zy33 ng22-cin33
　　　吴语文　就　是　讲　呀。箇点　黑人　一个个　侪　是　五斤

　　　　　猛厉害　　你　看　他　老是　被　伤病
　　　　　hen51 loh23- cin31 ne231 khoe523 li44 lae231-zy31 peh43 saon44- bin31
　　　　　狠　六　斤②，侬　看　俚　老是　畀　伤　病

---

① "单料"在苏州话中常用来形容人的身体单薄，"单料头身坏"正好与"大模坏"相对。

② "五筋狠六筋"的意思有四层：a. 凶猛厉害，此义同"场景对话2"中"个点黑人一个个侪是五筋狠六筋"。b. 比喻喜欢较真。"阿犯得着䏶，为仔一点点小事体五筋狠六筋。"（犯得吗，为了一点点小事那么较真。）c. 喜欢狠出头。"人家老大也弗出面，加二用弗着俚老末拖珈勒前八叉，五筋狠六筋。"（人家老大也不出面，更加用不着你老幺冲在前头去狠出头。）d. 白花大力气去做不值得的事。"喔唷，五筋狠六筋，原是朆做好。"（喔唷，花了大力气，还是没做好。）

缠 身， 这点 也 蛮 可 怜 的。
zoe22-kaeh3 feh43-tshin44 e44-tie31 ghaeh23 me44 tsoh43-nyih3-keh3
缠 夹 弗 清，哀点 也 蛮 作 孽① 个。

甲： Yao Ming seems a bit delicate. As soon as he appears on NBA court, I'm rather anxious about him.

乙： So do I. Look at the black giants who are as fierce as tigers. It was pathetic to watch the injury ruled him out.

3. 甲：普通话 丁 俊 辉 从 小 就 整 天 一 心 一 意
吴语音 tin44-tsin44-hue31 zon22-siae33 zeu231 ih43-nyih3-tae44-ia31 ih43-men33-sin44-sy31
吴语文 丁 俊 辉 从 小 就 一 日 到 夜、一 门 心 思

练 桌 球，连 小 学、中 学 都 没 系 统 地 上 过。
lie231 de22- jieu33 lie223 siae51-ghoh3 tson44-ghoh3 ze22-fen33 yi22-thon33 zaon231 kou523
练 台 球，连 小 学、中 学 俫 朆 系 统 上 过。

乙：普通话 是 的，他 父 母 这 样 做， 也 挺 特 别 的。
吴语音 zy231-keh3 li44-toh3 ya22-nyian33 zeh23- kan31 tsou523 gha223 me44 koh43-bih3 keh43
吴语文 是 个，俚 笃 爷 娘 实 梗 做， 也 蛮 角 别 个。

甲： Ding Junhui has committed himself to practising snooker since he was a child, and has received little formal education at a primary or a high school.

乙： Well, it's true that his parents are different from others.

---

① "作孽"的意思为：a. 可怜。此义同"场景对话2"中"俚看俚老是拨伤病缠夹不清，哀点也蛮作孽个"。b. 可惜。"作孽，马上到终点哉，临时完结一跤跟斗，冠军就此泡汤。"（可惜，马上到终点了，临到头摔了一跤，冠军就此泡汤。）c. 作恶。"倷朆再作孽哉，积点德吧。"（你不要再作恶了，积点德吧。）d. 罪过。"暴殄天物，作孽个啊。"（暴殄天物，罪过啊。）e. 遭罪受苦。"该着尔笃两个活宝，我真个作孽。"（得到你们两个活宝，我真的遭罪受苦。）

4. 甲：普通话 下 围棋 如果 按 照 定 式 循规蹈矩 来，虽
   吴语音 tsah43 we22-ji33 cia51-sy23 oe44-tsae31 din231- seh3 ih43-pe44-se44-nge31 le223 se44-
   吴语文 着① 围棋 假使 按 照 定 式 一板三眼② 来，虽

   然 赢 面 大 些， 但 看 着 没 啥意思。
   zoe31 yin22-mie33 dou231-tie31 de22-pih3-kou31 khoe523 leh23-he31 m22-peh3 sa523 i44-sy31 keh0
   然 赢 面 大 点，但不过 看 勒 嗨 朆 啥意思个。

   乙：普通话 大 多 数 棋手 还 是 选 择 与 式 定 一 模 一
   吴语音 da22-tou44-sou31 ji22-seu33 we22-zy33 sie51- zeh3 taeh43 din22-seh3 ih43-zy231 ih43-
   吴语文 大 多 数 棋手 还 是 选 择 搭 定式 一 似 一

   样， 毕 竟 赢 棋 是 硬 道 理
   theh3- seh43 pih43-cin523 yin223 ji223 zy231 ngan22-dae33- li31
   脱 式， 毕 竟 赢 棋 是 硬 道 理

甲：If you play Weiqi by formula, there are more chances of winning the game, but it is boring for the audience.

乙：However, most of the players will follow the formula. After all, to win the game is the most important thing.

5. 甲：普通话 高雅 的 昆 曲 艺 术 目 前 总 共
   吴语音 kae44-ia31 keh43 khuen44-chioh3 nyi22-zeh3 moh23-zie31 ih43-thaeh43-kuaeh43-tsy31
   吴语文 高雅 个 昆 曲 艺 术 目 前 一 塌 刮 子

   没 多 少 演员、 观 众 了。 昆 曲 说
   m22-peh3 ci51-ho31 ie51-yoe33 taeh43 kuoe44-tson31 tse44 khuen44-chioh3 kaon51-
   朆 不 几 许 演 员 搭 观 众 哉。 昆 曲 讲

---

① "着"字在苏州话中异常活跃，既可以等同于普通话中的助词"着"，又可以作为副词"最"（例："最外面"是"着着外头"，"最下面"是"着底"）解，这两类均读作zah23；更可以作为动词，例：下棋（着棋）、穿衣服（着衣裳），读作tsah43。

② "一板三眼"既指按部就班，循规蹈矩；也指做事过于顶真，呆板而不知变通。

起来曲高和寡，问题是雅俗共赏的评
chi44-le31 chioh43-kae44-ghou33- kua31 ven22-di33-zy31 ia51-zoh3-gon33-saon31 keh43 bin22-
起 来 曲 高 和 寡，问 题 是 雅 俗 共 赏 个 评

弹也面临观众老龄化的严峻现实。
de33 gha223 mie231-lin31 kuoe44-tson31 lae22-lin33-ho31 keh43 nyie231-tsin31 yie22-zeh3
弹 也 面 临 观 众 老 龄 化 个 严 峻 现 实。

乙：普通话 观　众　少，收　入　低，好　演　员　纷　纷　流　失　真
吴语音 kuoe44-tson31 sae51 seu44-zeh3 ti44　hae51-ie44- yoe31 fen44-fen31 leu22-seh3 tsen44-
吴语文 观　众　少，收　入　低，好　演　员　纷　纷　流　失　真

可惜。
keh3 tsoh43-nyih23 keh43-a0
个 作 孽 个 啊。

甲：There are few people who are performing or enjoying the local high art: Kunqu Opera. It is said to be caviar to the general, but the problem is that Pintan which was once the most popular attraction in Suzhou is now faced with the fact that its audience are growing old.

乙：Losing audience and money is losing good performers. What a pity!

6. 甲：普通话 冯　小　刚　拍　的　电　影《唐　山　大　地　震》非　常
吴语音 von22-siae44-kaon31 phah43-keh3 die22-in33 daon22- se33 da22-di33-tsen31 le22-teh43-
吴语文 冯　小　刚　拍　个　电　影《唐　山　大　地　震》来　得

感人，特别是救女儿还是救儿子
keh3 koe51 nyin223 deh23-bih3-zy31 cieu523 noe22-ng33 we22-zy33 cieu523 nyi22-tsy33
个 感 人，特 别 是 救 囡 儿 还 是 救 儿 子

的选择，那　　母亲真的心痛极了。
keh43 sie51-zeh3 geh23-keh3 m44-ma44-keh3 sin44 gha223 thon523 teh43-leh3 kae51-
个 选 择，箇 个　姆 妈 个　心 也 痛 得 勒 绞

第四单元　体育与艺术

```
                       tsoe31 le223 tse44
                        转   来   哉。
```

乙：普通话　儿子、女儿　哪　个　不　是　娘　的　心　头　肉　呢，
　　吴语音　nyi22-tsy33 noe22-ng33 lo231-keh3 feh43-zy231 nyian22-keh3 sin44-deu33-nyioh3 ne0
　　吴语文　儿　子、囡　儿　哪　个　弗　是　娘　个　心　头　肉　呢，

　　　　　　放　弃　任　何　一　个，都　是　舍不得　的，当　时
　　　　　　faon44-chi31 zen22-ghou33 ih43-keh43 ze22-zy33 nyioh23 thon523 keh43 taon44-zyu31
　　　　　　放　弃　任　何　一　个，侪　是　肉　痛　个，当　时

　　　　　　这　种　情　景，徐　帆　演　得　太　棒　了，我　是
　　　　　　ke44-tson31 zin22-cin33 zi22-ve33 ie51-teh3-leh3 theh43 hae51 tse44 ngou231- zy31
　　　　　　该　种　情　景，徐　帆　演　得　勒　忒　好　哉，我　是

　　　　　　泪　流　不　止　　啊。
　　　　　　nge231-li31 thaon44-thaon44-ti31 oh0
　　　　　　眼　泪　汤　汤　渧①　喔。

甲："Aftershock", directed by Feng Xiaogang, was very touching. There was a scene showed the mother informed by the rescuers that they can only save one out of her son and daughter. How she suffered when she made the choice.

乙：The son and the daughter are both part of mother's heart. Neither of them could she gave up. During the movie's screening, I was moved to tears by Xu Fan's great performance.

7.　甲：普通话　王　菲　明　摆　着　是　歌　坛　的　大　姐　大，你
　　　　吴语音　waon22-fi33 ngan22-phan33 ngan231 zy231 kou44-de33- keh3 da22-tsi44-da22 ne231
　　　　吴语文　王　菲　硬　碰　硬　是　歌　坛　个　大　姐　大，倷

---

① 也写作"眼泪答答渧"，表现眼泪流得连续不断的样子。

看　她　复出　巡演，　比　以前　　更加　火爆，
khoe523 li44 voh23- tsheh43 zin22-ie33 taeh43 lae22-tsae33 pi51 ka44- nyi31 hou51-bae33
看　俚　复出　巡演，　搭　老早　比加二　火爆

　　真　是　好　有　脸面　哦。
tse44 tsen44-keh3-zy31 tsheh43-tsoh43-tsy31 fon44-deu33-laeh3-li31
哉，真个是　出足仔风头①啦里。

乙：普通话　就　是，　虽然　她　不　善　炒作，回答问
吴语音 zeu22-zy33 kaon51 ia0　se44-zoe31 li44 feh43-zoe231 tshae51- tsoh3 we223-taeh3 ven22-
吴语文 就　是　讲呀，虽然　俚　弗　善　炒作，回答问

题　时　不够讨巧，不过　人家　实力
di33 zen22-kuaon33 moh23-tsyu44- moh3-koh3 pih43-kou523 nyin22-ka33 zeh23-lih3
题　辰光　木知木觉②，不过　人家　实力

摆　在那里，任凭　对手　再　怎么　不服气，拼
pa51-leh3 geh23-taeh3 ze22-bie33 te44-seu31 tse44 naeh23-han31 feh43 lin22-ben33 ciae523
摆　勒笪搭，随便　对手　再　哪哼　弗临盆③，叫

命作秀，　也　没用　的。
teh43 ng22-he44-loh3-tson31 ghah22-zy33 m22-ma33 yon231-keh3
得五虚六肿④，也　是　呒买用个。

① "出风头"指成为舆论注意的中心，出头露面，显示个人的表现。既可以当褒义词用，也可以作为贬义词，指故意引起别人注意，而且作为贬义词的情况较多。

② "木知木觉"与"木头木脑""木觉觉""木欣欣""木笃笃""木觉"均有"感觉迟钝，呆头呆脑，反应不灵敏"之意。而"木觉星宿"是在此基础上比喻迟钝的人。但两者一般都不含贬义。

③ "弗临盆"的意思绝对不能理解为普通话中"临盆"的反义词，其主要的意思就是"不服气，不服帖，不肯买账"；此外还有"不认错"和"不知世情"的意思。

④ "五虚（音海）六肿"有三层意思：a. 表示程度深。此义同"场景对话6"中"人家实力摆勒个搭，随便对手再哪哼弗临盆，叫得五虚六肿，也是呒买用个。"b. 形容肿得厉害。"啥体啊，倷个面孔五虚六肿啦里。"（干吗啊，你的脸肿得好厉害呀）。c. 形容身材臃肿、肥胖。"倷阿吃发酵粉，囔身体该场五虚六肿嗄。"（你吃没吃发酵粉，怎末身体这么臃肿呀？）

甲: Faye Wong was apparently the pop queen, whose come-back live tour was more popular than before. What a great success!

乙: As a famously private person, she is not very sociable, though. She is always one of the most influential pop performers of the last two decades despite of the deceptive show of those who are not quite reconciled.

8. 甲: 普通话　你　有没有买　　十　佳　中　青　年　评弹　演　员　演
吴语音　ne231　aeh43　ma231　zeh23-cia31　tson44-　tshin44-nyie31　bin22-de33　ie51-yoe31　ie51-
吴语文　倷　覅　买　十　佳　中　青　年　评弹　演　员　演

唱　　　精品　　　专辑，里　面　的　开篇　都　好　得　不
tshaon31　tsin44-phin44-tsoe44-zih3　li22-shian33-keh3　khe44-phie31　ze223　tse51-teh3　feh43
唱　　　精　品　　专　辑，里　向　个　开篇　佮　赞①　得　弗

得　了，听　起　来　真　　过　　瘾。
teh43　liae231　thin44-　chi44-le31　tsen44-keh3　saeh43-kheh43
得　了，听　起　来　真　个　煞　渴②。

乙: 普通话　我　是　个　老　听　客　了，那　末　好　的　碟片，
吴语音　ngou231-zy33-keh3　lae22-thin44-khah3　tse44　geh23-　zaon31　hae51-keh3　dih23-phie31
吴语文　我　是　个　老　听　客　哉，箇　状　好　个　碟　片，

怎么　会　　不　买　呢？第　一　只　就　是　袁小
naeh23-han31　ue523-teh3　feh43-ma231　ne0　di22-ih43-tsah43　zeu22-zy33　yoe22-siae44-
哪　哼　会　得　弗　买　呢？第　一　只　就　是　袁小

良、盛　小　云　　对唱　　　的《莺莺操琴》，唱　腔、
lian31　zan22-siae44-yiuin31　te44-tshaon44-keh3　in44-in31　tshae44　jin223　tshaon44-chian31
良、盛　小　云　　对唱　　个《莺莺操琴》，唱　腔、

①　苏州话里"赞"为"好"的意思，与普通话多为"赞扬"意义不同。
②　"煞渴"与"煞念"同义，意指"痛快；过瘾；某种欲望得到极度的满足"。"煞根"由此派生而来，虽然也是"痛快；过瘾；尽兴"之意，但程度上更进一步。

画面　都美极了，连我　　家那个　　对评弹
　　gho22-mie33 ze223 me51- teh3-le31 lie231-nyi31 oh43-li33-shian31 te523 bin22-de33
　　画　面侪美得来，连伲　屋里向　对 评 弹

　　不太感兴趣的　　　儿子也　喜　欢。
　　ga22-taeh43-taeh43-keh3 nyi22-tsy33 ghaeh23 huoe44-shi31 tseh0
　　茄　答　答①个儿 子　也　欢 喜 哉。

甲：Did you buy the album of Top 10 Best Pintan Performers? The Tanci arias sound so beautiful that it's a treat to have them.

乙：I am a huge fan of Pintan. I have bought the nice thing as soon as it released. The first aria is Cui Yingying Plays the Zither performed by Yuan Xiaoliang and Sheng Xiaoyun Both vocal presentation and pictures are gorgeous. Not only I but also my son who took no interest before likes it.

9. 甲：普通话　有　人　说　周　慧　敏　的　画　比　范　增　好，简
　　吴语音 yeu231 nyin223 kaon51 tseu44-we33-min31 keh43 gho231 pi51 ve22-tsen33 hae51 cie51-
　　吴语文 有　人　讲　周　慧　敏　个　画　比　范　增　好，简

　　　　直　在　胡　说。
　　zeh3 leh23-laon31 nyih23- huen23
　　直　勒浪　热　昏。

乙：普通话　范　增　倒　底　是　中　央　美　术　学　院　科　班　出
　　吴语音 ve22-tsen33 tae44-ti44-zy31 tson44-ian31 me51- zeh23 ghoh23-yoe31 khou44-pe31 tsheh43-
　　吴语文 范　增　倒　底　是　中　央　美　术　学　院　科　班　出

　　　　身　的　高　材　生，不　会　不　如　电　影　明　星　吧。
　　sen44-keh43 kae44-ze33-san31 feh43-ue523 feh43-zyu223 die22-in33 min22-sin33-keh3 ba0
　　身　个　高　材　生，弗　会　弗　如　电　影　明　星　个吧。

① "茄答答"主要的意思是"不起劲，不感兴趣"，还有"磨磨蹭蹭"和"不热心"之意。

甲：Zhou Huiming's pictures are said to be better than Fan Zheng's. That is sheer nonsense!

乙：Fang Zeng is a professional graduated from China Central Academy of Fine Arts after all. I don't think he will behind a film star in painting.

10. 甲：普通话 桃花坞年画名气响得很,是
　　　吴语音 dae22-ho44-ou31 nyie22-gho33 min22-chi33 shian51-teh3 kuaeh43-laeh43-laeh43 zy231
　　　吴语文 桃 花 坞 年 画 名 气 响 得 刮 辣 辣, 是

　　　　　吴 地 文 化 中 一 枝 独 特 的 艺 术 之 花。
　　　　　ghou22-di33 ven22- ho33 tson44 ih43-tsyu23 doh23-deh3-keh3 nyi22- zeh3-tsyu44-ho31
　　　　　吴 地 文 化 中 一 枝 独 特 个 艺 术 之 花。

乙：普通话 是的, 它与天津杨柳青年画齐名,
　　　吴语音 zy231-keh3 li44 taeh43 thie44-tsin31 yan22-leu44- tshin31 nyie22-gho33 zi22-min23
　　　吴语文 是 个, 俚搭 天 津 杨 柳 青 年 画 齐 名,

　　　　　有 "南 桃 北 杨" 之 称。
　　　　　yeu231 noe223 dae223 poh43 yan223 tsyu44 tshen44
　　　　　有 "南 桃 北 杨" 之 称。

甲：Suzhou Taohuawu Woodcutting New Year Pictures is one of the famous arts of Suzhou.

乙：Yes, it is as well known as the Woodcutting New Year Pictures of Yangliuqing. As the saying goes "The Taohuawu Woodcutting New Year Pictures to the south, the Woodcutting New Year Pictures of Yangliuqing to the north."

三 词语贴士

（一）坊间俗语

序号	英文	苏州话
1.	play Weiqi	tsah43 ji223
	下棋	着棋
2.	at a dead run	phin44-min31 pen44
	使劲跑	拼命奔
3.	throw forcibly	yon231-lih23 toh43, yon231-lih23 gue231
	用力掷	用力氐、用力掼
4.	produce an unexpected winner	lan231-ghoh3-tsy31 pae51-tsheh3 nyih23-lih3-tsy31
	爆冷门	冷镬子爆出热栗子
5.	perform Pintan	seh43-syu23
	演评弹	说书
6.	Pinghua (story-telling)	dou22-syu33
	评话	大书
7.	Suzhou Tanci (ballad-singing)	siae51-syu23
	弹词	小书
8.	commit oneself to	ih43-men33-sin44-sy31
	一心一意	一门心思
9.	Ghost in the machine	wan22-tshoh43-tshian31
	斜刺里闪出	横戳枪
10.	make a comic effect	tsheh43 shiueh43-deu23
	抖包袱	出噱头
11.	move to tears	nge231-li31 thaon44-thaon44-ti31
	眼泪直流	眼泪汤汤渧
		nge231-li31 taeh43-taeh43-ti31
		眼泪答答渧

（二）运动大类

序号	英文	苏州话
1.	track and field	die22-cin33
	田径	田径
2.	ball games	jieu22-le33
	球类	球类
3.	gymnastics	thi51-tshae23
	体操	体操

续表

序号	英文	苏州话
4.	weightlifting 举重	ciu51-zon31 举重
5.	shooting 射击	zo22-cih3 射击
6.	martial art 武术	vu22-zeh3 武术
7.	equestrian 马术	mo22-zeh3 马术
8.	water sports 水上项目	syu51-zaon31 ghaon22-moh3 水上项目
9.	ice sports 冰上运动	pin44-zaon31 yuin22-don33 冰上运动
10.	extreme sports 极限运动	jih23-ghe31 yuin22-don33 极限运动
11.	racing car 赛车	se51-tsho23 赛车
12.	men's event 男子项目	noe22-tsy33 ghaon22-moh3 男子项目
13.	women's event 女子项目	nyiu22-tsy33 ghaon22-moh3 女子项目
14.	team event 团体项目	doe22-thi33 ghaon22-moh3 团体项目
15.	individual event 单项	te44-ghaon31 单项

（三）各种运动会和参赛方

序号	英文	苏州话
1.	comprehensive sports 综合性运动会	tson44-gheh3-sin31 yuin22-don33-we31 综合性运动会
2.	the Olympic Games 奥运会	ae51-yuin33-we31 奥运会
3.	the Asian Games 亚运会	ia44-yuin33-we31 亚运会
4.	the National Games 全运会	zie22-yuin33-we31 全运会
5.	the Paralympic Games 残疾人运动会	ze22-zih3-nyin31 yuin22-don33-we31 残疾人运动会

续表

序号	英文	苏州话
6.	invitational tournament 邀请赛	iae44-tshin44-se31 邀请赛
7.	championship 锦标赛	cin51-piae44-se51 锦标赛
8.	wild and wacky sports 趣味运动会	tshi51vi31 yuin22-don33-we31 趣味运动会
9.	host country 东道国	ton44-dae33-kueh3 东道国
10.	seeded team 种子队	tson51-tsy33-de31 种子队
11.	national team 国家队	kueh43-cia44-de31 国家队
12.	home team 主队	tsyu51-de31 主队
13.	visiting team 客队	khah43-de223 客队
14.	cheering-section 啦啦队	la44-la44-de31 啦啦队

（四）体育组织和体育设施

序号	英文	苏州话
1.	IOC 奥委会	ae51-ue44-we31 奥委会
2.	sports club 体育俱乐部	thi51-yoh3 jiu22-loh3-bu31 体育俱乐部
3.	gymnasium 体育馆	thi51-yoh3-kuoe31 体育馆
4.	stadium 体育场	thi51-yoh3-zan31 体育场

（五）体育人员和竞技状态

序号	英文	苏州话
1.	athlete 运动员	yuin22-don33-yoe31 运动员
2.	coach 教练员	ciae51-lie33-yoe31 教练员

续表

序号	英文	苏州话
3.	referee, umpire 裁判员	ze22-phoe44-yoe31 裁判员
4.	chief judge 裁判长	ze22-phoe44-tsan31 裁判长
5.	good player 优秀选手	ieu44-seu31 sie51-seu23 优秀选手
6.	champion 冠军	kuoe51-ciuin31 冠军
7.	all-round champion 全能冠军	zen22-nen33-kuoe51-ciuin31 全能冠军
8.	record holder 世界记录保持者	syu44-ka31 ci51-loh3 pae51-zyu33-tse31 世界记录保持者
9.	competitive readiness 竞技状态	jin22-ji33 zaon231-the31 竞技状态
10.	dark horse 黑马	heh3-mo231 黑马
11.	draw 平局	bin22-jioh3 平局

（六）视觉艺术

序号	英文	苏州话
1.	painting 绘画	wo231 dou223 画图
2.	sculpture 雕塑	tiae44-sou31 雕塑
3.	photography 摄影	seh43-in51 摄影
4.	architecture 建筑	cie51-tsoh3 建筑
5.	craft 工艺	kon44-nyi31 工艺
6.	advertising 广告	kuaon51-kae31 广告
7.	animation 卡通	don22-gho33 动画

（七）表演艺术

序号	英文	苏州话
1.	picture arts 电影	die22-in33 电影
2.	television arts 电视	die22-zyu33 电视
3.	dance 舞蹈	vu231-dae31 舞蹈
4.	drama 戏剧	shi44-jiah3 戏剧
5.	music 音乐	in44-yoh3 音乐

（八）民间艺术

序号	英文	苏州话
1.	acrobatics 杂技	zeh23-ji31 杂技
2.	quyi 曲艺	chioh43-nyi31 曲艺
3.	puppet show 木偶	moh23-ngeu31 木偶
4.	Chinese shadow puppet show 皮影	bi22-in33 皮影

（九）流派和明星

序号	英文	苏州话
1.	classicism 古典主义	kou51-tie23 tsyu51-nyi31 古典主义
2.	romanticism 浪漫主义	laon231-me31 tsyu51-nyi31 浪漫主义
3.	realism 现实主义	yie22-zeh3 tsyu51-nyi31 现实主义
4.	symbolism 象征主义	zian22-tsen33 tsyu51-nyi31 象征主义
5.	impressionism 印象主义	in51-zian31 tsyu51-nyi31 印象主义

续表

序号	英文	苏州话
6.	abstractionism 抽象主义	tsheu44-zian31 tsyu51-nyi31 抽象主义
7.	naturalism 自然主义	zy22-zoe33 tsyu51-nyi31 自然主义
8.	comedy 喜剧	shi51-jiah3 喜剧
9.	tragedy 悲剧	pe44-jiah3 悲剧
10.	serious play 正剧	tsen44-jiah3 正剧
11.	artist 艺术家	nyi22-zeh3-cia31 艺术家
12.	star 明星	min22-sin33 明星
13.	idol 偶像	ngeu231-zian31 偶像

（十）中国戏剧

序号	英文	苏州话
1.	Beijing Opera 京剧	cin44-jiah3，cin44-shi31 京剧，京戏
2.	Kunqu Opera 昆曲	khuen44-chioh43 昆曲
3.	Pintan 评弹	bin22-de33 评弹
4.	Yue Opera 越剧	yiueh23-jiah3,zau22-shin44-shi31 越剧,绍兴戏
5.	Xi Opera 锡剧	sih43-jiah3,zan22-sih3 ven22-shi33 锡剧,常锡文戏
6.	Huai Opera 淮剧	wa22-jiah3 淮剧
7.	Huangmei Opera 黄梅戏	waon22-me33-shi31 黄梅戏
8.	farce 滑稽戏	waeh23-ci44-shi31 滑稽戏

四 对话中的特色词汇

序号	英文	苏州话
1.	voice 嗓子	ghoh23-lon31 喉咙
2.	(voice) sound clear and sweet 响亮清脆	kuaeh43-laeh3-son44-tshe31 刮辣松脆
3.	do 搞	lon44 弄
4.	hot 天热	nyih23-thie44-nyih3-seh3 热天热色
5.	on one's way to 路上	lou22-laon44-shian31 路浪向
6.	It's not a big deal 碍什么	nge231 tie51 sa523 碍点啥
7.	be sure 确定	tsen51-din31 准定
8.	real 实实在在	zah23-kueh3-thih3-ngan31 石骨铁硬
9.	real 的的确确	tih43-tih43-kuaeh43-kuaeh43 的的刮刮
10.	those in mane only 空心大佬倌	khon44-sin31 dou22-lae33-kuoe31 空心大佬倌
11.	be disappointed 拆供老寿星	tshah43-kon523 lae22-zeu33-sin31 拆供老寿星
12.	castles in the air 空心汤团	khon44-sin44-thaon44-doe31 空心汤团
13.	skinry 身材单薄	sen44-phe44-te44-liae31 身坯单料
14.	as fierce as a tiger 凶猛厉害	ng22-cin33 hen51 loh23-cin31 五筋狠六筋
15.	pity 可怜	tsoh43-nyih3 作孽
16.	different from others 特别	koh43-bih3 角别
17.	obey the laws 循规蹈矩	ih43-pe44-se44-nge31 一板三眼

第四单元 体育与艺术

续表

序号	英文	苏州话
18.	as like as two peas 一模一样	ih43-zy231 ih43-theh3-seh3 一似一脱式
19.	suffer 痛到极点	thon523 teh43 kae51-tsoe44-le31 痛得绞转来
20.	much more 更加	ka44-nyi31 加二
21.	slow 不灵敏，迟钝	moh23-tsyu44-moh3-cioh3 木知木觉
22.	not quite reconciled 不服气	feh43 lin223 ben223 弗临盆
23.	the deceptive show 拼命作秀	ciae523 teh43 ng22-he44-loh3-tson31 叫得五虚六肿
24.	not work 没用	m22-ma44-yon31 呒买用
25.	good 好	tse523 赞
26.	be a treat to have 过瘾	saeh43-kheh43 煞渴
27.	take less interest in 不起劲，不感兴趣	ga22-taeh3-taeh3 茄答答
28.	nonsense 胡说	huen44-seh3-loe33-gho31 昏说乱话
29.	behind sb 不如	feh43-zyu223 弗如
30.	famous 名气很响	min22-chi33 shian523 teh43 kuaeh43-laeh3-laeh3 名气响得刮辣辣
31.	as..as 和，跟	taeh43 搭

五 巩固练习

1 甲：体育比赛，有时候啦啦队也很要紧的。

乙：是的，他们的的确确起到了为运动员起到呐喊助威的作用。

甲：不过有些啦啦队队员在场上喊得声嘶力竭，看着够可怜的。

乙：这个你就不懂了，就是要这样才过瘾呀。

2 甲：昨天，我到园区的科文中心看杂技演出了，太好了！
乙：我不大敢看惊险的项目，难得看看，心都跳到嗓子眼了。
甲：卖相倒是个十足的男子汉，哪里知道胆子这么小。
乙：被你夹住一筷子了，男儿胆子小是好事，不容易闯祸。你不要不服气。

六 参考答案

甲：普通话 体育 比赛，有 时候 啦啦队 也 很 要 紧 的。
　　吴语音 thi51-yoh3 pi51-se31 yeu22-zen33-kuan31 la44- la44-de31 gha223 me44 zon231-iau31 keh0
　　吴语文 体育 比赛，有 辰光 啦啦队 也 蛮 重 要 个。

乙：普通话 是 的，他们 的 的 确 确 为运动员 起 到
　　吴语音 zy231-keh3 li44-toh3 tih43-tih43-kuaeh43-kuaeh43 chi51-tae44-tsy31 we231 yuin22-don33-
　　吴语文 是 个， 俚笃 的 的 刮 刮 起 到 仔 为 运 动

　　　　　　呐 喊 助 威 的 作用。
　　　　　　yoe31 naeh23- he31 zou22-ue33-keh3 tsoh43-yon231
　　　　　　员 呐 喊 助 威 个 作用。

甲：普通话 不 过 有 些 啦啦队 队 员 在 场 上
　　吴语音 pih43-kou523 yeu231-tson31 la44-la44-de31 de22- yoe33 leh23-he31 zan22-laon33
　　吴语文 不 过 有 种 啦啦队 队 员 勒嗨 场 浪

　　　　　　喊 得 声 嘶 力 竭，看 着 够 可 怜 的。
　　　　　　he51-teh3 ng22- he44-loh23-tson31 khoe51-tsy31 gha223 me44 tsoh43- nyih3-keh3
　　　　　　喊 得 五 虚 六 肿， 看 仔 也 蛮 作 孽 个。

乙：普通话 这 个 你 就 不 懂 了，就 是 要 这样 才
　　吴语音 e44-keh3 ne231 zeu231 feh43-ton51 tse44 zeu22- zy33 iae523 e44-zan33-meh3 tse44
　　吴语文 哀个 㑚 就 弗 懂 哉，就 是 要 哀场 末 再

　　　　过　瘾　呀。
　　　　saeh43-kheh43 ue0
　　　　煞　渴　啘。

甲：The cheerleaders sometimes are important at a sports contest.
乙：Their cheers in support of the players are really working.
甲：But it was pathetic to watch some cheerleaders shout at the top of their voice in the field.
乙：It's beyond your understanding. That was fun.

2

甲：普通话 昨天，　　我 到 园 区 的 科 文 中 心
　　吴语音 zoh23-nyih3-tsy44-taeh3 ngou231 tae523 yoe22-chiu44 keh43 khou44-ven33-tson44-sin31
　　吴语文 昨 日 仔 搭，我 到 园 区 个 科 文 中 心

　　　　看 杂 技 演 出 的，　太 好 了！
　　　　khoe523 zeh23-ji31 ie51-tsheh3-keh3 fiau523 theh43 tse523 oh0
　　　　看 杂 技 演 出 个，勿 忒 赞 喔！

乙：普通话 我 不 大 敢 看 惊 险 的 项 目，难 得
　　吴语音 ngou231 feh43-da231 koe51 khoe523 cin44-shie44-keh3 ghaon22-moh3 ne22-teh3
　　吴语文 我 弗 大 敢 看 惊 险 个 项 目，难 得

　　　　看 看 心 都 跳 到 嗓 子 眼 了。
　　　　khoe51-khoe31 sin44 gha223 thiae523 tae44 ghoh23-lon33-kheu31 tse44
　　　　看 看 心 也 跳 到 喉 咙 口 哉。

甲：普通话 外 表 倒 是 个 十 足 的 　 男 子 汉
　　吴语音 ma22-sian33 tae44-zy-keh3 zah23-kueh43-thih43- ngan33-keh3 noe22-tsy44-hoe31
　　吴语文 卖 相 倒 是 个 石 骨 铁 硬 个 男 子 汉

　　　　哪 里 知 道 胆 子 这 么 小。
　　　　lo22-taeh3 shiae51-teh3 te51-tsy31 zeh23-kan31 siae523
　　　　哪 搭 晓 得 胆 子 实 梗 小。

乙：普通话 被 你 夹 住 一 筷 子 了，男 儿 胆 子 小 是
吴语音 peh43 ne231 cie44-lae31 ih43-khue44-ng23 tse44 noe22-nyin33 te51-tsy31 siae523 zy231
吴语文 曱 俚 攓 牢 一 筷 儿 哉，男 人 胆 子 小 是

好 事， 不 容 易 闯 祸。 你 不 要 不 服 气。
hae51-zy33- thi31 feh43-yon33-yi31 tshaon51 ghou231 ne231 fiae523 feh43 lin22-ben33
好 事 体， 弗 容 易 闯 祸。 俚 覅 弗 临 盆。

甲：I saw an acrobatic show at Suzhou Science and Cultural Arts Centre yesterday. Wonderful!

乙：I rare not to watch daring feats, which make my heart on my mouth.

甲：You seem like a man, but I didn't know you were so timid.

乙：Now you have something on me. But you should acknowledge that a timid man doesn't make trouble.

第五单元

饮食与服务

一 情景引入

甲：普通话 十一 长 假 马 上 到 了, 你 有 什 么 打 算?
　　吴语音 zeh23-ih3 zan22-ka33 tsih43-moh3 tae523 tse44 ne231 aeh43-yeu231 sa523-keh3 tan51-soe31
　　吴语文 十 一 长 假 即 目① 到 哉, 倷 阿 有 啥 个 打 算?

---

① "即目"等同于普通话中的"马上",指相对较短的时间,这里的马上,既可以指"立即"(还有一分钟,即目出发。),也可以指"几天后"(如同"情景引入")。

乙：普通话 民以食为天，我么今天松鹤楼、明天
　　吴语音 min223 i51 zeh23 we231 thie44 ngou231-meh3 cin44-tsae31 son44-ngoh31-leu31 min22-tsae33
　　吴语文 民以食为天，我末今朝松鹤楼、明朝

得月楼、后天川福楼、大后天贵宾
teh43-nyuih3- leu31 gheu231-nyih3 tshoe44-foh3-leu31 da22-gheu33- nyih3 kue523-pin44-
得月楼、后日川福楼、大后天贵宾

楼，一天一家吃过来。你愿不愿意与我
leu31 ih43-nyih3 ih43-ka44 chih43-kou44-le31 ne231 aeh43-kae44-shin31 taeh43 ngou231
楼，一日一家吃过来。倷阿高兴搭我

一起去？
ih43-dae231 chi523 aeh0
一淘去啊？

甲：普通话 别开玩笑了，你会天天去酒店吃饭？
　　吴语音 fiae523 tan51 ban223 tse44 ne231 ue523-teh nyih23-zoh3 chi523 tseu51-tie31 chih43 ve231
　　吴语文 覅打棚①哉，倷会得日逐去酒店吃饭？

平时，你恨不得一个钱掰成
bin231-zan33-nyih3-ciah3 ne231 ghen231-feh3-teh3 ih43- keh43 don22-die33 pe44-zen31
平常日脚，倷恨弗得一个铜钿掰成

两个用，真的有事情万不得已请客，也
lian231-keh3 yon231 tsen44-keh3 yeu231 zy22-thi33 ve22-peh3-teh3-i31 tshin51-khah3 gha223
两个用②，真个有事体万不得已请客，也

心疼得吃不下，哪里会没有事情舍得到
nyoh23 thon523-teh3 chih43-feh3-loh3 aeh43-zy231 m22-peh3 zy22-thi33 so51-teh3 tae523
肉痛得吃弗落，阿是呒不事体舍得到

---

① "打棚"意思为"开玩笑"，基本上都是带有善意的。
② "一个铜钿掰成两个用"与"场景对话6"中的"做人家"均有褒贬两重含义，褒义指"非常节俭"，贬义指"十分小气"。

第五单元　饮食与服务　109

```
            酒  店  去  大  吃  特  吃?
            tseu51-tie31 chi523 da22-chih3-deh3-chih3-keh3-a0
            酒  店  去  大  吃  特  吃  个 啊?
```

乙：普通话　跟　你　逗着玩　呢！我　是　去　这种　有　名　气　的
　　吴语音 taeh43 ne231 leu231-leu31 ia0 ngou231-zy31 chi523 geh23-tson31 yeu231 min22-chi44-keh3
　　吴语文　搭　侬　搂搂　呀！我　是　去　箇种　有　名　气　个

```
            大  酒  店  的  网  页  上  看  看, 顺  便  依  样
            da22- tseu44-tie44-keh3 maon22-yeh3-laon31 khoe523-khoe31 zen22-ta44-bie31 i44-yan31
            大  酒  店  个  网  页  浪  看  看, 顺  带  便  依  样

            画  葫  芦  学  几  只  他  们  的  拿  手  菜。
            gho231 ghou22-lou33 ghoh223 ci51-tsah3 li44-toh3-keh3 no22-seu44-tshe31
            画  葫  芦  学  几  只  俚笃  个  拿  手  菜。
```

甲：普通话　哦，原　来　你　是　这样　　天　　天　到　酒
　　吴语音 oh43 nyioe231-le31 ne231-zy31 zeh23-kan31 yan22-tsy33 me44-nyih3-thie31 tae523 tseu51-
　　吴语文　喔，原　来　侬　是　实梗样子　每日天　到　酒

```
            店  吃  饭  啊, 这  倒  要  好  好  谢 谢  酒  店  的
            tie31 chih43 ve231 a0 geh23-tae44-iae31 hae51-hae44-ciae31 zia22- zia33 tseu51-tie44-keh3
            店  吃  饭  啊, 箇  倒  要  好  好较 谢 谢  酒  店  个

            网  上  服  务  呢。
            maon231-laon31 voh23-vu31 tse0
            网  浪  服  务  哉。
```

甲：The National Day holiday is approaching. What's your program?

乙：Bread is the staff of life. I am going to take turns to enjoy the decilious food in local restaurants, including Songhelou Restaurant, Deyuelou Restaurant, Chuanfu Restaurant, and Guibinlou Restaurant. Would you like to go with me?

甲：No kidding. You can't possibly go to eat at a restaurant every day. You always watch every penny. Unless absolutely compelled, you will not treat us. If you have to, it will make you lose your appetite to see such waste. How could you have splurged on big meals at restaurants?

乙: I am only joking. I am just going to web sites of some famous restaurants and copy some of their specialties.

甲: I see. It was so that you can eat at a restaurant every day. Thanks to the restaurants' online service.

 二 场景对话

1. 甲: 普通话　我　的　孙女　　　暑假　天　天　在　　我　家　　吃
      吴语音 nyi231-keh3 sen44-noe33-n31 syu44-ka31 thie44-thie31 leh23-he31 nyi231 oh43-li231 chih43-
      吴语文　伲　个　孙　囡　儿　暑　假　天　天　勒　嗨　伲　屋　里　吃

      饭，嘴　巴　刁　得　不　得　了，为　了　配　他　胃　口，我
      ve231 tsyu51-po23 tiae44-teh3 feh43-teh43-liae231 we22-tsy33 phe523 li44 we22-kheu33 ngou231
      饭，嘴　巴　刁　得　弗　得　了，为　仔　配　俚　胃　口，我

      天　天　买　洗　烧，忙　得　晕　头　转　向。
      nyih23-zoh3 ma231 da231 sae44 maon22-teh3 tshih43-huen44-poh43- sou31
      日　逐　买　汏　烧，忙　得　七　荤　八　素①。

   乙: 普通话　我　与　你　一　样，日　日　煎　炒　爆　熬，给　小
      吴语音 ngou231 taeh43 ne231 ih43-yian231 nyih23-nyih3 tsie44 tshae51 pae523 ngae223 paon44 siae51-
      吴语文　我　搭　侬　一　样，日　日　煎　炒　爆　熬，帮　小

      皇帝　准　备　齐　全，他　还　爱吃不吃　的，而且
      waon33-ti31 tshih43- toe44-poh43-tsen31 n44-ne31 we223 ga22-leh3- ga31 leh3 we22-ka33
      皇　帝　七　端　八　正②，尔　侬　还　茄　勒　茄　了，还　加

---

① "七荤八素"是夸张地形容手忙脚乱，头昏脑胀，甚至晕头转向到连东南西北也分辨不清。

② "七端八正"比喻准备齐全，而且十分妥帖。

一 个　劲　地　横挑鼻子竖挑眼。
ih43-mah3-lou44- sou31 tshih43-kan44-phoh43-diae31
一 脉 啰 唆① 七 更 八 调②。

甲：My granddaughter had dinner at my home everyday during her summer holiday. She is so fastidious about her food that I was busy all day preparing food to her taste. I was rushed off my feet.

乙：I am, like yourself, cooking in many ways every day — baking, frying, and boiling. Although I have got everything ready for my "little emperor", he always turns his head away and picks on me.

2. 甲：普通话　昨天　　　去　听　了　一　个　有　关　健　康　饮
吴语音 zoh23-nyih3-tsy44-taeh3 chi523 thin44-tsy31 ih43-keh43 yeu22-kue33 jie22-khaon33 in51-
吴语文　昨　日　仔　搭　去　听　仔　一　个　有　关　健　康　饮

食的讲座，有个听众很讨厌，　老是
zeh3-keh3 kaon51-zou31 yeu231-keh3 thin44-khah3 me44 thae51-za33-ie33-keh3 lae231-zy31
食个讲座，有个听客蛮讨惹厌个，老是

好显摆抢着发言，　但　　常常是答
shie44-kaeh43-kaeh43 ga22- leh3 zie22-poh3-tsha31 de22-pih3-kou31 cin44-zan31 tshih43-
妗夹夹③茄勒前八叉，但不过经常七

非所问，真的不像样。
tsyu44-poh43-taeh3 tsen44- keh3 tshih43-feh43-lae33-se44-chie31
嘴八答④，真个七弗老三牵。

---

① "一脉啰唆"是"啰唆"的比较级，比"啰唆"的程度更深。

② "七更八调"是指横挑鼻子竖挑眼，含有故意找茬、挑刺的意思，下面场景对话4中"象牙筷浪扳雀丝"、"扳错头"也是这个意思。

③ "妗夹夹"与下页的"茄勒前八叉"均带有贬义，指不是行家却常常自以为是，在众人面前好显摆发表见解，结果却往往是错误的。

④ "七嘴八搭"除了具有场景对话2中"答非所问"的意思，另外还有"胡说八道"以及"七嘴八舌"两层意思。"七弗老牵"除了具有场景对话2中"不像样"的意思，另外还有"不成体统、不伦不类"的意思。

乙：普通话 现 在 有 些 人，就 喜欢 不懂 装 懂，
　　吴语音 yie22-ze33 yeu231-tson31 nyin223 zeu22-zy33 huoe44-shi31 feh43-ton44-tsaon44-ton31
　　吴语文 现 在 有 种 人，就 是 欢 喜 弗 懂 装 懂，

　　　　冒充行家。
　　　　aeh43-ghou33-loe31 mae22-tshon33 cin44-kaon44-tsoe31
　　　　阿 胡 卵 冒 充 金 刚 钻①。

甲：I attended a lecture on healthy eating yesterday. There was an unpleasant audience who always tried to get a word in first to show him off. But he always gave the wrong answers. What a disgrace!

乙：Those who like pretending to know what they don't know are actually fake experts.

3. 甲：普通话 上 个 星 期 天 去 农 家 乐 吃 饭，点 了 个 松
　　吴语音 zaon231-keh3 li22-pa33 nyih23 chi523 non22-cia44-loh3 chih43-ve231 tie51-tsy44-tsah3 son44-
　　吴语文 上 个 礼 拜 日 去 农 家 乐 吃 饭，点 仔 只 松

　　　　鼠 鳜鱼，味 道 与 松 鹤 楼 比 是 天 差 地 远。
　　　　tshyu44-kue44-ng31 mi22-dae33 taeh43 son44-ngoh3-leu31 pi51 zy231 dou22-the44-yoe33-pan31
　　　　鼠 鳜鱼，味 道 搭 松 鹤 楼 比 是 大 推 远 蹦。

乙：普通话 你 去 那 种 地 方 吃 松 鼠 鳜鱼，真 是
　　吴语音 ne231 tae523 geh23-tson31 zan22-ho33 chi523 chih43 son44-tsyu44-kue44-ng31 tsen44-keh3
　　吴语文 倷 到 箇 种 场 化 去 吃 松 鼠 鳜鱼，真 个

　　　　的 脑子进水了。
　　　　zy31 aeh43-chioh43-si31
　　　　是 阿 屈 死②。

甲：I made a pleasure-in-farmhouse tour last week. The squirrel-shaped mandarin fish we ordered in a small restaurant was entirely different from that of in Songhelou Restaurant.

乙：How come you ate squirrel-shaped mandarin fish in a place like that. What were you thinking?

---

① "阿胡乱冒充金刚钻"是骂人的话，意指外行冒充内行。
② "阿屈死"又写作"阿屈西"，"屈死"。专称见识少、眼界浅而容易上当受骗或被人愚弄的人。

第五单元 饮食与服务

4. 甲：普通话 经理，顾客是上帝没错，可　　有的顾
　　　吴语音 cin44-li31 kou523-khah3 zy231 zaon22-ti33 feh43-tsho23 pih43-kou523 yeu231-keh3 kou523-
　　　吴语文 经理，顾客是上帝弗错，不过 有个顾

　　　　　客就好 鸡蛋里挑骨头，怎么办？
　　　　　khah3 zeu231 huoe44-shi31 zian22-nga33-khue44-laon31 pe44 tshiah43-sy44 naeh23-han31 be231
　　　　　客就欢喜 象牙筷浪扳雀丝，哪哼办？

　　乙：普通话 如果 顾客 挑刺， 我们应该以更加周
　　　吴语音 cia51-sy33 kou523-khah3 pe44 tsho44-deu31 nyi231 in44-taon31 no223 ka44-nyi33-dae33-
　　　吴语文 假使 顾客 扳错头， 倷应当 拿 加二道

　　　　　到的服务来让 他们满意。
　　　　　di33-keh3 voh23-vu31 le223 nyian231 li44-toh3 moe231-i31
　　　　　地①个服务来让 俚笃满意。

　甲：It's perfectly true that customer goes first. Yet there are customers who always love finding quarrel in a straw. What should we do about it?
　乙：We should provide good service to satisfy the nitpickers.

5. 甲：普通话 哎，你们几个小朋友吃得慢些，又不是
　　　吴语音 ghe223 n22-toh3 ci51-keh3 siae51-ban33-yeu31 chih43-teh3 me231-tie31 yih23 feh43-zy231
　　　吴语文 欸，尔笃几个小朋友吃得慢点，亦弗是

　　　　　争夺 祭鬼的饭菜，干吗 这么 狼吞虎咽的？肠
　　　　　tshian51 kan44-ve31 tsoh43-sa523 geh23-zaon31 laon22-then44-hou44-ie44-keh3 zan22-
　　　　　抢 羹饭②，作啥 箇状 狼吞虎咽个？肠

---

① "道地"有三层含义：a. 周到，地道。此义同"场景对话4"中"倷应当拿加尼道地个服务来让唔笃满意"。b. 真正，纯粹。哀只虾子鲞鱼个味道是道地个采芝斋味道。（这个虾子鲞鱼的味道是真正的采芝斋味道。c. 实在。老张做人蛮道地个。（老张做人很实在。）

② "羹饭"在苏州话中特指祭奠死者的饭菜。"抢羹饭"通常对人们吃相不雅、迫不及待地争食时讲，一般是长辈训斥小辈时用。

胃 要 受 不 了 的。
we33 iae523 chih43-feh43-siae44-keh3
胃 要 吃 弗 消 个。

乙：普通话 奶奶，我们 下午 一点钟 前 必须 赶到 体
吴语音 ae44-bu31 nyi231 gho22-me33-tseu31 ih43-tie51 tson44 zie223 pe51-iae31 bae22-tae33 thi51-
吴语文 媪婆，倷 下晚昼 一点钟 前 板要 跑到 体

育馆集训，否则 要 挨罚 的。
yoh3-kuoe31 zih23-shiuin31 feu44-tseh3 iae523 chih43 mae22-lih3-tsy3 lih23 pih43-koh43 keh0
育馆集训，否则 要 吃毛栗子、立壁角① 个。

甲：普通话 你 不应该 在背后说老师坏话 的。
吴语音 ne231 feh43-in44-taon31 tshoh43 lae44-sy31 pih43- ciah43 keh0
吴语文 倷 弗应当 戳老师鳖脚② 个。

甲：Eat it slowly, kids. Don't snarf down the meal as if you were grabbing the sacrifice for ghosts. You would get sick after downing so many things in so little time.

乙：Grandma, we must arrive at the stadium before 1 p.m. to attend the training camp, or we will be punished.

甲：Don't speak ill of our coach behind his back.

6. 甲：普通话 老板，你的 油条 价格 怎么 比别人 贵呀。
吴语音 lae22-pe33 ne231-keh3 yeu22-diae33 ka44-die31 naeh23-han31 pi51 nyin22-ka33 keh3-ciu51 cia44
吴语文 老板，倷个 油条 价钿 哪哼 比 人家个 贵③ 嘎。

---

① 把中指卷起来，用凸出的顶端敲别人脑袋一下叫做"吃毛栗子"。贴墙而立地被罚站称之为"立壁角"。这两个词语，通过动作形象地表明挨罚的样子，其实不一定真的挨罚。

② "戳鳖脚"主要意思为"背后说人坏话"，此外，还有"挖墙角"的意思。

③ 苏州话中"贵"在表示"价格高"的意义时，写法与普通话完全相同，但读音大不一样，读作ciu523。场景对话9中的"嗰"的意义则与"贵"相对，指价格便宜。

第五单元　饮食与服务

乙：普通话　我　用　的　油　都　是　到　超　市　买　的，而且　每
　　吴语音　ngou231 yon22-keh3 yeu223 ze22-zy33 tae523 tshae44- zy31 ma231-keh3 r44-tshi31 nyih23-
　　吴语文　我　用　个　油　侪　是　到　超　市　买　个，而且　且

　　　　　　天　倒　掉，不　重　复　使　用，你　放　心　　　吃，
　　　　　　zoh3 tae523-theh3 feh43 zon22-voh3 sy51-yon31 ne231 faon44- sin31 thoh43 te51 chih43
　　　　　　逐　倒　脱，弗　重　复　使　用，㑚　放　心　托　胆　吃

　　　　　　丝　毫　　　　不用　担　心。
　　　　　　hae51-leh3 ih43-tie44-tie31 gha223 fiae523 te44-sin31
　　　　　　好　勒，一点点　也　朆　担　心。

甲：普通话　一　般　　开　店　的　人　都　蛮　精打细算的　　你
　　吴语音　ih43-pe44-sin31 khe44 tie523 keh43 nyin223 ze223 me44 tsou44-nyin33-ka44-keh3 ne231
　　吴语文　一　般　性　开　店　个　人　侪　蛮　做　人　家　个　㑚

　　　　　　倒　　　　与众不同。
　　　　　　tae523 le22-teh3-keh3 koh43-bih3-keh3
　　　　　　倒　　来得个　角　别　个。

甲：Boss, why are your fried dough sticks more expensive than others'.

乙：The oil I use comes from supermarket,and I change it every day. Take it easy. Just eat as much as you want.

甲：People who own their business pinch pennies all the time. You are different.

7. 甲：普通话　老　板　娘，我　这　里　是　工　学　院　公　共　教　学　部
　　　吴语音　lae22-pe44-nyian31 nyi231 e44-taeh3-zy31 kon44- yoh3-yoe31 kon44-gon31 ciae51-yoh3-bu31
　　　吴语文　老　板　娘，倷　哀搭　是　工　学　院　公　共　教　学　部

　　　　　　　社　科　教　研　室，我们　要　5　份　宫　保　鸡　丁　盖
　　　　　　　zo22-khou33 ciae51-nyie44-seh3　nyi231 iae523 ng231- ven31 kon44-pae44-ci44-tin31 ke51-
　　　　　　　社　科　教　研　室，倷　要　5　份　宫　保　鸡　丁　盖

浇饭, 能　　　　快 点 吗?
ciae44-ve31 aeh43 khou51-i31 khua51-tie23
浇饭, 阿 可 以 快 点?

乙: 普通话 老 生 意 了, 马 上　　　　就 到。
吴语音 lae22-san44-i31 tse44 tsheh43 ih43-keh43 phi44-deu31 zeu231 tae523
吴语文 老 生 意 哉, 出 一 个 披 头① 就 到。

甲: Madame, this is Social Science Teaching and Research Office of Public Education Department, Engineering College. Five rice with saute diced chicken and peanuts to take away, please. Could you hurry up? I don't have time.
乙: You are a regular customer of our restaurant. I will bring that right away.

8. 甲: 普通话 老李, 你 不 应 该　　呀! 你 说 你们 亲 戚 裹
吴语音 lae22-li33 ne231 feh43-tsoh43-shin44-keh3-a31 ne231 kaon51 n22-toh3 tshin44-cioe31 pae44-
吴语文 老李, 俫 弗 作 兴 个 啊! 俫 讲 尔 笃 亲 眷 包

的 粽 子 价 钱 便 宜 质 量 又 好, 我 非 但 自 己
keh3 tson44-tsy31 ka44-die31 jian223 tseh43-lian231 yih23 hae51 ngou231 fi44-de31 zy22-ka33
个 粽 子 价 钿 嘸 质 量 亦 好, 我 非 但 自 家

买 了 不 少, 还 动 员 亲 朋 一 起 买, 结 果
ma231-tsy31 feh43-sae51 we223 don22-yoe33 tshin44-ban31 ih43-dae231 ma231 cih43-kou523
买 仔 弗 少, 还 动 员 亲 朋 一 淘 买, 结 果

肉 粽 里　　都 是 大 肥 肉。
nyioh23-tson44-li44-shian31 ze22-zy33 lae22-phaon44-nyioh3
肉 粽 里 向 侪 是 老 胖 肉。

---

① "出披头"同"出辔头", 本指骑马飞奔, 现在大多指人飞快地跑, 习惯上加进数量词, 变为"出一个披头"。

乙：普通话 老张，我 与 你 是 几 十 年 的 老 朋 友 了，
　　吴语音 lae22-tsan33 ngou231 taeh43 ne231 zy231 ci51-seh3- nyie33-keh3 lae22-ban33-yeu31 tse44
　　吴语文 老张，我 搭侬 是 几 十 年 个 老 朋 友 哉，

　　　　　我 怎 么 会 作弄 你 呢！我 来 打 电
　　　　　ngou231 naeh23- han31 ue523 teh43 lon44-son31 ne231 neh0 ngou231 le223 tan51 die22-
　　　　　我 哪哼 会 得 弄松① 侬 呢！我 来 打 电

　　　　　话 问 问 到 底 怎 么 回 事。
　　　　　gho33 men231-men31 tao44-ti31 naeh23-han31 tsaon44 zy22-thi33
　　　　　话 问 问 到 底 哪哼 桩 事体。

甲：普通话 我 也 想 你 不 至 于 哄 我 受骗上当 吧。
　　吴语音 ngou231 gha223 sian523 ne231 feh43-tshae44 tsyu51-yu31 peh43 ngou231 jie223 moh23-sae31 ba0
　　吴语文 我 也 想 侬 弗 超 至 于 畀 我 掮木梢② 吧。

乙：普通话 哦，拿 错 了，那 两 大 包 是 一 个 饭店 特 意
　　吴语音 oh43 no223 tsho44 tse44 geh23-lian33-dou33-pae31 zy231 ih43-keh3 ve22-tie33 dih23-we31
　　吴语文 喔，拿 错 哉，箇 两 大 包 是 一 个 饭店 特 为

　　　　　订 的。不 好 意思，我 亲 戚 说 会 照 原
　　　　　din231- keh3 feh43-hae51 i44-sy31 nyi231 tshin44-cioe31 kaon51 ue523 tsae523 nyioe22-
　　　　　定 个。弗 好 意思，伲 亲 眷 讲 会 照 原

　　　　　数 再 送 过 来 一 份 的。
　　　　　sou33 tse44 son523 kou44- le31 ih43-ven231 keh0
　　　　　数 再 送 过 来 一 份 个。

---

① "弄松"的程度有轻重之别，轻者意为"作弄、戏弄"，重者是指背后放黑枪，拍黑砖，使坏，比较阴险。

② "掮木梢"喜欢帮闲事，受人哄骗、被人利用，做吃力不讨好的蠢事。"掮水浸木梢"进一步指上当程度更深，做的事情更蠢。

甲：Li, you had me fooled. You said the the zongzi made by your relatives are of high quality and not expensive either. Not only I have bought a great many zongzi, but also my family and friends. It then turned out that they were full of fat meat.

乙：Zhang, we have been friends for more than a decade. How could I make a fool of you? Let me make a call to check what it was all about.

甲：You won't go so far as to cheat me, will you?

乙： There are some mistakes. The two packages you've got are prepared for a restaurant. My relative promised to send another one according to the original amount soon.

9. 甲：普通话 胥 门 那 儿 的 饭店 锦绣 天堂 最近
　　吴语音 si44-men31 geh23-mie33-tie33-keh31 ve22-tie31 cin51-seu44-thie44-daon31 tse51-jin31
　　吴语文 胥 门 箇 面 点 个 饭店 锦绣 天 堂 最近

　　　　　　招牌菜 打 5 折 供应，很 划 算 的。
　　　　　　tsae44-ba33-tshe31 tan51 te44-tseh3 kon51-in23 keh43-soe523 teh43-le0
　　　　　　招 牌 菜 打 对 折 供 应，合 算 得 来。

乙：普通话 那 今天 晚上 就 去 大 大 地 吃一顿，如何？
　　吴语音 geh23-meh3 cin44-tsae31 ia44-li31 zeu22-chi33 hae51-hae44-ciae31 chih43 ih43-ten523 naeh23-han31
　　吴语文 箇 末 今朝 夜里 就 去 好 好 较 吃 一 顿， 哪哼？

甲：普通话 我 多么 想 现 在 就 去 呀！
　　吴语音 ngou231 ghen22-feh3-teh3 yie22-ze33 zeu231 chi523 neh0
　　吴语文 我 恨 弗 得 现 在 就 去 呢！

乙：普通话 你 几 岁了，还 这样 急 性子。
　　吴语音 ne231 ci51-se31 tse0 we223 e44-zaon31 seh43- zah3-fon31 zeu231 tsha51 bon223
　　吴语文 倷 几 岁 哉， 还 哀 状 说 着 风 就 扯 篷①。

甲：The specialties of Jinxiu Tiantang Restaurant near Xumen are sold at a 50% discount, which is a good bargain.

乙： Let's have a big meal there tonight, shall we?

甲：How I wish I could go there right now.

乙：Come on. You're no longer a child. Be patient.

---

① "说着风就扯篷"是对性子特别急的形象比喻。

三 词语贴士

（一）餐具

序号	英文	苏州话
1.	spoon	tshae44
	汤勺	㮾
2.	chopsticks	khue44-ng31
	筷子	筷儿
3.	bowl	uoe51
	碗	碗
4.	soup bowl	thaon44-tson31
	小碗	汤盅
5.	plate	ben22-tsy33
	盆子	盆子

（二）厨房调料

序号	英文	苏州话
1.	kitchen	tsae44-ghoh3-ke31
	厨房	灶镬间
2.	ginger	lae22-cian33
	姜	老姜
3.	garlic	da22-soe33
	蒜	大蒜
4.	scallion	tshon44
	葱	葱
5.	soy sauce	tsian44-yeu31
	酱油	酱油
6.	rice wine	waon22-tseu33
	料酒	黄酒
7.	vinegar	tshou523
	醋	醋
8.	starch	lin22-fen33
	生粉，淀粉	菱粉
9.	monosodium glutamate	vi22-tsy44-sou31
	味精	味之素

续表

序号	英文	苏州话
10.	salt	yie223
	盐	盐
11.	sugar	daon223
	糖	糖

(三)正餐

序号	英文	苏州话
1.	breakfast	tsae51-ve31
	早餐	早饭
2.	lunch	tson44-ve31
	午餐	中饭
3.	supper	ia44-ve31
	晚餐	夜饭
4.	Chinese food	tson44-tshoe31
	中餐	中餐
5.	western food	si44-tshoe31
	西餐	西餐
6.	combo	thae44-tshoe31
	套餐	套餐
7.	staple food	tsyu51-zeh3
	主食	主食
8.	non-staple food	fu44-zeh3
	副食	副食
9.	hors d'oeuvres	lan22-ben33
	冷盘	冷盆
10.	fried food	nyih23-tshae31
	热炒	热炒
11.	pot-stewed food	lou22-tshe33
	卤菜	卤菜
12.	rice	bah23-mi33-ve31
	米饭	白米饭
13.	porridge	phae44-ve31
	稀饭	泡饭

（四）点心

序号	英文	苏州话
1.	Chinese pie 大饼	da22-pin33 大饼
2.	fried dough sticks 油条	yeu22-taeh3-kue31　yeu22-diae33 油煠桧　油条
3.	baozi（steamed buns with stuffing） 包子	moe22-deu33 馒头
4.	steamed dumpling 汤包	thaon44-pae31 汤包
5.	won ton（stuffed thin dumplings served with soup） 馄饨	wen22-den33 馄饨
6.	dumpling 饺子	ciae51-tsy23 饺子
7.	tangyuan (glutinous rice balls) 汤圆	thaon44-doe31 汤团
8.	sweet dumpling 元宵	nin22-po44-thaon44-doe31 宁波汤团
9.	spring roll 春卷	tshen44-cioe31 春卷
10.	noodles 汤面	yan22-tshen44-mie31 阳春面
11.	mooncake 月饼	ngeh23-pin31 月饼
12.	corn 玉米	yu22-mah3 雨麦
13.	sweet potato 红薯	se33-yu31 山芋
14.	food 可吃的东西（泛指）	chih43-jioh43 吃局

（五）烹饪方法

序号	英文	苏州话
1.	fry 煎	tsie44 煎
2.	saute 炒	tshae51 炒

续表

序号	英文	苏州话
3.	fry at high temperature very quickly	pae523
	爆	爆
4.	stew	ngae223
	熬	熬
5.	fry	tso523
	炸	炸
6.	boil	men44
	煮	闷
7.	steam	tsen44
	蒸	蒸
8.	roast	khae51
	烤	烤
9.	bake	hon44
	烘	烘
10.	thicken by starch	tsah43-nyi231
	勾芡	着腻

（六）菜肴

序号	英文	苏州话
1.	potato	yan22-yu33-na31
	土豆	洋芋艿
2.	tomato	fe44-ka31
	西红柿	番茄
3.	cabbage	cioe51- sin44-tshe31
	包菜	卷心菜
4.	ipomoea aquatica	on44-tshe31
	空心菜	蕹菜
5.	ham	zou22-den33
	腿肉	坐臀
6.	fat	lae22-phaon44-nyioh3, tsan44-nyioh3
	肥肉	老胖肉，胀肉
7.	herring	tsi44-ng31
	青鱼	鲭鱼
8.	ctenopharyngodon idellus	we22-ng31
	草鱼	鲩鱼

续表

序号	英文	苏州话
9.	chicken	ci44-koh43-koh3
	鸡	鸡咯咯
10.	duck	aeh43-lie33-lie31
	鸭	鸭唼唼
11.	goose	bah23-ou44-ciu31
	鹅	白乌龟

（七）水果

序号	英文	苏州话
1.	apple	bin22-kou33
	苹果	苹果
2.	pear	li223
	梨	梨
3.	grape	beh23-dae31
	葡萄	葡萄
4.	watermelon	si44-ko3
	西瓜	西瓜
5.	banana	shian44-tsiae31
	香蕉	香蕉
6.	loquat	bih23-bo31
	枇杷	枇杷
7.	waxberry	yan22-me33
	杨梅	杨梅
8.	apricot	ghan22-tsy33
	杏子	杏子
9.	shaddock	ven22-te33
	柚子	文旦

（八）餐饮场所

序号	英文	苏州话
1.	restaurant	ve22-tie33
	饭店	饭店
2.	restaurant	tshoe44-thin31
	餐厅	餐厅
3.	canteen	zeh23-daon31
	食堂	食堂

续表

序号	英文	苏州话
4.	snack bar 快餐店	khua44-tshoe44-tie31 快餐店
5.	cafe 咖啡馆	kha44-fi44-kuoe31 咖啡馆

（九）服务与消费

序号	英文	苏州话
1.	greeter 迎宾员	nyin22-pin44-yoe31 迎宾员
2.	usher 引导员	yin22-dae33-yoe31 引导员
3.	waiter 招待员	tsae44-de33-yoe31 招待员
4.	waiter 服务员	voh23-vu33-yoe31 服务员
5.	banquet 宴会	ie44-we31 宴会
6.	menu 菜谱	tshe44-pu31 菜谱
7.	order 点菜	tie51 tshe523 点菜
8.	serve 上菜	zaon231 tshe523 上菜
9.	bill v. 结账	cih43-tsan523 结账
10.	bill n. 账单	tsan44-te31 账单
11.	take-out 外卖	nga22-ma33 外卖
12.	rip off customers 宰客	tse44-khah3 宰客

（十）苏州名店

序号	英文	苏州话
1.	Songhelou Restaurant 松鹤楼	son44-ngoh3-leu31 松鹤楼
2.	Deyuelou Restaurant 得月楼	teh43-nyueh3-leu31 得月楼
3.	Huangtianyuan Pastry Store 黄天源	waon22-thie44-nyioe31 黄天源
4.	Zhuhongxing Noodle House 朱鸿兴	tsyu44-ghon33-shin31 朱鸿兴
5.	Lugaojian Sauced Meat Store 陆稿荐	loh23-kae44-tsie31 陆稿荐
6.	Caizhizhai Candy Store 采芝斋	tshe51-tsyu44-tsa31 采芝斋
7.	Yeshouhe Food Store 叶受和	yeh23-zeu33-ghou31 叶受和

四 对话中的特色词汇

序号	英文	苏州话
1.	soon 马上	tsih43-moh3 即目
2.	kidding 开玩笑	tan51-ban223 打棚
3.	money 钱	don22-die33 铜钿
4.	feel sick 心疼	nyoh23 thon523 肉痛
5.	do not have 没有	m22-peh3 呒不
6.	make fun of 逗着玩	leu231-leu31 搂搂
7.	granddaughter 孙女	sen44-noe33-ng31 孙囡儿
8.	wash 洗	da231 汏

续表

序号	英文	苏州话
9.	rushed off one's feet 晕头转向	tshih43-huen44-poh43-sou31 七荤八素
10.	get everything ready 准备齐全	tshih43-toe44-poh43-tsen31 七端八正
11.	always 一个劲	ih43-mah3-lou44-sou31 一脉啰唆
12.	picks on sb 横挑鼻子竖挑眼	tshih43-kan44-poh43-diae31 七更八调
13.	show off 好显摆	shie44-kaeh43-kaeh43 妡夹夹
14.	get a word in first 挤在前面	ga23-leh3 zie22-poh3-tsha31 茄勒前八叉
15.	give an irrelevant answer 答非所问	tshih43-tsyu44-poh43-taeh43 七嘴八答
16.	be disgrace 不像样	tshih43-feh4-lae33-chie51 七弗老牵
17.	fake expert 冒充行家	aeh43-ghou33-loe31 mae22-tshon33 cin44-kaon44-tsoe31 阿胡卵冒充金刚钻
18.	entirely different from 天差地远	dou22-the44-yoe33-pan31 大推远蹦
19.	fool 铳头	aeh43-chioh43-si31 阿屈死
20.	find quarrel in a straw 找茬	zian22-nga33-khue44-laon31 pe44 tshiah43-sy44 象牙筷浪扳雀丝
21.	good 周到	dae231-di31 道地
22.	nitpicker 挑刺	pe44 tsho44-deu31 扳错头
23.	the sacrifice for ghosts 祭鬼的饭菜	kan44-ve31 羹饭
24.	be punished 挨罚	chih43 mae22-lih3-tsy31.lih23 pih43-koh43 吃毛栗子.立壁角
25.	speak ill of sb behind one back 背后说坏话	tshoh43 pih43-ciah43 戳蹩脚
26.	empty out 倒掉	tae523 theh43 倒脱

续表

序号	英文	苏州话
27.	Take it easy. 丝毫不用担心	faon44-sin31 thoh43 te51 放心托胆
28.	pinch pennies 精打细算，抠门	tsou44-nyin33-ka31 做人家
29.	hurry up 快点	ghae22-sae44-tie31 豪惵点
30.	right away 很短的时间	tsheh43 ih43-keh3 phi44-deu31 出一个披头
31.	less expensive 便宜	jian223 噱
32.	make a fool of sb 作弄	lon44-son31 弄松
33.	be cheated 受骗上当	jie223 moh23-siae31 掮木梢
34.	specially 特意	dih23-we31 特为
35.	How I wish I could... 多么想	ghen231- feh3-teh3 恨不得
36.	a quick temper 急性子	seh43-zah3 fon44 zeu231 tsha51 bon223 说着风就扯篷

五、巩固练习

1 甲：老张，你这个清炒虾仁烧得真的好极了，味道无可挑剔，得月楼的特级厨师也不过这点水平哦。

乙：老李你不要开玩笑了。你说清炒虾仁吃口不错，我听着蛮开心。什么我的水平与特级厨师居然不相上下哟，我假使相信，真的昏头了。

甲：是非自有公论，大家尝尝看，看我有没有说错。

2 甲：今天到饭店吃饭，吃出一肚子火来。

乙：消消火，发火对身体不利的。

甲：我去消费，照理我是上帝，谁知道碰到个服务员从头到尾摆出了一副后娘脸来，真的讨厌。你说要不要生气。

乙：是蛮惹人生气的，不过你犯不着为别人的错误不开心，把自己的身体弄坏不合算的哟。

六 参考答案

1

甲：普通话 老张，你 这个 清 炒 虾 仁 烧得 真的
　　吴语音 lae22-tsan33 ne231 ke44-tsah3 tshin44-tshae44-ho44-nyin31 sae44-teh3 tsen44-keh3
　　吴语文 老张，倷 该 只 清 炒 虾 仁 烧 得 真 个

　　　　　好极了，味 道 无 可 挑 剔， 特 级 厨 师
　　　　　tse51-theu31 mi22-dae33 m22-peh3 ghe22-gho33 hae51 kaon51 deh23-cih3 zyu22-sy33
　　　　　赞 透，味 道 呒 不 闲 话 好 讲， 特 级 厨 师

　　　　　也 不 过 这 点 水 平 哦。
　　　　　gha223 pih43-kou523 ke44-zaon33-tie31 ho44-deu33-cin31 ue0
　　　　　也 不 过 该 状 点 花 头 经 唲。

乙：普通话 老李你 不要 开玩笑 了。你 说 清 炒 虾 仁
　　吴语音 lae22-li33 ne231 fiae523 tan51-ban223 tse44 ne231 kaon51 tshin44-tshae44-ho44--nyin31
　　吴语文 老李 倷 朆 打 棚 哉。倷 讲 清 炒 虾 仁

　　　　　吃 口 不 错，我 听 着 蛮 开心。什么
　　　　　chih43-kheu51 feh43-tsho23 nou231 thin44-leh3-he31 me44 ou44-sin31 sa523 keh43
　　　　　吃 口 弗 错，我 听 勒 嗨 蛮 窝 心 啥 个

　　　　　我 的 水 平 与 特 级 厨 师 居 然 不 相
　　　　　ngou231-keh3 syu51-bin23 taeh43 deh23-cih3 zyu22-sy33 ciu44-zoe31 ban22-tshih43-
　　　　　我 个 水 平 搭 特 级 厨 师 居 然 碰 七

　　　　　上 下 么。我 假 使 相 信， 真 的 昏 头 了。
　　　　　ban33-poh3-meh3 ngou231 ciae51-sy23 sian44-sin44-meh3 tsen44-keh3 nyih23-huen31 tse44
　　　　　碰 八 末 我 假 使 相 信 末， 真 个 热 昏 哉。

甲：普通话 是 非 自 有 公 论， 大 家 尝 尝
　　吴语音 yeu231-li31 m22-li33 tsheh43-leh3 tson51-nyin23 tsyu51-li31 da22-ka33 zaon22-zaon33-
　　吴语文 有 理 呒 理 出 勒 众 人 嘴 里，大 家 尝 尝

看，看 我 有没有说 错。
khoe31 khoe523 ngou231 aeh43 - seh43 tsho44
看，看 我 阿 说错。

甲：Zhang, you are a wonderful cook. The shrimps saute tastes delicious. It could have been done by a special-grade chef.

乙：Li, don't make fun of me. I am glad to hear you like it. If I believe that I runs the special-grade chef close in cooking, I must be off my head.

甲：Public opinion is the best judge. You guys just try yourself please.

2

甲：普通话 今天 到饭店里去吃饭，吃出 一
吴语音 cin44-tsae31 tae523 ve22-tie44-li31 chi523 chih43- ve231 chih43-tsheh43-tsy31 ih43-
吴语文 今朝 到饭店里去吃饭，吃 出 仔 一

肚 子 火来。
dou33-bi31 hou51 le223
肚 皮 火 来。

乙：普通话 消消火，发火 对身体不利的。
吴语音 ne231-ne31 chi523 kuan44-hou31 te523 sen44-thi31 feh43-lin223 keh0
吴语文 耐耐气，光 火 对身体弗灵个。

甲：普通话 我 去 消费，照理 我 是 上 帝，谁 知
吴语音 ngou231 chi523 siae44-fi31 tsae51-li31 ngou231-zy31 zaon22-ti33 sa523-nyin23 shiae51-
吴语文 我 去 消费，照理 我 是 上 帝，啥 人 晓

道 碰到 个 服务员 从 头 到尾 摆出 了
teh3 ban22-zah3- keh3 voh23-vu33-yoe31 zon22-deu33-tae44-meh3 pa51-tsheh3-tsy31
得 碰 着 个 服务员 从 头 到 末 摆出 仔

一 副 后 娘 脸 来，真 的 讨 厌。你 说
ih43-fu523 me22-nyian33-mie33- khon31 tsen44-keh3 tshoh43-chi523 ne231 kaon51
一 副 晚 娘 面 孔，真 个 触 气。倷 讲

要 不 要 生 气。
aeh43-iae523 hou51-mae31
阿 要 火 冒。

乙：普通话 是 蛮 惹人生气的，不 过 你 犯不着 为 别 人
吴语音 zy231 me44 za231-chi44-keh3 pih43-kou523 ne231 ve22-feh3-zah3 we231 nyin22-ka44-
吴语文 是 蛮 惹 气 个，不 过 倷 犯 弗 着 为 人 家

的 错 误 不 开心，把 自 己 的 身 体 弄
keh3 tsho44-ngou31 feh43-khe44-sin31 no223 zy22--ka44-keh3 sen44-thi31 lon44-teh3
个 错 误 弗 开 心，拿 自 家 个 身 体 弄 得

坏　　　　不 合 算 的 哟。
wa22-wa33-tsa44-tsa31 feh43 keh43-soe523 keh43-a0
坏 坏 喳 喳 弗 合 算 个 啊。

甲：I went to a restaurant for dinner today. What happened to me there really made my blood boil.

乙：Calm down, getting ticked off about it won't do you any good.

甲：Customers first. As a customer, I deserve good service. However, the waitress worked up a most sarcastic expression of countenance all through dinner. What a nice guy. I think in that case anyone would get pretty ticked off, don't you?

乙：Sure. But that's not worth getting so upset about the mistakes of others, which will not do you any good.

第六单元

交通与旅游

一 情景引入

甲：普通话　今　年　中　秋　节　天　公　　　不　作　美，紧
　　吴语音　cin44-nyie31　tson44-tsheu44-tsih3　lae22-thie44-ya31　feh43　paon44-maon223　kaeh43-
　　吴语文　今　年　中　秋　节　老　天　爷　弗　帮　忙，夹

　　　　　　要　时　刻　下　雨　了，本　来　一　家　子　说　好　要　去
　　　　　　maon44-deu33-li31　loh23-yu31　tse0　pen51-le23　ih43-ka44-men31　kaon51-hae31　iae44-chi31
　　　　　　忙　头　里　落　雨　哉，本　来　一　家　门　讲　好　要　去

看 石 湖 串 月 的，这 一 来 只 好 泡 汤 了。
khoe523 zah23-ghou31 tshoe523 ngeh23 keh0 geh23-ci44-meh3 tseh43-hae51 tshah51-kon44 tse44
看 石 湖 串 月 个，箇 记 末 只 好 拆 贡 哉。

乙：普通话 石 湖 反 正 在 苏 州，又 逃 不 了 的。
吴语音 zah23-ghou31 fen51-tsen31 leh23-laon31 sou44-tseu31 yih23 dae22-feh43-theh43-keh3
吴语文 石 湖 反 正 勒 浪 苏 州，亦 逃 弗 脱 个。

今 年 看 不 成， 还 有 明 年 呢。
cin44-nyie31 khoe523 feh43 zen223 meh0 we22-yeu33 min22-nyie33 le0
今 年 看 弗 成 末， 还 有 明 年 唻。

甲：普通话 你 知 道 我 儿 子 盼 望 了 好 久 了，到 底
吴语音 ne231 shiae51-teh3 nyi231 nyi22-tsy33 po44-maon33- tsy31 zan231-yoe31 tse0 tae44-ti31
吴语文 俚 晓 得 伲 儿 子 巴 望① 仔 长 远 哉，到 底

还 小，跟 他 说 下 雨 看 不 到 月 亮，他 就 是 不
siae51 le0 taeh43 li44 kaon51 loh23-yu31 khoe523 feh43-zah3 ngeh23-lian31 li44 zeu22 feh43-
小 唻，搭 俚 讲 落 雨 看 弗 着 月 亮，俚 就 弗

相 信，死 活 纠 缠 着 要 去。嗬 哟，哭
sian44-sin31 kaeh43-kaeh3-nyiae33-nyiae31 tsoh43-tsy51 iae523 chi523 hoh43-yoh3 khoh43-
相 信，夹 夹 绕 绕② 作 仔 要 去。嚯 唷，哭

得 气 都 喘 不 过 来，连 脸 上 也 面 无 血 色，
teh43-le31 ah43-teh3-feh3-tsoe31 lie22-teh3 mie22-khon33 ghaeh23 kaeh43-leh3 sy44-bah3
得 来 曷 得 弗 转，连 得 面 孔 也 夹 勒 丝 白，

---

① "巴望"有两层意思：a. 希望，盼望。这种希望往往带有急切的心情在里面。此义同情景引入中"俚晓得伲儿子巴望仔长远哉"。b. 指望，盼头。例：尔笃伲子哀趟考进清华大学，曩末俚有巴望哉。(你儿子这次考进清华大学，这下你有盼头了。)

② "夹夹绕绕"有三层意思：a. 死活纠缠。这种纠缠有点没完没了的意味。此义同情景引入中"夹夹绕绕作仔要去"。b. 搞七搞八。例：我勒讲张三，俚缠仔李四，真个夹夹绕绕，冬瓜缠勒茄门里。(我在说张三，你搞成李四，真的搞七搞八，风马牛不相及。) c. 形容男女之间关系暧昧。如：俚笃两家头有点夹夹绕绕。(他们两个关系暧昧。)

第六单元　交通与旅游

弄　得　我　们　束　手　无　策。事　到　头　来　只　好　撑　了
lon44-teh3-nyi31 m22-seu33 sa44-lou31 lin22-zyu33 woe22-cih3 tseh43- hae51 tshian44-tsy44-
弄　得　伲　呒　手　筛　锣①。临　时　完　结　只　好　撑　仔

把　伞　陪　他　到　山　塘　街　兜　了　一　圈，这　样　总
po31 se51 be22-li33 tae523 se44-daon33-ka31 deu44-tsy31 ih43-chioe23 ke22-zan31 tson44-
把　伞　陪　俚　到　山　塘　街　兜　仔　一　圈，该　场　总

算　太　平。嘿，你　倒　别　说，晚　上　游　山
soe31 oe44-yih3 e0 ne231 tae523 fiae523 kaon51 ia44-li44-shian31 beh23-sian31 se44-
算　安　逸②！哎，侬　倒　麳　讲，夜　里　向　𡍼　相　山

塘　街　的　人　很　　　多。
daon33-ka44-keh3 nyin223 le22-teh3-keh3 tou44
塘　街　个　人　来　得　个　多。

乙：普通话　山　塘　街　的　夜　景　是　很　美　的，下　雨　天　味　道
吴语音 se44-daon33-ka44-keh3 ia44-cin31 zy231 me44 tse523 keh0 loh23-yu33-thie31 mi22-dae33
吴语文　山　塘　街　个　夜　景　是　蛮　赞　个，落　雨　天　味　道

尤　其　好。　　不　过　以　后　不　凑　巧
zah23-zeh3 lin22-kuaon33 pih43-kou523 gho22-thaon33 chih43-sou523 ban22-zah3
着　实　灵　光。　不　过　下　趟　吃　素　碰　着

---

①　"呒手筛锣"也写作"呒手筛箩"，原来指腾不出手来敲锣，腾不出手来筛箩筐。后来引申为：a. 束手无策。此义同情景引入中"弄得伲呒手筛锣"。b. 比喻很无奈。例：我弗是弗想做班干部，实在是有种事体呒手筛锣。（我不是不想做班干部，实在是有些事情很无奈。）c. 很忙，腾不出时间做其他事情。例：侬麳喊我去参加演讲比赛哉，我已经忙得呒手筛锣哉。（你不要叫我去参加演讲比赛了，我已经非常忙碌了。）

②　"安逸"的词义比较丰富：a. 太平，安稳。此义同情景引入中"临时完结只好撑仔把伞陪俚到山塘街兜仔一圈，该场总算安逸！"。b. 舒适，满意。例：哀个房子弗大，住勒嗨倒蛮安逸个。（这个房子不大，住在里面倒蛮舒适的。）c. 安静。例：侬阿好安逸点勒，嘴巴到现在呱嗒呱嗒勄停过勒。（你安静点吧，嘴巴到现在吧嗒吧嗒没停过。）d. 省省。例：外头雪落得蛮大，侬么就安逸点麳出去哉，到辰光跌着仔末要日脚好过。（外面雪下得很大，你就省省吧不要出去了，到时摔倒了日子就不好过了。）e. 收敛。例：侬安逸点着唲，就勄阿胡卵冒充金刚钻哉。（你收敛点吧，就不要外行冒充内行了。）

的 事 情 多 得 很,难 道 你 们 都 样 样
ngeh23-dou33-keh3 nyih23-ciah3 tou44 le0 ne22-sin44-dae31 n22-toh3 ze223 yan22-yan33
月 大① 个 日 脚 多 来,难 信 道 尔 笃 侪 样 样

顺 着 小 孩 呀。
sa523 zen231 siae51-noe31 aeh0
啥 顺 小 囡 啊。

甲：普通话 这个 只 有 等 他 大 了 再 收 拾 他 了。
吴语音 e44-keh3-zy33 tseh43-yeu231 ten51 li44 dou231-tsy31 tse44 seu44-tsoh3 kueh43-due231 tse44
吴语文 哀个 是 只 有 等 俚 大 仔 再 收 作 骨 头② 哉。

....

甲：We were going to Shihu Lake to enjoy the moon this Mid-Autumn Day, and then all of a sudden, it clouded over and began to rain. Our plan was thwarted by the weather.

乙：Anyway, Shihu Lake is in Suzhou, which won't run away. You missed out on a good time this year, there is always next year.

甲：My son has been looking forward to it for a long time. He is a kid after all, who didn't believe that the moon is not visible on a rainy day, and simply teased me to take him to Shihu Lake. He cried so bitterly that he could hardly breathe and there was no color in his face, which had rendered us helpless. As a result, we walked about Shantang Street with him in the rain. Now, everything is back to normal. We are enjoying some peace and quiet. There are quite a few people who travel Shantang Street at night.

乙：The night scene there is beautiful, particularly when it is raining and humid. There will be other inopportune occurrences hereafter. Will you always indulge his every whim?

甲：We will teach him a lesson when he grows up.

....

① "吃素碰着月大"本来指准备吃一个月素食,正好碰上大月,就得多吃一天素。后来常用这句俗语来比喻事不凑巧或者比喻难得有事相求正好不凑巧而难以办成。

② "收骨头"就是教训,收拾,对人严加管束,使人把放松散漫的心思收起来,不能胡说乱动或松松垮垮。

二、场景对话

1. 甲： 普通话 以前 苏州 的 交通 主要 是 靠
　　　　吴语音 lae22-ti44-tsy31 sou44-tseu44-keh3 ciae44-thon31 tsyu51-iae44-zy31 khae523
　　　　吴语文 老底子 苏州 个 交通 主要 是 靠

　　　　　　　三 横 四 纵 的 河 道 来 维 持 的。
　　　　　　　se44-wan31 sy523-tson31 keh0 ghou22-dae33 le223 vi22-zyu33-keh3
　　　　　　　三 横 四 纵 个 河 道 来 维 持 个。

乙： 普通话 正 是 呀，居 民 的 房 子 也 都 是 沿 河 造 的。
　　　吴语音 me44 tsen523 ia0 ciu44-min44-keh3 vaon22-tsy33 gha223 ze22-zy33 yie22-ghou33 zae231-keh3
　　　吴语文 蛮 正 呀，居 民 个 房 子 也 侪 是 沿 河 造 个。

甲： Traditionally, the traffic of Suzhou was maintained by the network composed of four lengthwise and three transverse channels.

乙： And the houses of locals were built along the streams.

2. 甲： 普通话 在 水 乡 苏州 生活， 最 好 要 学
　　　　吴语音 leh23-he31 syu51-shian23 sou44-tseu31 kou523 nyih23-ciah3 tse51-hae23 iae523 ghoh23-
　　　　吴语文 勒嗨 水 乡 苏州 过 日 脚，最 好 要 学

　　　　　　会 游 泳。
　　　　　　ue31 yeu22-ion33
　　　　　　会 游 泳。

乙： 普通话 为 什么？
　　　吴语音 tsoh43-sa51 neh0
　　　吴语文 作 啥 呢？

甲： 普通话 前 天 晚上， 我 做 完 小 生意 推 着
　　　　吴语音 zie22-nyih3-tsy44-taeh3 ia44-li31 ngou231 tsou523 woe223 siae51-san44-i31 the44-tsy31
　　　　吴语文 前日 仔 搭 夜里， 我 做 完 小 生意 推 仔

板车回家，一　　不小心滑到河里。
pe51-tsho23 tsoe51-chi31 ih43-keh43 feh43 taon44-sin31 waeh23 tae523 ghou22-pan44-
板车 转去，一个 弗当心 滑到 河浜

　　　　幸亏　有人路过，总算没有淹死。
li33 yin22-chiu44-teh3 yeu231 nyin223 lou22-kou31 tson44-soe31 fen44 zen231-saeh3
里。幸亏得有人路过，总算朆沉煞

　　　可是　那些谋生工具都扑通扑通掉
de22-pih3-kou31 geh23-tie31 chih43-ve231 ka44-san31 ze223 bih23-lih3-boh3-loh3 deh23-
但不过簹点吃饭家生侪别栗卜落①敁

入河里　了。你说我是不是个倒霉鬼。
leh3 ghou22-li33-shian31 tse44 ne231 kaon51 ngou231 aeh43- zy231 keh0 me22-taeh4-ciu31
勒河里向哉。倷讲我阿是个霉搭鬼

乙：普通话 不算 倒霉，　命保住就是大幸。
吴语音 soe523 feh43 zaon231 feh43-seh43-deu31 min231 pae51-lae31 zeu22-zy33 da231-yin31
吴语文 算弗上 弗色头②，命保牢就是大幸

　　　　赶紧去把游泳学会吧。
ghae22-sae33 chi523 no223 yeu22-ion33 ghoh23 ue523 ba0
豪慜去拿游泳学会吧

甲：To live in a water town such as Suzhou, it is better to learn to swim.

乙：Why?

甲：The night before last, I finished my small business and trundled my wheelbarrow home. Unfortunately, I fell into the river by accident. But luckily, someone passed by so that I hadn't got drowned. My implements for living were all in the water. It just wasn't my day.

乙：Let's look on the bright side. Your life is still yours. Go to learn swimming at once.

---

① "别栗卜落"是个拟声词，苏州话中的拟声词还有霹雳啪啦、乞栗壳落、悉粒缩落、咣当咣当、哐啷啷等。

② "弗色头"也写作"弗色骰"、"弗失头"、"弗识头"，主要意思为"倒霉"、"晦气"。

3. 甲： 普通话 现在 马路上 的 汽车 多得很。 那
　　 吴语音 yie22-ze33 mo22-lou33-laon33-keh3 chi44-tsho31 tou44-teh3 feh43 teh43 liae231 ue44-
　　 吴语文 现在 马路 浪 个 汽车 多得 弗得 了。 弯

　　　　　　　天　　　　我 开车　　时 有 很 短 一会
　　 nyih3-tsy44-taeh43 ngou231 khe44 tsho44-tsy31 zen22-kuaon33 tsen44-tsen31 ih43-shih43-
　　　　　　　日 仔 搭 我 开 车子 辰 光 真正 一 歇

　　　　　　　儿 没集中注意力， 差 点 儿 跟 对 面　　　　正
　　 shih43 khoe44 ya22-nge33 shie51-cia44-hou31 taeh43 te44-kou31 phih43-ciu44-taon44-
　　　　　　　歇 看 野眼①， 险 家 伙 搭 对过 劈 居 当

　　　　　　　中 开 来　　 的 卡 车 相 撞。
　　 tson31 khe44-kou44-le33-keh3 kha51-tsho23 shian44 beh23-deu31 tse0
　　　　　　　中 开 过 来 个 卡 车 香 鼻 头 哉。

乙： 普通话 算 算 你 也 一 把 年 纪了， 怎 么 还 这
　　 吴语音 soe523-soe31 ne231 ghaeh23 ih43-po51 nyie22-ci33 tse44 naeh23-han31 we2321 ke44-
　　 吴语文 算 算 侬 也 一 把 年 纪哉， 哪 哼 还 该

　　　　　　　样 不 明事理。
　　 zan31 m22-tshin44- deu31 cia0
　　　　　　　场 呒 清 头 嘎。

甲： There are so many cars on the road that I just missed hitting the other car when my mind blanked out momentarily.

乙： You are not a kid any more and should know what's what. It's dangerous to be absent-minded while driving.

---

① "看野眼"指注意力不集中，但分两种情况：一种是随意闲适的，比如"坐勒草坪浪望望野景，看看野眼，来得个惬意"；另一种是不该分神时分神，如场景对话3中"弯日仔搭我开车辰光真正一歇歇看野眼"的情形。

4. 甲：普通话 苏州的公交车班次、线路都不少，
    吴语音 sou44-tseu44-keh3 kon44-ciae44-tsho31 pe44-tshy31 sie44-lou31 ze223 feh43-sae51
    吴语文 苏州个公交车班次、线路侪弗少，

    但 一到上下班高峰，乘公交
    pih43-kou523 ih43-tae523 zaon22-gho33-pe31 kae44-fon31 tshen523 kon44--ciae44-
    不过一到上下班高峰，乘公交

    车的人多得不得了。今天我发急
    tsho44-keh3 nyin223 tou44-teh3-le44m22-dae33-zen31 cin44-tsae31 ngou231 faeh43-cih43
    车个人多得来吭淘成①。今朝我发急

    了 才好不容易挤上去。
    pon523-tsy23 tse44 hae51-feh3-yon33-yi31 gaeh23-zaon33-chi31
    蹦② 仔再好弗容易轧上去。

乙：普通话 所以要发展轨道交通呀。
    吴语音 we22-tsy44-kaon31 iae523 faeh43-tsoe51 kue51-dae33 ciae44-thon44 ia0
    吴语文 为仔讲要发展轨道交通呀。

甲：普通话 倒是让人急死了， 建了几年
    吴语音 tae44-zy31 cih43-cin44-fon31 ban22-zah3 me22- laon33-tson31 gae231-tsy31 ci51 nyie223
    吴语文 倒是急惊风碰着慢郎中③，搞仔几年

    了，还没建好。
    tse44 we22-fen44 lon44-hae31 le0
    哉，还飏弄好唻。

---

① "数量多，数不清"是最常用的意义。苏州话中表示"数量多"的词还有"弗弗少少""几几许许""交交关关""行情行市""吭多吭少"等。此外，"吭淘成"还有"没有规矩"、"没有出息"、"不正经"等义项。

② "发急蹦"是指发急到极点了。

③ "急惊风碰着慢郎中"原意指得了急病却偏偏碰到一个行动迟缓的医生，一般比喻为"干着急"。

乙：普通话 你是 站 着 说 话不 腰 疼，这是 一个大
　　吴语音 ne231-zy31 cie523 nyin223 thiae44-te31 feh43-chih43- lih3 e44-keh3-zy31 ih43-keh3 dou22-
　　吴语文 倷 是 见 人 挑 担 弗 吃力①，哀个是 一个大

　　　　工 程， 怎 么 可 能 一蹴而就？
　　　　kon44- zen31 naeh23-han31 khou44-nen31 ih43-le33-shin31 zeu231 zen22-kon33
　　　　工 程， 哪 哼 可 能 一来兴 就 成功？

甲：Although there are a lot of bus lines in Suzhou, the buses are too crowded to get on at rush hour. My patience is pretty well exhausted today and push my way aboard with all the strength.

乙：That's the reason why rail transit should be built.

甲：It has been constructing for many years, I am getting impatient.

乙：Nothing is easier than fault-finding. Such a major project cannot be done at one go.

5. 甲：普通话 请 问， 到 西 园 怎 么 走？
　　　吴语音 tshin51-men31 tae523 si44-yoe31 naeh23-han31 tseu51
　　　吴语文 请 问， 到 西 园 哪 哼 走？

乙：普通话 前 面 一 条 弄 堂 拐 进 去 转 一个 弯
　　吴语音 zie22-deu33 ih43-diae23 lon22-daon33 zaeh23-tsin44-chi31 tsoe523 ih43-keh43 ue44
　　吴语文 前 头 一 条 弄 堂 直 进 去 转 一 个 弯

　　　　就 到。
　　　　zeu231 tae523
　　　　就 到。

甲：Excuse me, how can I get to Xiyuan Temple?

乙：Turn into the lane ahead, you'll find it after the second turning.

---

① "见人挑担弗吃力"指不干某事不知道这事的辛苦，而且还说风凉话。

6. 甲：普通话 拙政园 正在 举行 荷花展， 大 的 很
　　吴语音 tseh43-tsen44-yoe31 leh23-laon31 ciu51-yin33 ghou22-ho44-tsoe31 dou231-zy31 dou231-
　　吴语文 拙 政 园 勒 浪 举 行 荷 花 展， 大 是 大

　　　　大， 　　　　小 的 很 小。　　　　 有 一 种
　　　　teh3 tsha44-tsha44-yi31 siae51-zy31 siae51-teh3 shi44-shi44-ji31 yeu231 ih43-tson51
　　　　得 诧 诧 异, 小 是 小 得 稀 稀 奇①。 有 一 种

　　　　碗 莲 特别 神奇， 最 小 的 　　 荷 花 只
　　　　uoe51-lie23 ka44-nyi31 shi44-ji33-keh3 zy231 tse51 siae523-keh3 ghou22-ho33 tseh43-
　　　　碗 莲 加 二 稀 奇 个 是 最 小 个 荷 花 只

　　　　有 指 甲 　　 那 样 大。
　　　　yeu231 tsih43-khaeh43-be31 zeh23-kan23 dou231
　　　　有 节 掐 瓣 实 梗 大。

乙：普通话 真 的！虽然 最 近 我 很 忙， 但
　　吴语音 tsen44-keh3 se44-zoe31 ke44-tshian31 ngou231 maon22-saeh3-tse31 de22-pih3-kou31
　　吴语文 真 个！虽然 该 饿 我 忙 煞 哉, 但 不 过

　　　　无 论 如 何 也 要 抽 空 去 看一看。
　　　　ze22-bie33 naeh23-han31 gha22-iae33 tsheu44-khon44-chi31 kho523-khoe31
　　　　随 便 哪 哼 也 要 抽 空 去 看 看。

甲：There is a lotus show in the Humble Administrator's Garden. Some of the lotus there are large while some are very small. What impressed me most is bowl lotus which is as small as a human's nail.

乙：Really? Though I've been quite busy recently, I will go there.

---

① "大是大得诧诧异，小是小得稀稀奇"指大的大到令人诧异的地步，小的小到使人惊叹的程度。"诧诧异"、"稀稀奇"通过叠词来进一步强调。

第六单元　交通与旅游

7. 甲：普通话 世界 著 名 建 筑 大 师 贝 聿 铭 设 计 的
　　　吴语音 syu44-ka31 tsyu523-min23 cie51-tsoh3-da33-sy44 pe44-yuih3-min31 seh43-ci44-keh3
　　　吴语文 世 界 著 名 建 筑 大 师 贝 聿 铭 设 计 个

　　　　　　苏 州 博 物 馆 新 馆 漂 亮 得 很。
　　　　　　sou44-tseu44 poh43-veh3-kuoe31 sin44-kuoe31 phiae-lian33-teh3 he51-he44-ue31
　　　　　　苏 州 博 物 馆 新 馆 漂 亮 得 海 海 威。

　 乙：普通话 是的，它 不 愧 为 贝大师的"封刀之作"。
　　　吴语音 zy231-keh3 li44 feh43-gue231 we231 zy231 pe44- da33-sy44-keh3 fon44-tae44-tsyu44-tsoh3
　　　吴语文 是个，俚 弗 愧 为 是 贝大师个 "封刀之作"。

　 甲：The new Suzhou Museum designed by world-famous architect Pei Leoh Ming is gorgeous.

　 乙：It does deserve to be the final work of Mr. Pei's.

8. 甲：普通话 不要 不开心 了，明 天 就 带 你 去 玩
　　　吴语音 fiae523 chiae523-tsyu44-toh43-zeh3 tse44 men22-tsae33 zeu231 ta523-ne31 chi523 beh23-
　　　吴语文 覅 翘 嘴 笃舌① 哉，明 朝 就 带 侬 去 孛

　　　　　　水 乡 一 日 游。
　　　　　　sian31 syu51-shian44- ih43-zeh3-yeu31
　　　　　　相 水 乡 一 日 游。

　 乙：普通话 你 总 归 喜 欢 闹 别 扭、唱 反 调，今 天
　　　吴语音 ne231 tson51-kue23 huoe44-shi31 kan51-kan44-ciae31 tih43-koh43-jiae31 cin44-tsae31
　　　吴语文 侬 总 归 欢 喜 梗 梗 交②、跌 角 翘，今 朝

　　　　　　就 不 该 到 这种 偏僻 的 地方来玩。
　　　　　　zeu231 feh43-ke23 tae523 e44-tson31 iae44-nyi33-koh3-loh3-keh3 zan22-ho33 le223 beh23-sian31
　　　　　　就 弗 该 到 哀种 妖泥 角落 个 场化 来 孛 相。

---

① "翘嘴笃舌"用嘴巴、舌头的变异形态来表明内心的不开心。

② 喉咙里哽住东西总归是不舒服的，"梗梗交"就是形象地表明"闹别扭"的意思。

甲：Come, come, cheer up, We will set out for the water town on a one-day trip.

乙：You are always taking against me. We ought not to have come to such a lonely place.

9. 甲：普通话　玄　妙　观　　　小　吃　摊　一　摆，老　苏　州　的　味
　　　吴语音　yoe22-miae33-kuoe31-keh3siae51-chih3-the31 ih43 pa51 lae22-sou44-tseu44-keh3 mi22-
　　　吴语文　玄　妙　观　个　小　吃　摊　一　摆，老　苏　州　个　味

　　　　　　　道　就　出　来　了。外　地　的　游　客　也　多　了。
　　　　　　　dae33 zeu231 tsheh43-le223 tse0 nga22-di33-keh3 yeu22-khah3 gha223 tou44 tse44
　　　　　　　道　就　出　来　哉　外　地　个　游　客　也　多　哉。

　乙：普通话　真　叫　肚　子　的　容　量　有　限，否　则　是　实
　　　吴语音　tsen44 ciae523 dou22-bi33-keh3 yon22-lian33 yeu231 ghe231 feu44-tseh3-zy31 zeh23-
　　　吴语文　真　叫　肚　皮　个　容　量　有　限，否　则　是　实

　　　　　　　在　想　一　种　种　吃　过　来。
　　　　　　　deu31 sian523 ih43-tsah43-tsah3 chih43-kou44-le31 tse0
　　　　　　　头　想　一　只　只　吃　过　来　哉。

　甲：普通话　我　最　记　挂　　那　个　很　薄　　的　千　层　饼
　　　吴语音　ngou231 tse51-tse31 chi44-ci31 ue44-keh3 boh23- shiae44-shiae44-keh3 tshie44-zen33-pin31
　　　吴语文　我　最　最　牵　记　弯　个　薄　噩　噩　个　千　层　饼

　　　　　　　好　吃　得　打　耳　光　都　不　肯　放。
　　　　　　　hae51-chih43-teh3 ha44 nyi22-kuan33 gha223 feh43 khen51 faon523-theh3
　　　　　　　好　吃　得　夯①耳　光　也　弗　肯　放②脱。

甲：Snack bars of Temple of Secrets have the distinctive flavour of Suzhou, They are attracting more visitors from other towns.

乙：How I wish I could have a gigantic appetite so that I could try the snacks one by one. The most memorable of all is layer cakes which is very tasty.

---

① 鼻化脱落后读 ha。

② "夯耳光侪不肯放"带点夸张地形容东西美味到挨耳光都不肯放弃的地步。

三 词语贴士

（一）交通工具

序号	英文	苏州话
1.	automobile 汽车	chi44-tsho31 汽车
2.	bus 公交车	kon44-ciae44-tsho31, kon44-gon33-chi44-tsho31 公交车，公共汽车
3.	taxi 出租车	tsheh43-tsou44-tsho31 出租车
4.	coach 大客车	dou22-khah3-tsho31 大客车
5.	train 火车	hou51-tsho23 火车
6.	maglev 磁悬浮列车	zy22-yoe33-veu31 lih23-tsho31 磁悬浮列车
7.	high-speed railway 高铁	kae44-thih3 高铁
8.	ship 轮船	len22-zoe33 轮船
9.	yacht 快艇	khua44-thin31 快艇
10.	airplane 飞机	fi44-ci31 飞机
11.	airliner 客机	khah43-ci23 客机
12.	transport aircraft 运输机	yuin22-syu44-ci31 运输机

（二）交通设施

序号	英文	苏州话
1.	subway 地铁	di22-thih3 地铁
2.	stop 停车站	din22-tsho44-ze31 停车站
3.	traffic island 安全岛	oe44-zie33-tae31 安全岛

续表

序号	英文	苏州话
4.	parking lot 停车场	din22-tsho44-zan31 停车场
5.	traffic lights 红绿灯	ghon22-loh3-ten31 红绿灯
6.	traffic post 交通岗	ciae44-thon44-kaon31 交通岗
7.	probe 探头	thoe44-deu31 探头
8.	main road 主干道	tsyu51-koe44-dae31 主干道
9.	car lane 机动车道	ci44-don33-tsho44-dae31 机动车道
10.	bicycle lane 非机动车道	fi44-ci44-don33-tsho44-dae31 非机动车道
11.	sidewalk 人行道	zen22-yin33-dae31,zaon22-ka44-yie31 人行道，上街沿
12.	overpass 立交桥	lih23-ciae44-jiae31 立交桥
13.	pedestrian bridge 人行天桥	zen22-yin33-thie44-jiae31 人行天桥

（三）交通规则

序号	英文	苏州话
1.	sign post 路标	lou22-piae33 路标
2.	one-way street 单行线	te44-ghan33-sie31,te44-ghan33-dae31 单行线，单行道
3.	crosswalk 斑马线	pe44-mo33-sie31, wan22-dae33-sie31 斑马线,横道线
4.	speed limit 限速	ghe22-soh3 限速
5.	speeding 超速	tshae44-soh3 超速
6.	loop 回路	we22-lou33· 回路

续表

序号	英文	苏州话
7.	stop sign 停车标志	din22-tsho44-piae44-tsyu31 停车标志
8.	No parking. 禁止泊车	cin523-tsyu44-beh3-tsho31 禁止泊车
9.	Stop. 禁止通行	cin523-tsyu44-thon44-yin31,feh43-nyian231 kou523 禁止通行, 弗让过

（四）路况和驾驶

序号	英文	苏州话
1.	flat 平整	bin22-tsen33 平整
2.	uneven 不平整	tshih43-kae44-poh3-ti31 七高八低
3.	crowded 拥挤	gaeh23 轧
4.	uncrowded 稀疏	khon44-daon33-daon31 空荡荡
5.	give way to 让路	nyian231 lou231 让路
6.	drive without a license 无证驾驶	vu231-tsen31 cia523-sy31 无证驾驶
7.	hit-and-run 肇事逃逸	zae22-zy33 dae22-yih3 肇事逃逸
8.	traffic accident 车祸	tsho44-ghou31 车祸

（五）交通从业人员

序号	英文	苏州话
1.	traffic police 交警	ciae44-cin31 交警
2.	traffic inspector 稽查员	ci44-zo33-yoe31 稽查员
3.	driver 驾驶员	cia523-sy44-yoe31 驾驶员

续表

序号	英文	苏州话
4.	chief conductor	lih23-tsho44-tsan31
	列车长	列车长
5.	conductor	lih23-tsho44-yoe31
	列车员	列车员
6.	captain	ci44-tsan31
	机长	机长
7.	airhostess	khon44-tsia31
	空姐	空姐
8.	captain	zoe22-tsan33
	船长	船长
9.	sailor	syu51-seu23
	水手	水手
10.	first mate	dou22-fu33
	大副	大副

（六）出游

序号	英文	苏州话
1.	hiking	yoe22-tsoh3，tsheh43-yoe22-men31
	远足	远足，出远门
2.	tour route	li22-yin33-lou33-sie31
	旅行路线	旅行路线
3.	guide book	li22-yin33 tsyu51-noe23
	旅行指南	旅行指南
4.	outbound tour	tsheh43-cin51-yeu31
	出境游	出境游
5.	inbound tour	kueh43-ne33-yeu31
	国内游	国内游

（七）旅游从业人员和游客

序号	英文	苏州话
1.	guide	dae22-yeu33
	导游	导游
2.	local guide	di22-be33
	地陪	地陪
3.	tour	li22-yeu33-doe31
	旅游团	旅游团

续表

序号	英文	苏州话
4.	individual traveler	se51-khah3
	散客	散客
5.	tour pals	li22-yeu33
	驴友	驴友

（八）旅游景观

序号	英文	苏州话
1.	natural scenery	zy22-zoe33-cin44-kuoe31
	自然景观	自然景观
2.	artificial scenery	zen22-ven33-cin44-kuoe31
	人文景观	人文景观
3.	holiday resort	dou22-ka44-chiu31
	度假区	度假区
4.	former residences of celebrities	min22-zen33-kou44-ciu31
	名人故居	名人故居
5.	summer resort	bi22-syu23-sen44-di31
	避暑胜地	避暑胜地

（九）苏州名街

序号	英文	苏州话
1.	Guanqian Street	khuoe44-zie33-ka31
	观前街	观前街
2.	Shantang Street	se44-daon33-ka31
	山塘街	山塘街
3.	Pingjiang Road	bin22-kaon44-lou31
	平江路	平江路
4.	Taohuawu	dae22-ho44-ou31
	桃花坞	桃花坞
5.	Nanhao Street	noe22-ngae33-ka31
	南浩街	南浩街
6.	Daoqian Street	dae22-zie33-ka31
	道前街	道前街
7.	Shiquan Street	zeh3-zie33-ka31
	十全街	十全街

续表

序号	英文	苏州话
8.	Renming Road	zen22-min33-lou31
	人民路	人民路
9.	Ganjiang Road	koe44-tsian44-lou31
	干将路	干将路
10.	Ligong Causeway	li22-kon44-di31
	李公堤	李公堤
11.	Modern Avenue	yie22-de33-da33-dae31
	现代大道	现代大道
12.	Shilu Shopping Mall	zah23-lou31 bu22-yin33-ka31
	石路步行街	石路步行街

（十）苏州名胜

序号	英文	苏州话
1.	Tiger Hill	hou51-chieu23
	虎丘	虎丘
2.	Humble Adminstrator's Garden	tseh43-tsen44-yoe31
	拙政园	拙政园
3.	Lion Grove	sy44-tsy44-lin31
	狮子林	狮子林
4.	Garden of the Canglangting Pavilion	tshaon44-laon33-din31
	沧浪亭	沧浪亭
5.	Garden of the Master of the Nets	maon22-sy44-yoe31
	网师园	网师园
6.	Lingering Garden	leu22-yoe33
	留园	留园
7.	Joyous Garden	yi22-yoe33
	怡园	怡园
8.	Garden of Couple's Retreat	ngeu22-yoe33
	藕园	藕园
9.	Mountain Villa with Embracing Beauty	gue22-seu44-se44-tsaon31
	环秀山庄	环秀山庄
10.	West Garden	si44-yoe31
	西园	西园

续表

序号	英文	苏州话
11.	Cold Mountain Temple Monastery	gho22-se44-zy31
	寒山寺	寒山寺
12.	North Temple Pagoda	poh43-zy33-thaeh3
	北寺塔	北寺塔
13.	Temple of Secrets	yoe22-miae33-kuoe31
	玄妙观	玄妙观
14.	Town God's Temple	zen22-waon33-miae31
	城隍庙	城隍庙
15.	Mountain of the Wonderful Rocks	lin22-nge33-se31
	灵岩山	灵岩山
16.	Sacred Hill	thie44-bin33-se31
	天平山	天平山
17.	Shangfang Hill	zaon22-faon44-se31
	上方山	上方山
18.	Taihu Lake	tha44-ghou31
	太湖	太湖
19.	Shihu Lake	zah23-ghou31
	石湖	石湖
20.	Jinji Lake	cin44-ci44-ghou31
	金鸡湖	金鸡湖
21.	Guangfu	kuaon44-foh3
	光福	光福
22.	Zhouzhuang	tseu44-tsaon31
	周庄	周庄
23.	Luzhi	loh23-zeh3
	甪直	甪直

四 对话中的特色词汇

序号	英文	苏州话
1.	look forward to	po44-vaon31
	希望	巴望

续表

序号	英文	苏州话
2.	tease sb to 死活纠缠	kaeh43-kaeh3-nyiae33-nyiae31 夹夹绕绕
3.	pale 面色苍白	mie22-khon33 kaeh43-leh3 sy44-bah3 面孔夹勒丝白
4.	helpless 束手无策	m22-seu33 sa44-lou31 呒手筛锣
5.	as a result 事到临头	lin22-zyu33 woe22-cih3 临时完结
6.	put up an umbrella 撑伞	tshian44 se51 撑伞
7.	Everything is back to normal 太平	oe44-yih3 安逸
8.	particularly 尤其	zah23-zeh3 着实
9.	inopportune occurrences 事不凑巧	chih43-sou523 ban22-zah3 ngeh23-dou31 吃素碰着月大
10.	settle with sb 收拾	seu44 kueh43-deu231 收骨头
11.	indeed 正是	me44-tsen31 蛮正
12.	live 生活	kou523 nyih23-ciah3 过日脚
13.	go home 回去	tsoe51-chi31 转去
14.	drown 淹死	zen231-saeh3 沉煞
15.	luckily 幸亏	yin22-chiu44-teh3 幸亏得
16.	plump into 扑通扑通	bih23-lih3-boh3-loh3 别栗卜落
17.	fall 掉	deh23 敛
18.	cooler 倒霉鬼	me22-taeh3-ciu31 霉搭鬼
19.	bad luck 倒霉	feh43-seh3-deu31 弗色头

续表

序号	英文	苏州话
20.	lose one's concentration 注意力不集中	khoe44-ya33-nge31 看野眼
21.	numerous 数量多	m22-dae33-zen31 呒淘成
22.	beyond endurance 发急	faeh43-cih3-pon31 发急蹦
23.	to be anxious but unable to do anything 干着急	cih23-cin44-fon31 ban22-zah3 me22-laon33-tson31 急惊风碰着慢郎中
24.	Nothing is easier than fault-finding. 站着说话不腰疼	cie523 nyin223 thiae44-te31 feh43 chih43-lih3 见人挑担弗吃力
25.	be done at one go 一蹴而就	ih43-le33-shin31 zeu231 zen22-kon33 一来兴就成功
26.	turn into 拐进去	zah23-tsin44-chi31 直进去
27.	of all sizes 大的很大，小的很小	dou231-zy31 dou231-teh3 tsha44-tsha44-yi31, siae523-zy31 siae523-teh3 shi44-shi44-ji31 大是大得诧诧异，小是小得稀稀奇
28.	nail 指甲	tsih43-khaeh3-be31 节掐瓣
29.	anyway 无论如何	ze22-bie33 naeh23-han31 随便哪哼
30.	sad 不开心	chiae44-tsyu44-toh3-zeh3 翘嘴笃舌
31.	bicker 闹别扭	kan51-kan44-ciae31 梗梗交
32.	take against sb 唱反调	tih43-koh43-jiae31 跌角翘
33.	lonely place 偏僻的地方	iae44-nyi33-koh3-loh3 妖泥角落
34.	tasty 打耳光都不肯放	ha44 nyi22-kuan33 gha223 feh43-khen51 faon523 夯耳光也弗肯放

五 巩固练习

1 甲：环太湖马路造得棒极了，汽车在上面开太爽了。
乙：也要注意安全呀，千万不要飙车呀！
甲：当然，我已经不是青涩的小伙子了，不会这样不懂事的。
乙：这样就好。祝你玩得开心。

2 甲：听说旅行社在整治黑导游了。
乙：早就该这么做了。那些黑导游的所作所为是败坏苏州人的名声，丢苏州人的脸。
甲：是的，名胜古迹不带游客去，专挑那些高回扣的、鬼头鬼脑的地方。
乙：希望旅行社一以贯之，不要走过场哦。

六 参考答案

甲：普通话　环　太　湖　马　路　造　得　　棒　极 了，汽车
　　吴语音 gue22-tha44-ghou31 mo231-lou31 zae231-teh3-le31tse523- teh3-le31 chi44-tsho31
　　吴语文　环　太　湖　马　路　造　得　来　赞　得 来，汽车

　　　　　 在　　上　　面　开　　太　爽　　　　　 了。
　　　　　 leh23-he31 zaon22-deu33 khe44-zy31 sia51-i23 teh3 feh43-teh43-liae231
　　　　　 勒　嗨　上　头　开　是　惬意　得　弗　得　了。

乙：普通话　也要　注意　安全　呀，千　万　不要　飙　车呀！
　　吴语音 gha22-iae33 tsyu51-i31 oe44-zie31 keh43 a0 tshie44- ve31 fiae523 piae44-tsho44 a0
　　吴语文　也要　注意　安全　个　啊，千　万　勿　飙　车啊！

甲：普通话　当　然，我　已　经　不　是　青涩的小伙子　了，不　会
　　吴语音 taon44-zoe31 ngou31 i44-cin31 feh43-zy231 tshin44- deu33-ciu31 tse0 feh43-ue523
　　吴语文　当　然，我　已　经　弗　是　青　头　鬼　哉，弗　会

这样不懂事的。
zeh23-kan23 m22-tshin44-deu33-keh3
实梗朆青头个。

乙：普通话 这样 就 好。祝 你 玩 得 开心。
吴语音 ke44-zaon31 zeu231 hae51 tshoh43 ne231 beh23-sian523 kha44-weh3
吴语文 该状 就 好。祝 侬 孛 相 快活。

甲：The road going around Taihu Lake is great. It's fantastic to drive down it.
乙：For your safety, don't drive fast.
甲：Of course not. I've grown up and seen sense.
乙：OK. Have a good time!

2

甲：普通话 听说 旅行社 在 整治 黑导游 了。
吴语音 thin44-seh3 li22-yin33-zo31 leh23 tsen51-zyu31 heh43-dae33-yeu31 tse44
吴语文 听说 旅行社 勒 整治 黑导游 哉。

乙：普通话 早 就 该 这么 做 了。那些 黑 导游
吴语音 lae231-tsae31 zeu22-ke33 e44-zaon31 tsou523 tse44 geh23-tie31 heh43-dae33-yeu31-
吴语文 老早 就 该 哀状 做 哉。箇点 黑 导游

的 所作所为 是 败坏 苏州 人 的 名
keh3 sou51-tsoh3-sou44-we31 zy231 ba231-wa31 sou44-tseu44-nyin33- keh3 min231-
个 所作 所为 是 败坏 苏州 人 个 名

声，给 苏州 人 丢脸。
sen31 the44 sou44-tseh44-nyin33-keh3 de223
声，坍 苏州 人 个 台。

甲：普通话 是的，名胜古迹 不 带 游客 去，专
吴语音 zy231-keh3 min231-sen31 kou51-tsih3 feh43 ta523 yeu22-khah3 chi523 tsoe44-men31
吴语文 是个，名 胜 古 迹 弗 带 游 客 去，专 门

挑 那 些 回 扣 高 的、乱 七 八 糟 的 地 方。
ke51 geh23-tie31 we22- kheu33 kae44-keh3 ciu51-deu44-ciu44-nae33-keh3 zan22-ho33
拣 简 点 回 扣 高 个、鬼 头 鬼 脑 个 场 化。

乙：普通话 希 望 旅 行 社 一 以 贯 之，不要 走 过 场 哦。
吴语音 shi44-vaon31 li22-yin33-zo31 ih43-i44-kuoe44-tsyu31 fiae523 tseu51 kou523-zan31 oh43
吴语文 希 望 旅 行 社 一 以 贯 之， 勿 走 过 场 喔。

甲：Travel agencies are cleaning up black guides in a bid to stop the disarray in tourism industry.

乙：It's about time. What they had done brought dishonor to Suzhou and discredited to Suzhouness

甲：Quite right, they show the tourists the spots where they can get the rebate instead of famous places of interest.

乙：I hope the travel agencies can finish what is started and don't just go through the motions.

第七单元

一 情景引入

甲：普通话 老 张，你有没有觉 得，现 在 一 年 四 季 气 候
　　吴语音 lae22-tsan33 ne231 aeh43 koh43-zah43 yie22-ze33 ih43-nyi23 sy523-ci31 thie44-chi31
　　吴语文 老 张，傢 阿 觉 着，现在 一 年 四 季 天 气

变 化 没 有 我们 小 时 候 分 明 了。因为 极 端
pie523-ho31 m22-peh3 nyi231 siae51-haeh3-li31 fen44-min31 tse44 in44-we31 jih23-toe44-
变 化 呒 不 伲 小 呷 里 分 明 哉。因为 极 端

天 气, 洪 水、风 暴、干 旱、地 震、海 啸 和
thie44-chi31 ghon22-syu33 fon44-bae31 koe44-ghoe31 di22-tsen33 he51-siae23 taeh43
天 气, 洪 水、风 暴、干 旱、地 震、海 啸 搭

各 种 自 然 灾 害 接 二 连 三 出 现, 地 球
koh43-tson51 zy22-zoe33 tse44-ghe31 tsih43-nyi33--lie33-se31 tsheh43- yie231 di22-jieu33-
各 种 自 然 灾 害 接 二 连 三 出 现, 地 球

上 到 处 乱 七 八 糟。
laon31 tae44-tsyu31 ih43-thie44-syu44-ka31
浪 到 处 一 天 世 界①。

乙: 普通话 是 这样, 我们 苏 州 还 算 是 人 间 天 堂
吴语音 zy231 zeh23-kan33-ia0 nyi231 sou44-tseu31 we22- soe44-zy31 zen22-cie44-thie44-daon31
吴语文 是 实 梗 呀, 伲 苏 州 还 算 是 人 间 天 堂

呢, 大 的 自 然 灾 害 估 计 短 时 间 内 轮 不
le0 dou231-keh3 zy22-zoe33-tse44-ghe31 kou51-ci23 ih43-zyu33-se44-kheh3 len22-feh3-
唻, 大 个 自 然 灾 害 估 计 一 时 三 刻② 轮 弗

到 我们 头 上, 不 过 四 季 分 明 的 日 子 也
tae31 nyi231 deu22-laon33 pih43-kou523 sy44-ci44-fen44-min33- keh3 nyih23-ciah3 gha223
到 伲 头 浪, 不 过 四 季 分 明 个 日 脚 也

是 一 去 不 复 返 了。
ih43-ciah3-chi31 feh43- we22-tsoe44-deu31 tse44
一 脚 去③ 弗 回 转 头 哉。

---

① "一天世界"形容差到极点, 它与前文中提到的"一塌糊涂"是一个意思。
② "一时三刻"绝对不是普通话中一个小时四十五分钟的意思, 而是指"时间很短", 甚至是"立时立刻"。
③ "一脚去"有三层意思: a.一去不回。此义同"情景引入"中"必过四季分明个日脚也一脚去弗回转头哉"。b.把剩下的东西全部包下, 类似于苏州话中"折倒"的意思。例: 锢点吆, 哀点青菜我一脚去哉。(便宜点吧, 这些青菜我全买了。) c.死, 此时为贬义词, 等同于苏州话中的"翘辫子"。例: 箇杀千刀总算一脚去哉。(那该死的家伙总算死了。)

甲： 普通话　节　气　上　老　早　立　秋　了，天　还　是　热　得　天
　　　吴语音　tsih43-chi44-laon31 lae231-tsae33 lih23-tsheu31 tse44 thie44 we22-zy33 nyih23-teh3-le31
　　　吴语文　节　气　浪　老　早　立　秋　哉，天　还　是　热　得　来

　　　　　　　天　要　开　了　空　调　　　才　能　睡　觉。中
　　　　　　　thie44-thie31 iae523 khe44-tsy31 khon44-diae31-leh3 tse44-hae31 khuen44-kae31 tson44-
　　　　　　　天　天　要　开　仔　空　调　勒　再　好　睏　觉。中

　　　　　　　秋　这　天　突　然　一　　天　里　　温　度　降
　　　　　　　tsheu31 geh23-nyih3 zah23-san44-deu31 ih43-nyih3-tsy44-taeh3 uen44-dou31 kaon523-
　　　　　　　秋　箇　日　眚　生　头　一　日　仔　搭　温　度　降

　　　　　　　了　十　七　度，衣　服　一　口　气　　从　短　袖　衫
　　　　　　　tsy23 zeh23-tshih3-dou31 i44-zaon31 ih43-ciah43-loh3-seu31 zon231 toe51-zeu33-tsy31
　　　　　　　仔　十　七　度，衣　裳　一　脚　落　手①　从　短　袖　子

　　　　　　　到　两　用　衫。
　　　　　　　tae523 lian22-yon33- se31
　　　　　　　到　两　用　衫。

乙： 普通话　是　呀，　这　种　神　鬼　天，谁　　吃　得　消？为
　　　吴语音　zy231-keh3-ia31 ke44-tson31 zen22-ciu44-thie31 sa523- nyin31 chih43-teh3-siae31 we22-
　　　吴语文　是　个　呀，该　种　神　鬼　天，啥　人　吃　得　消？为

　　　　　　　了　自　己　身　体　健　康，大　家　也　要　爱　护　地　球，
　　　　　　　tsy33 zy22-ka33 sen44-thi31 jie22-khaon33 da22-ka33 gha22-iae33 e51-ghou31 di22-jieu33
　　　　　　　仔　自　家　身　体　健　康，大　家　也　要　爱　护　地　球，

　　　　　　　过　低　碳　生　活。
　　　　　　　kou523 ti44-the31 sen44- weh3
　　　　　　　过　低　碳　生　活。

---

① "一脚落手"有两层意思：a. 一口气。此义同情景引入中"衣裳一脚落手从短袖子到两用衫"。b. 一竿子到底。例：该桩事体倷做也做则，就一脚落手做完吧。（这件事情你做也做了，就一竿子做到底吧。）

甲：Zhang, we wouldn't have the dramatic changes of season on our childhood, do you think so? Extreme weather such as flood, storm, drought, earthquake, tsunami and natural disasters come in clusters. The earth is in chaos.

乙：Suzhou is "the paradise on earth", so we won't have a tragedy like that in a short time. On the other hand, the four distinct seasons will never return.

甲：Autumn Begins was long past now. It was still so hot that I would not sleep well without the air conditioner. There was a sharp fall of 17 degrees in temperature on Mid - Autumn Day. We had to take off T-shirts and put on coats.

乙：Oh, Gosh! What awful weather we're having! For our health, we should take care of the earth and lead a low-carbon life.

二 场景对话

1. 甲：普通话　张　家　阿　婆，你　身　体　好　棒，　　　　都
   吴语音　tsan44-ka44-ae44-bu31 ne231 sen44-thi31 zah23-zeh3 jie231 leh0 ue0 i44-cin31
   吴语文　张　家　媪　婆，倷　身　体　着　实　健了畹，已经

   立　冬　了，还　喝　凉　开　水！
   lih23-ton44 tse44 we223 chih43 lan22-khe44-syu31
   立　冬　哉，还　吃②冷　开　水！

---

① "健"有三层含义：a. 指身板结实硬朗，行动灵活自如，往往对中老年人而言。此义同"场景对话1"中"倷身体着实健畹"。b. 指发展态势良好。例：该个一歇倷风头健得来。（最近一阵你春风得意哇。）c. 过分热心，反不讨好。例：倷拎错个秤纽绳勒嗨，夠瞎管健呢。（你领会错了意思，不要瞎管闲事了。）

② "吃"除了与普通话一样用于"吃饭，吃官司，吃不消"等处外，它在苏州话中有着非常宽泛的使用范围。a. 喝。此义同"场景对话1"中"还吃冷开水"。b. 吸。例：该搭是无烟区，弗许吃香烟。（这里是无烟区，不许吸烟。）c. 挨揍，挨打，找打。例：小鬼，说弗听啊，想吃生活阿是个？（小鬼，说不听，想挨打是吗？）d. 踏空，算错。例：倷箇次是老鬼失匹，吃添哉。（你这次是精明人失着，算错了。）e. 喜欢。例：俚蛮吃倷个。（他很喜欢你的。）f. 接受。例：就梗吧，我弗吃倷箇一套。（歇着点吧，我不接受你那一套。）g. 固定。例：倷用力吃牢凳子，夠让俚翻脱。（你用力固定住凳子，别让它翻倒。）h. 欺负，常用叠词表示。例：倷只会吃吃我。（你只会欺负我。）

第七单元　气象与节气

乙：普通话　现在温度有 20 多度呢，以前早
　　吴语音　yie22-ze33 uen44-dou31 yeu231 nyie22-ci44-dou31 laeh43-li31 lae22-ti44-tsy31 lae231-
　　吴语文　现在温度有廿几度拉里，老底子老

　　　　　　就冷了有些时候了。
　　　　　　tsae31 zeu231 lan231- tsy33-yeu31 lian231-nyih3 tse44
　　　　　　早就冷仔有两日哉。

甲：Ms. Zhang, it's already Winter Begins and you still drink cold water. How hale and hearty!

乙：The temperature is up in the twenties now. In other days it would have been cold for some weeks.

2. 甲：普通话　可恶的天气，立秋了还这么热。昨天
　　吴语音　doe22-min33-thie31 lih23-tsheu31 tseh43 we223 e44-zaon31 nyih23 zoh23-nyih3-tsy44-
　　吴语文　断命①天，立秋则还哀状热。昨日仔

　　　　　　做得板栗烧鸡味道不错，没放在冰
　　　　　　taeh3 sae44-keh3 lih23-tsy44-sae44-ci31 mi22-dae33 feh43-tsho23 fen44 pa51-leh3 pin44-
　　　　　　搭烧个栗子烧鸡味道弗错，朆摆勒冰

　　　　　　箱里，结果坏了。
　　　　　　sian44-li31 cih43-kou51 seu44-theh3 tse44
　　　　　　箱里，结果嗖脱哉。

乙：普通话　那可不爽了。
　　吴语音　geh23-ci31 on44-tson31 tse44
　　吴语文　箇记翁肿②哉。

---

① "断命"并非早死的意思，它常常被人们用来表示一种不满的情绪，但并不含有恶意的诅咒。

② "翁肿"一词与普通话的意思相去甚远，意为"不愉快，不爽"，而这种不开心的心情又无法发泄。

甲: This damned weather. It's already Autumn Begins, we are still suffering from the heat. Not having been kept in the refrigerator, the Braised Chicken with Chinese Chestnut I cooked yesterday went off in this hot weather.

乙: Oh, you must be upset.

3. 甲: 普通话 刚才那场雷雨真厉害,又是闪
   吴语音 kaon44-chiae31 geh23-zan31 le22-zen33-yu31 tsen44-cia44- hou31 yih23-zy31 hoh43-
   吴语文 刚巧 箇场雷阵雨真家伙,② 亦是嚯

   电,又是打雷,而且是炸雷。
   shie51 yih23-zy31 le22- shian33 nga22-ka44-zy31 zah23-di33-le31
   显,亦是雷响,外加是着地雷。

   乙: 普通话 是的,轰隆隆打雷的时候,我正好
   吴语音 zy231-keh3 kuaon44-laon44-laon31 tan51 le223 keh43 zen22-kuaon33 ngou231 Zi22-chiae33
   吴语文 是个,咣啷啷打雷个辰光,我齐巧

   走在路上,吓得魂灵儿差点飞走。
   tseu51-leh3 lou22-laon33 hah43-teh3 wen22-lin33-deu31 the44-pe44-tie31 tsheh43 chiae51
   走勤路浪,吓得魂灵头推板点出窍。

甲: The thunderstorm just now was terrible. The lightening and the heavy thunder both occurred simultaneously.

乙: I was walking down the road when it thundered. I was scared.

4. 甲: 普通话 这个天气真是奇怪, 开春了 倒
   吴语音 ke44-keh3 thie44-chi31 tsen44-keh3 ji22-tsheh3- kua44-yan31 khe44 tshen44 tse44 tae523
   吴语文 该个天气真个奇出怪样,开春哉倒

---

① "真家伙"除了集褒贬于一体,既有"真讨厌,真烦,真不能让人省心,真够呛"等贬义外,同时又有"真佩服,真不容易,真厉害"等褒义。

第七单元　气象与节气

冷 得 让 人 受 不 了 了。
lan231-teh3 nyian231 nyin223 chih43-feh43- siae31 tse0
冷 得 让 人 吃 弗 消 哉。

乙：普通话　你 也 算 年 纪 不 小 了，白 活 喽， 居
　　吴语音　ne231 gha22-soe33 nyie22-ci33 ih43-dou33-po51 tse0 uaon44-khon31 weh23-tsy31 e44-
　　吴语文　侬 也 算 年 纪 一 大 把 哉，枉 空① 活 仔

然 连 倒 春 寒 也 不 知 道。
e44-tie31 se44-sou31 tseh43-oh43 ciu44-zoe31 lie223 ae523-tshen44-lan31 gha223 feh43 shiae51-teh3
哀点 岁 数 则 喔，居 然 连 奥 春 冷 也 弗 晓 得。

甲：The weather is so changeable. It is still chilly in early spring.
乙：I can't believe you have no idea about "Dao Chun Han" which means the weather is cold in the late spring here.

5. 甲：普通话　节 气 是 我们 祖 先 历 经 千 百 年 的
　　　吴语音　tsih43-chi523 zy231 nyi231 lae22-tsou44-tson31 lih23-cin31 tshie44-pah3-nyie31-keh0
　　　吴语文　节 气 是 伲 老 祖 宗 历 经 千 百 年 个

实 践 创 造 出 来 的 宝 贵 科 学 遗 产，
zeh23-zie31 tshaon523-zae31 tsheh43-le33-keh3 pae51-kue31 khou44--yoh3 yi22-tshe33
实 践 创 造 出 来 个 宝 贵 科 学 遗 产，

是 反 映 天 气 气 候 和 物 候 变 化、掌
zy231 fe51-in31 thie44-chi31 chi523-gheu31 taeh43 veh23-gheu31 pie523-ho31 tsan51-
是 反 映 天 气 气 候 搭 物 候 变 化、掌

握 农 事 季 节 的 工 具。
oh3 non22-zy33 ci523-tsih3-keh3 kon44-jiu31
握 农 事 季 节 个 工 具。

---

① "枉空"除了"场景对话5"中"白白地"意思外，还有"不像话"之意。例：侬该种样子像受过高等教育个人啊，简直枉空喔！(你这种样子像受过高等教育的人吗，简直不像样呀！)

乙：普通话 春 秋 战 国 时 期，中 国 就 已 经 通
吴语音 tshen44-tsheu31 tsoe523-kueh3 zen22-kuaon33 tson44-kueh3 zeu231 i44-cin31 thon44-
吴语文 春 秋 战 国 辰 光，中 国 就 已 经 通

过 测 量 正 午 太 阳 影 子 的 长 短，
kou31 tsheh43-lian223 tson44-laon44-shian31 tha44-yan31 in51-tsy23-keh0 zan22-toe33
过 测 量 中 浪 向 太 阳 影 子 个 长 短，

来 确 定 冬 至、夏 至、春 分、秋 分 四
le223 chioh43-din231 ton44-tsyu31 gho22-tsyu33 tshen44-fen31 tsheu44-fen31 sy523-
来 确 定 冬 至、夏 至、春 分、秋 分 四

个 节 气。
keh3 tshih43-chi523
个 节 气。

甲：Jieqi is a precious scientific legacy created by our ancestors on the basis of thousands of years of practice. It was used to indicate the climate and phenology changes in ancient China and decide the time for farming.

乙：In the Spring and Autumn period, ancient Chinese people measured the length of the shadow under the sunshine to find the winter solstice, the summer solstice, the spring and autumnal equinoxes.

6. 甲：普通话 老 和 尚 过 江 那 天，狂 风 大 作，
吴语音 lae22-ghou33-zaon31 kou523 kaon44 geh3-nyih3 fon44 zy231 dou231-teh3-le31 ya22-
吴语文 老 和 尚 过 江 箇 日，风 是 大 得 来 野

我 家 那 个 简 易 遮 雨 棚 彻
huah3-huah3 nyi231 oh43-li33-shian31 geh23-keh3 cie51-yi31 tso44-yu33-ban31 peh43
豁豁①，伲 屋 里 向 箇 个 简 易 遮 雨 棚 畀

---

① "野豁豁"是指程度深，往往用来形容指大的程度，也可以比喻说话夸张。

　　　　　　　底 完 蛋。
　　　　　tshe51-tsy33-keh3 ve22- zyu33
　　　　　　　铲 仔 个 饭 除①。

乙：普通话 有没有 砸 到 人？
　　吴语音 an44　hah43-wa231 nyin223
　　吴语文 酾 吓 坏 人？

甲：普通话 总 算 老天有眼， 没 出 事 故。
　　吴语音 tson44-soe31 thie44-khe44-nge31 fen44 tsheh43 zy22-thi33
　　吴语文 总 算 天 开 眼②，酾 出 事 体。

甲：On Feburary 28th in the Chinese lunar calendar, which is called the day of "The old monk crosses the river" by locals in Suzhou, my shelter was destroyed in the gale.

乙：Did it get anyone? Fortunately, nobody got hurt.

7. 甲：普通话 明 天 下 雨 吗？
　　　吴语音 men22-tsae33 aeh43-loh3-yu31
　　　吴语文 明 朝 阿 落 雨？

乙：普通话 多 云， 局 部 地 区 有 时 有 小 到 中 雨。
　　吴语音 tou44-yuin31 jioh23-bu31 di22-chiu33 yeu22-zen33-kuaon31 yeu231 siae51-tae23 tson44-yu31
　　吴语文 多 云， 局 部 地 区 有 辰 光 有 小 到 中 雨。

甲：普通话 你 这 话 模 棱 两 可， 根 本
　　吴语音 ne231 ken44-pen44-zy31 weh23-len31 jieu22-jieu33 pie51-thaeh3-thaeh3 ken44-pen31
　　吴语文 俫 根 本 是 囫 囵 球 球 扁 塌 塌③，根 本

---

① "铲饭除"形象地通过铲光锅底的锅巴来形容"彻底完蛋，一锅端"的情景。

② "天开眼"等同于普通话中"苍天有眼，报应分明"的意思，但不像普通话中用于感情强烈、悲怆的语境里，只是表达说话者一种小小的得意之情。

③ "囫囵球球扁塌塌"以外部形态的不确定，来表示一件事情或者一句话有点模棱两可，叫人琢磨不透。

不 负 责 任。
feh43 te44 cie44-ka31
弗 担 肩 胛。

甲：Will it rain tomorrow?
乙：Most of the area will be cloudy, and partly small rain will turn to middle rain.
甲：Your answer was slightly ambiguous the final work of Mr. Pei's.

8. 甲：普通话 不 知 不 觉，冬 至 到 了，一 年 快 过 去 了。
吴语音 ih43-ta523 feh43 ta523 ton44-tsyu31 tae523 tse44 ih43-nyie23 khua523 kou523-theh3 tse0
吴语文 一 带 弗 带，冬 至 到 哉，一 年 快 过 脱 哉。

乙：普通话 起 九 了，日 短 天 冷，晚 上 就 尽
吴语音 chi51 cieu51 tse44 nyih23-toe31 thie44 lan231 ia44- deu31 me22-ke33 zeu231 zin231-
吴语文 起 九 哉，日 短 天 冷，夜 头 慢 间 就 尽

量 少 出 去 吧。一 切 安 排 好 就 早
lian31 sae51 tsheh43- chi523 ba0 ih43-tshih43 oe44-den31 syu44-zi31 zeu231 tsae51-
量 少 出 去 罢。一 切 安 顿 舒 齐 就 早

点 钻 到 被 窝 里 去 吧。
tie23 tsoe44-tae31 bi22-fon44-don33-li31 chi523 ba0
点 钻 到 避 风 洞 里 去 吧。

甲：Soon, before anyone was aware of it, the winter solstice came and a year is gone.
乙：The nights are drawing out as it's getting colder. Try to stay at home and go to bed early.

9. 甲：普通话 你 怎 么 吃 这 么 少？
吴语音 ne231 naeh23-han31 chih43 zeh23-kan31 sae51
吴语文 倷 哪哼 吃 实 梗 少？

乙：普通话 我 疰 夏 的，一 到 夏 季，身 上 不 舒 服，
吴语音 ngou231 gho22-tsyu33-keh3 ih43-tae523 nyih23-thie31 sen44-laon31 iu44-syu31 ou44-
吴语文 我 夏 疰 个，一 到 热 天，身 浪 淤 水 乌

心 里 就 烦躁， 就 吃 不 下 饭。
sou44-teh3-le31 sin44-li31 zeu231 tsi44-tsae31 zeu231 chih43-feh43-loh3 ve231
苏① 得 来，心 里 就 济糟②， 就 吃 弗 落 饭。

甲：How come you lose your appetite？

乙：I am suffering from summer fever, which is a summer disease with symptoms of fever, loss of appetite, etc.

三 词语贴士

（一）常见气象

序号	英文	苏州话
1.	lightening	hoh43-shie51
	闪电	喔显
2.	foggy	mi22-lou33
	雾	迷露
3.	frosty	saon44
	霜	霜
4.	dew	lou22-tsyu33
	露珠	露珠
5.	ice run	lin22-daon33
	冰棱	凌宕
6.	snowy	loh23 sih43
	下雪	落雪
7.	rainy	loh23 yu231
	下雨	落雨
8.	windy	chi51 fon44
	刮风	起风
9.	thunder	tan51 le23
	打雷	打雷
10.	freeze	cih43 pin44
	结冰	结冰

① "淤水、乌苏"主要是指皮肤上不舒服的感觉。
② "济糟"指内心里说不出的烦躁，由此引发人的表情、语气、态度等发生一连串的不良连锁反应。

(二) 自然灾害

序号	英文	苏州话
1.	earthquake 地震	di22-tsen33 地震
2.	tsunami 海啸	he51-siae23 海啸
3.	typhoon 台风	de22-fon33 台风
4.	debris flow 泥石流	nyi22-zah3-leu31 泥石流
5.	flash flood 山洪暴发	se44-ghon31 bae22-faeh3 山洪暴发
6.	hail 冰雹	pin44-bae31 冰雹
7.	drought 干旱	koe44-ghoe31 干旱
8.	landslide 山体滑坡	se44-thi31 waeh23 phu31 山体滑坡

(三) 日常天气

序号	英文	苏州话
1.	sunny 晴天	zin22-thie33，tsheh43-tha44-yan31 晴天，出太阳
2.	cloudy 阴天	in44-thie31，in44-tsy44-thie31 阴天，阴子天
3.	rainy 雨天	loh23-yu33-thie31 落雨天
4.	cloudy 多云	tou44-yuin31 多云

(四) 气候种类

序号	英文	苏州话
1.	mountain climate 山地气候	se44-di31 chi523-gheu31 山地气候
2.	monsoon climate 季风气候	ci44-fon31 chi523-gheu31 季风气候
3.	forest climate 森林气候	sen44-lin31 chi523-gheu31 森林气候

续表

序号	英文	苏州话
4.	highland climate 高地气候	kae44-di31 chi523-gheu31 高地气候
5.	ocean climate 海洋气候	he51-yan23 chi523-gheu31 海洋气候
6.	continental climate 大陆气候	da22-loh3 chi523-gheu31 大陆气候
7.	desert climate 沙漠气候	so44-moh3 chi523-gheu31 沙漠气候
8.	polar climate 极地气候	jih23-di31 chi523-gheu31 极地气候
9.	subtropical climate 亚热带气候	ia44-nyih3-ta31 chi523-gheu31 亚热带气候
10.	tropical climate 热带气候	nyih23-ta31 chi523-gheu31 热带气候
11.	temperate climate 温带气候	uen44-ta31 chi523-gheu31 温带气候
12.	tropical rain forest climate 热带雨林气候	nyih23-ta31 yu22-lin33 chi523-gheu31 热带雨林气候

（五）气象术语

序号	英文	苏州话
1.	Centigrade 摄氏度	seh43-zy33-dou31 摄氏度
2.	zero 零度	lin22-dou33 零度
3.	below zero 零度以下	lin22-dou33 i51-gho31 零度以下
4.	meteorology 气象学	chi523-zian33-yoh3 气象学
5.	weather forecast 天气预报	thie44-chi31-yu22-pae33 天气预报
6.	atmosphere 大气	da22-chi33 大气
7.	low-pressure 低气压	ti44-chi44-ah3 低气压

续表

序号	英文	苏州话
8.	atmospheric pressure 气压	chi44-ah3 气压
9.	climate 气候	chi523-gheu31 气候
10.	temperature 气温	chi523-uen33 气温

（六）春季节气

序号	英文	苏州话
1.	Spring begins 立春	lih23 tshen44 立春
2.	The rains 雨水	yu22-syu33 雨水
3.	Insects awaken 惊蛰	cin44-tseh3 惊蛰
4.	Vernal Equinox 春分	tshen44-fen31 春分
5.	Clear and bright 清明	tshin44-min31 清明
6.	Grain rain 谷雨	koh43-yu231 谷雨

（七）夏季节气

序号	英文	苏州话
1.	Summer begins 立夏	lih23-gho31 立夏
2.	Grain buds 小满	siae51-moe31 小满
3.	Grain in ear 芒种	maon22-tson33 芒种
4.	Summer solstice 夏至	gho22-tsyu33 夏至
5.	Slight heat 小暑	siae51-syu31 小暑
6.	Great heat 大暑	dou22-syu33 大暑

（八）秋季节气

序号	英文	苏州话
1.	Autumn begins 立秋	lih23 tsheu44 立秋
2.	Stopping the heat 处暑	tshyu51-syu31 处暑
3.	White dews 白露	bah23-lou31 白露
4.	Autumn Equinox 秋分	tsheu44-fen31 秋分
5.	Cold dews 寒露	ghoe22-lou33 寒露
6.	Hoar-frost falls 霜降	saon44-kaon31 霜降

（九）冬季节气

序号	英文	苏州话
1.	Winter begins 立冬	lih23 ton44 立冬
2.	Light snow 小雪	siae523-sih3 小雪
3.	Heavy snow 大雪	dou22-sih3 大雪
4.	Winter Solstice 冬至	ton44-tsyu31 冬至
5.	Slight cold 小寒	siae51-ghoe23 小寒
6.	Great cold 大寒	dou22-ghoe33 大寒

（十）节气起源

序号	英文	苏州话
1.	midspring 仲春	zon22-tshen33 仲春
2.	midsummer 仲夏	zon22-gho33 仲夏

续表

序号	英文	苏州话
3.	midautumn	zon22-tsheu33
	仲秋	仲秋
4.	midwinter	zon22-ton33
	仲冬	仲冬

四 对话中的特色词汇

序号	英文	苏州话
1.	on one's childhood	siae51-haeh3-li31
	小时候	小呷里
2.	be in chaos	ih43-thie44-syu44-ka31
	乱七八糟	一天世界
3.	in a short time	ih43-zyu33-se44-kheh3
	短时间	一时三刻
4.	never return	ih43-ciah3-chi31
	一去不回	一脚去
5.	in a short while	ih43-ciah3-loh3-seu31
	一口气	一脚落手
6.	hale and hearty	zah23-zeh3-jie31
	好棒	着实健
7.	drink	chih43
	喝	吃
8.	for some weeks	yeu22-lian33-nyih3
	有些时候	有两日
9.	damned	doe22-min33
	可恶	断命
10.	go bad	seu44
	坏	馊
11.	angry	on44-tson31
	不爽	翁肿
12.	terrible	tsen44-cia44-hou31
	真厉害	真家伙
13.	rumble	khuaon44-laon33-laon31
	轰隆隆	咣啷啷

续表

序号	英文	苏州话
14.	feel scared 魂灵儿飞走	wen22-lin33-deu31 tsheh43 chiae523 魂灵头出窍
15.	strange 奇怪	ji22-tsheh3-kua44-yan31 奇出怪样
16.	vain 白白地	uaon44-khon31 枉空
17.	fiercely 极大	dou231-teh3 ya22-huah3-huah3 大得野豁豁
18.	house 家	oh43-li33-shian31 屋里向
19.	dead 彻底完蛋	tshe51-ve22-zyu31 铲饭除
20.	fortunately 老天有眼	thie44-khe44-nge31 天开眼
21.	accident 事故	zy22-thi33 事体
22.	ambiguous 模棱两可	weh23-len31 jieu22-jieu33 pie51-thaeh3-thaeh3 囫囵球球扁塌塌
23.	irresponsible 负责任	te44 cie44-ka31 担肩胛
24.	unconsciously 不知不觉	ih43 ta523 feh43- ta523 一带弗带
25.	at night 晚上	ia44-deu33-me33-ke31 夜头晚间
26.	get ready 安排好	oe44-den33-syu44-zi31 安顿舒齐
27.	bed 被窝	bi22-fon44-don31 避风洞
28.	feel sick 不舒服	iu44-syu31 ou44-sou31 淤水、乌苏
29.	fretful 烦躁	tsi44-tsae31 济糟

五 巩固练习

1 甲：前天雷允上药店赠送人体骨架图,你有没有去领？
乙：到的时候已经发完了,没拿到。
甲：你肯定被那场大雨拖住脚了,是雨停后才出门的。
乙：是的,雨一停我要紧赶过去,还是晚了。

2 甲：张阿姨,你在编什么东西？怎么那么小？
乙：哦,我在编放咸鸭蛋的绳袋,不知不觉,立夏马上要到了。
甲：我们小时候倒是个个都在头颈里挂上咸鸭蛋的,现在是看不大见了。
乙：我也想让我孙子稍稍感受一下传统文化的味道。

六 参考答案

1

甲：普通话 前天　　　雷允上药店赠送人体
吴语音 zie22-nyi3-tsy44-taeh3 le22-iuin44-zaon31 yah23- vaon31 zen231-son31 nyin22-thi33
吴语文 前日仔搭 雷允上药房赠送人体

骨架图,你去领？
kueh43-ka44-dou31 ne231 an44 chi523 lin231
骨架图,倷齆去领？

乙：普通话 到的时候已经发完了,没拿到。
吴语音 tae523-keh3 zen22-kuaon33 i44-cin31 faeh43 kuaon44 tse0 fen44 no22-zah3
吴语文 到个辰光已经发光哉,朆拿着。

甲：普通话 你肯定被那场大雨拖住脚了,
吴语音 ne231 khen51-din31 peh43 geh23-zan31 dou22-yu33 thou44-lae31 ciah43-deu231 tse44
吴语文 倷肯定畀箇场大雨拖牢脚头哉,

　　　　　　雨　停　后　　　　　才　出　门　的。
　　　　　　yu231 din22-tsy33 kou523-gheu31 tse44 tsheh43-men33-keh3
　　　　　　雨　停　仔　过　后　再　出　门　个。

乙：普通话 是 的，雨 一 停 我 要 紧 赶　过 去，还 是 晚 了。
　　吴语音 zy231-keh3-ia31 yu231 ih43-din23 ngou231 iae44-cin31 shieu44-kou44-chi31 we22-zy33 e523 tse44
　　吴语文 是 个 呀，雨 一 停 我 要 紧 休 过 去，还 是 晏 哉。

甲：Did you get the human skeleton drawing as a gift from Leiyunshang Pharmaceutical Store?

乙：It had been run out when I arrived.

甲：You must have been kept by the heavy rain, and didn't go out until it stopped.

乙：As soon as it stopped raining, I rushed all the way to the store only to miss it.

2

甲：普通话 张 阿 姨，你 在　编 什 么 东 西？ 怎 么
　　吴语音 tsan44-a44-yi31 ne231 leh23-he31 pie44 sa523-keh3 meh23-zy31 cia0 naeh23-han31
　　吴语文 张 阿 姨，㑚 勒 嗨 编 啥 个 物 事 嗄？ 哪 哼

　　　　　　那　么　小？
　　　　　　geh23-zaon31 siae51-keh3
　　　　　　箇　状　小　个？

乙：普通话 哦，我　在　编 放 咸 鸭 蛋 的 绳 袋，不 知
　　吴语音 oh43 ngou231 leh23-he31 pie44 faon523 ghe22-aeh3-de33-keh3 zen22-de33 ih43 ta523
　　吴语文 喔，我　勒 嗨 编 放 咸 鸭 蛋 个 绳 袋，一 带

　　　　　　不　觉，立　夏　马　上　要　到　了。
　　　　　　feh43 ta523 lih23-gho31 tsih43-moh3 iae523 ta523 tse0
　　　　　　弗　带，立　夏　即　目　要　到　哉。

甲：普通话 我们 小　时　候　倒 是 个 个 都 在　　头 颈
　　吴语音 nyi231 siae51-zen33-kuaon31 tae44-zy31 kou44-kou31 ze223 leh23-laon31 deu22-cin44-
　　吴语文 伲　小　辰　光　倒 是 个 个 赕 勒 浪 头 颈

里　　挂上　咸　鸭　蛋的，现　在　是　不　常　见　　了。
li31-shian44 ko523 tsah43 ghe22-aeh3-de33-keh3 yie22-ze33-zy31 khoe523-feh3-da33-cie31 tse0
里向　挂只　咸　鸭　蛋个，现　在　是　看　弗　大　见　哉。

乙：普通话　我　也　想　让　　我　孙　子　稍　稍　感　受　一
　　吴语音 ngou231 gha22-sian33 nyian231-nyi31 sen44-tsy31 sae44-shiu31 koh43-taeh43 ih43-
　　吴语文　我　也　想　让　　伲　孙　子　稍　许　觉　搿　一

　　　　　下　传　统　文　化　的　味　道。
　　　　　tie51 zoe22-thon33 ven22-ho44-keh3 mi22-dae33
　　　　　点　传　统　文　化　个　味　道。

甲：Aunt Zhang, what are you knitting? It looks so small.
乙：A bag for a salted duck egg. The Summer Begins is coming.
甲：As a child, I used to hang a bag with a salted duck egg round my neck, which is uncommon now.
乙：I'd like to make one for my grandchild so that he can touch the traditional culture in Suzhou.

第八单元

邻里与家常

一 情景引入

甲：普通话　王　爷爷，听　说　你的孙子　　真　有出息
吴语音　waon22-aeh3-tia31 thin44-seh3 n22-toh3 sen44-tsy44 yeu231 tsheh43-sih43-teh43 feh43-
吴语文　王　阿爹，听　说　尔笃孙子　有　出　息　得　弗

　　　　　　　　留　学　回来，自己　开起了　公司，生意
　　　　　teh3-liae231 leu22-ghoh3 tsoe51-le33 zy22-ka33 khe44-tsy33-pe31 kon44-sy31 san44-i31
　　　　　得了，留　学　转来，自家　开仔爿　公司，生意

做 到 了 国 外。
tsou44-tae44-tsy31 kueh43-nga231 chi523 tseh43 ueh0
做 到 仔 国 外 去 则 唲。

乙：普通话 你 过 奖 了。 他 是 刚 刚 起 步， 根 本 不 成
吴语音 ne231 kou44-tsian31 tse44 n44-ne33-zy31 ih43- lih3 mi231 toh43 tsoh43 mi22-chi31 gha223
吴语文 倷 过 奖 哉。 尔 倷 是 一 粒 米 笃 粥， 米 气 也

气 候。
m22- peh3 leh0
呒 不 嘞。

甲：普通话 我 想 和 你 商 量 个 事 情， 我 儿 子 最
吴语音 ngou231 sian51 taeh43 ne231 san44-lian31 tsaon44 zy22-thi33 nyi231 nyi22-tsy33 ke44-
吴语文 我 想 搭 倷 商 量 桩 事 体， 伲 儿 子 该

近 下 岗 在 家 里， 托 你 和 你 孙 子
tshian31 gho22-kaon33-leh3 oh43-li231 iae523 thoh43 ne231 taeh43 n22-toh3 sen44-tsy31
歁 下 岗 勒 屋 里， 要 托 倷 搭 尔 笃 孙 子

说 说， 让 我 儿 子 到 他 公 司 里 去 干干活。
kaon51-kaon31 nyian231 nyi231 nyi22-tsy33 tae523 li44 kon44-sy44-li31 chi523 tsou523 san44-weh3
讲 讲， 让 伲 儿 子 到 俚 公 司 里 去 做 生 活①。

乙：普通话 你 儿 子 从 小 做 事 就 特 别 细 心，
吴语音 n22-toh3 nyi22-tsy33 zon231 siae523 tsou523 zy22-thi33 zeu231 deh23-bih3 po51-si23
吴语文 尔 笃 儿 子 从 小 做 事 体 就 特 别 把 细②，

正 好 我 孙 子 这 一 阵 公 司 里 缺 个 保 安，
zi22-chiae33 nyi231 sen44-tsy31 ke44-tshian31 kon44-sy44- li31 huah43-keh43 pae51-oe23
齐 巧 伲 孙 子 该 歁 公 司 里 豁 个 保 安，

---

① "生活"有四层含义：a. 活计。此义同"情景引入"中"让伲儿子到尔倷公司里去做做生活"。
b. 苦头、伤害。例：倷想讨吃生活？（你想挨揍吗？）c. 货真价实。例：该记真生活则唲？（这次货真价实了吧？）d. 够呛。例：倷结棍个啊，哀记真生活。（你厉害的，这次够呛。）

② "把细"主要是"仔细、小心"的意思，还带着"谨慎"的味道。

第八单元　邻里与家常

这 个 职 位 一 个 月　　　工 资、奖 金、补 贴,
ke44-tsah3 we22- tsy33 ih43-keh3 ghae22-deu33 kon44-tsy31 tsian51-cin23 pu51-thih3
该 只 位 子 一 个 号 头　工 资、奖 金、补 贴,

合 起 来 总 共　　　　　　有　2000　元
lou44-lou44-kuaeh43-kuaeh4 goh23-loh3--se44-men31 yeu231 lian231-tshie44-khue44-
啰 啰 刮 刮、榈 落 山 门① 有　2000　块

左 右, 你　儿 子 愿 意 做 吗?
mo33-yan31 n22-toh3 nyi22-tsy33 aeh43-khen51 tsou523
模 样, 尔 笃 儿 子 阿 肯 做?

甲: 普通话 愿意的　愿意的。　真 的　　太 感谢　　你 了。
　　吴语音 khen51-keh3-a0 khen51-keh3-a0 tsen44-keh3-zy31 tshie44-tou44- me33-zia33-ne31 se0
　　吴语文 肯 个 啊 肯 个 啊。真 个 是　千 多 万 谢 侬 哉!

甲: Mr. Wang! I heard your grandson is very successful. He has started his own business after he studied abroad. His business has expanded to foreign countries.

乙: You give him more credit than he deserves. He just got a good start on business. But there is a long way to go.

甲: I have something personal to talk over you. My son is out of job now. Would it possible for you to ask your grandson to offer a position in his company to my son?

乙: Your son was careful when he was a little boy. My grandson's company has a vacancy on security. Its monthly pay amounts to about $2000, which includes salary, bonus and allowance. Would he like to take this job?

甲: Of course. Thank you so much.

---

① "啰啰刮刮""榈落山门"与前面碰到的"一塌刮子"都是总共的意思。

二 场景对话

1. 甲：普通话 李阿姨，我们 明天 要 搬家 了，今天 跟
吴语音 li22-a44-yi31 nyi231 men22-tsae33 iae523 poe44 zan223 tse44 cin44-tsae31 taeh43
吴语文 李阿姨， 倷 明朝 要 搬 场 哉，今朝 搭

你 告别 一 下。
ne231 we22-deu33 ih43-san31
倷 回头 一声。

乙：普通话 几十年 的 好 邻居 了，真的是 远 亲 不
吴语音 ci51-seh3-nyie33-keh3 hae51-shian44-lin31 tse44 tsen44-keh3-zy31 cin44-shian44-lin31
吴语文 几十年 个 好 乡邻 哉，真个是 金 乡邻、

如 近邻， 我 心里 真 舍不得。
nyin22-tshin44-cioe31 ngou231 sin44-li31 ciae44-kue31 so51-feh3-teh3- teh3
银 亲眷， 我 心里 交关 舍弗得个。

甲：普通话 我 也是呀，但愿 搬了新家 以后，邻居
吴语音 ngou231 gha22-zy33 ia0 de22-nyioe33 poe44-tsy31 zan223 kou523-gheu31 shian44-lin31
吴语文 我 也是呀，但愿 搬仔场 过后，乡邻

关系 也 像我们一样，如同 亲戚，千万
kue44-yi31 gha223 zian231 nyi231 ih43-yan23 se523-kou31 tshin44-cioe31 tshie44-ve31
关系 也 像 倷一样， 赛过① 亲眷， 千万

不要 像 几世仇人 哦。
fiae523 lon44-teh3-leh3 zian231 tshih43- syu44-ioe44-ka31 zeh23-kan31
覅 弄得勒像 七 世 冤家② 实梗。

---

① "赛过"在苏州话中多指"好像、如同"之意，与普通话多指"胜过、超过"不同。
② "七世冤家"有两层意思：a. 积怨很深的仇人。此义同"场景对话1"中"千万不要像七世冤家喔"。b. 泛指似恨实爱、给自己带来苦恼而又舍不得的人，通常是情人、亲人，为爱至极的反语。例：倷真个是我个七世冤家，我前世欠倷个，今世来还。（你真是我的讨债鬼，我前世欠你的，今世来还。）

甲：Ms. Le, we will move tomorrow. So we come to say goodbay to you.

乙：We have been neighbors for several decades. The proverb says neighbors are gold and relatives are silver. I will miss you so much.

甲：I will miss you too. I hope we will get along well with our new neighbors like relatives.

2. 甲：普通话 你知道吗，昨天下午 1 3 幢
吴语音 ne231 aeh43 shiae51-teh3 zoh23-nyih3-keh3 gho22-me33-tseu31 zeh23-se44-zaon31
吴语文 倷 阿 晓 得，昨 日 个 下 晚 昼 1 3 幢

4 0 5 室被贼 光顾了，家里
sy44-lin33 ng231 seh3 peh3 zeh23-kueh3-deu31 le22-kou33 tse44 oh43-li33-shian31
4 0 5 室畀贼骨头来过哉，屋里向

一片狼藉。
loh23-loh3-loe31
络络乱①。

乙：普通话 光 天 化 日 入 室 偷 盗，那 小 偷 也
吴语音 tshin44-thie31 bah23-zeh3 zeh23-seh3 theu44-dae31 geh23 zeh23-kueh3-deu31 gha223
吴语文 青 天 白 日 入 室 偷 盗，箇 贼 骨 头 也

太嚣张了。
theh43 he44-ue31 tseh43-ba0
忒海威则吧。

甲：Do you know the Room 405 in Buliding 13 was burgled yesterday afternoon? The house was in a mess.

乙：I can't believe the burglary happened during the day. The thieves are extremely audacious.

---

① "络络乱" 形容十分杂乱。它除了描绘物品杂乱至极外，还用来描摹人的心里七上八下，毫无方寸。

3. 甲：普通话 张爷爷，跟你商量个事，你家
   吴语音 tsan44-aeh3-tia31 taeh43 ne231 san44-lian31 tsaon44 zy22-thi33 n22-toh3 oh43-li33-
   吴语文 张 阿爹，搭倷 商量 桩 事体，尔笃屋里

   空调外机的位置能否 往 右
   shian31 khon44-diae31 nga22-ci44-keh3 we22-tsy33 aeh43 khou51-i23 maon231 yeu22-
   向 空 调 外 机 个 位 子 阿 可 以 望 右

   边 移 半 米 距离，因为 那 水滴 正 好
   mie33 yi22-theh3-keh3 poe523-mi31 jiu22-li33 in44-we31 Geh23-syu31 zi22-chiae33
   面 移 脱 个 半 米 距离，因为 箇 水 齐 巧

   滴在 遮雨棚上，晚上 滴里搭拉，
   ti523-leh3-keh3 tso44-yu33-ban33-laon31 ia44-li33-shian31 tih43-lih3-toh3-loh3-keh3
   滴 勒 个 遮 雨 棚 浪，夜 里 向 滴 沥 笃 落 个，

   我 觉也 睡不着。
   ngou231 kae523 ghaeh23 khuen523-feh3-zah3-tseh3
   我 觉 也 睏 弗 着 则。

乙：普通话 真受罪， 怪不得你 一脸 没睡醒的样子。
   吴语音 tsen44-keh3 ze231-kou31 kua44-feh3-teh3 ne231 ih43-tsah3 kah43-ia44-mie33-khon33-
   吴语文 真 个 罪过， 怪 弗 得 倷 一只 隔夜 面 孔①

   我 一定尽 快 移 位。
   -ue0 ngou231 khen51-din31 zin231-khua31 thon51-tsah3 we22-tsy33
   唵。我 肯 定 尽 快 捅② 只 位 子。

---

① "隔夜面孔"有两层意思：a. 没睡醒的脸。此义同"场景对话3"中"怪弗得倷一只隔夜面孔唵"。b. 比喻陈旧过时的样子。例：已经冷天哉，该只橱窗里摆个还是春秋衫，一副隔夜面孔。（已经冬天了，这个橱窗里摆的还是春秋衫，一副过时的样子。）

② "捅"在苏州话中主要是"移动，挪动"的意思，与普通话中主要是"用棍、棒、刀、枪等戳刺"的意思不同。

甲：Mr. Zhang, I'd like to talk to you about your air conditioner. Would it possible for you to move the outside part of your air conditioning to the right for half a meter? The water from the drain pipe dropped on my rain shelter. I was kept up by the noise all night.

乙：I'm so sorry. You look so tired and sleepy. I will restall it as soon as possible.

4. 甲：普通话 小张，怎么今天你送孩子上学了？平时不 一直是你老婆 管的吗？
   吴语音 siae51-tsan23 naeh23-han31 cin44-tsae31 ne231 son523 siae51-kuoe23 tae44-ghoh3-daon31 tseh43-cia0 bin231-zan33- zen33-kuaon31 feh43-zy31 ih43-ciah43 zy231 n22-toh3 ka44-tsyu44-bu31 kuoe51-keh3 meh0
   吴语文 小张，哪嚑今朝倷送小倌到学堂则嘎？平常辰光 弗是一脚是尔笃家主婆 管个末？

乙：普通话 哦，老伯 早。老婆 单位破天荒 组织旅游两天，害得我们家的生活全部打乱。
   吴语音 oh43 lae22-pah3-pah3 tsae51 ka44-tsyu44-bu31 te44-we31 phu44-thie44-huaon31-keh0 tsou51-tseh3-chi31 li22-yeu33-lian33-thie31 ghe231-teh3-nyi31 oh43-li33-keh3 nyih23- ciah3 zie22-bu33 tan51-loe31
   吴语文 喔，老伯伯早。家主婆单位破天荒个组织去旅游两天，害得伲屋里个日脚全部打乱。

甲：普通话 你们父子俩的晚饭肯定没有着落吧，就
   吴语音 n22-toh3 ya22-lian33-keh3 ia44-ve31 khen51-din31 fen44-zah3-kaon44-leh3-ue0 zeu231
   吴语文 尔笃爷两个夜饭肯定朆着缸勒哇，就

到 我 家 　　来 吃 吧。
tae523 ngou231 oh43-li231 le223 chih43 ba0
到 我 屋 里 来 吃 罢。

乙：普通话 那么 我 　就 厚着 　　　　脸 皮 来吃饭 了。
　　吴语音 geh23-meh3 ngou231-zeu33 mie22-bi33 lae231-lae31 dou22-bi33 pae51-pae31 tse44
　　吴语文 箇 末 我 　就 面 皮 老 老，肚 皮 饱 饱 哉。

甲：Good morning, Mr. Zhang. How come you take your child to school today? Usually your wife takes in charge of this job.

乙：Good morning. My wife is having a 2-day trip organized by her company. When she isn't at home, we are living in a mess.

甲：I guess you haven't prepared your supper. How about coming to my house and having dinner with us?

乙：Thank you for inviting us. We really appreciate that.

5. 甲：普通话 我们 社 区 的 小 李 说话 态 度 和 气 就
　　吴语音 nyi231 zo22-chiu44-keh31 siae51-li31 cie523 nyin223 hae51-seh3-hae44-gho31 zeu22-
　　吴语文 伲 社 区 个 小 李 见 人 好 说 好 话 就

　　　　是 有 时 　　说 话 啰 唆，
　　zy33 yeu22-zen33-kuaon31 kaon51-chi31 ghe22-gho33-le31 gheu22--tsyu44-naeh3-teh3
　　　　是 有 辰 光 讲 起 闲 话 来 厚 嘴 呐 得。①

　　　　好 管　　 闲 事。
　　tsou523-chi31 zy22-thi33-le31 yeu231-tie31 mo22-jie33-jie33-keh3
　　　　做 起 事 体 来 有 点 马 健 健② 个。

乙：普通话 是 个 小 屄 头 吧，不 过 好 人 常 有 几 分 屄头的味道。
　　吴语音 zy231-keh3 siae51-zeu33-deu31 ue0 pih43-kou523 hae51-nyin23 zan22-ta31 se44-fen31 zeu223
　　吴语文 是 个 小 寿 头 啘，不 过 好 人 常 带 三 分 屄。

①"厚嘴呐得"有两层意思：a. 说话啰唆。此义同"场景对话5"中"就是有辰光讲起闲话来厚嘴呐得"。b. 不善表达。例：对弗起，伲男人厚嘴呐得，弗大会讲闲话个。（对不起，我丈夫不善表达，不太会讲话的。）

②"马健健"指好管闲事又没管好，与上一单元的"健"中"过分热心，反而不讨好"的意思接近。

甲：Mr. Le in our community is gentle and polite. But sometimes he is garrulous and inquisitive.

乙：I think he is a little bit silly. A nice man always shows a bit silliness.

6. 甲：普通话 老婆， 你 这 件 新 买 的 衣服 款 式、
　　　吴语音 ka44-tsyu44-bu31 ne231 ke44-jie231 sin44 ma231-keh3 i44-zaon44-keh3 khuoe51-seh3
　　　吴语文 家主婆，倷 该 件 新 买 个 衣裳 个 款 式、

　　　　　　面 料 都 不 错， 就 是 颜 色 艳 丽 了 些， 大
　　　　　　liae22-tsoh3 ze223 feh43-tsho23 zeu22-zy33 nge22-seh3 ie523-zah3-tsy33-tie31 shiueh43-
　　　　　　料 作 侪 弗 错， 就 是 颜 色 艳 着 仔 点， 血

　　　　　　红 的， 好 像 与 你 的 年 纪 不 相 符 合。
　　　　　　phan44-da33-ghon31 zian22-saeh3 taeh43 ne231-keh3 nyie22-ci33 feh43-sian44 vu22-gheh3 ue0
　　　　　　嘭 大 红， 像 煞 搭 倷 个 年 纪 弗 相 符 合 啘。

乙：普通话 你 个 老 鬼 为 人 最 坏， 怎 么，
　　　吴语音 ne231-tsan3 lao22-si44-nyin31 lou231-kueh3-tin44- chieu44-keh3 naeh23-han31
　　　吴语文 倷 只 老 死 人 露骨① 顶 丘 个， 哪 哼

　　　　　　嫌 我 年 纪 大 了？
　　　　　　yie22-pi44-ngou231 nyi22-ci33 dou231-tseh3-a0
　　　　　　嫌 比② 我 年 纪 大 则 啊？

甲：Honey, the style and material of your new cloth are good in quality. But the color is loud. I don't think the bright red suits your age.

乙：Hum, are you reminding me of my age?

---

①"露骨"不是指表面的、显现的，恰恰是指骨子深处的。"丘"是"坏"的意思。
②"嫌比"除了"嫌弃"的意思外，还有"不称心、不顺眼"之意。例：倷勤横嫌比竖嫌比哉。(你不要横不称心竖不称心了。)

7. 甲：普通话 妈妈，你 这个 鸡 根 炸 得 真 棒， 外 脆 里
　　　吴语音 m44-ma31 ne231 e44-keh3 ci44-ken31 then51-teh3 hae51-teh3-le31 nga22-tshe44-li33-
　　　吴语文 姆妈，倷 哀个 鸡 根 佘①得 好 得来， 外 脆 里

　　　　　　嫩， 颜 色 焦 黄 味 道 喷 香， 馋 得
　　　　　　nen31 tshah43-laeh3-tsiae44-waon31 mi22-dae33 phen44-phen44--shian31 ze22-teh3-
　　　　　　嫩， 赤 辣 焦 黄， 味 道 喷 喷 香， 馋 得

　　　　　　我 口 水 直 流。
　　　　　　ngou31 ze22-thou44-syu44-gha31 taeh43- taeh43-ti31 te44
　　　　　　我 馋 吐 水 也 答 答 滴 哉。

乙：普通话 你 个 馋 鬼， 别 转 悠 个 不 停，
　　　吴语音 ne231-tsah3 ze22-lae33-phe31 fiae523 toh43-toh43- tsoe31 zi22-zi33-tsoe44-keh3-tse0
　　　吴语文 倷 只 馋 痨 胚②，勠 笃 笃 转 齐 齐 转③个 哉，

　　　　　　坐 下 来 好 好 地 吃， 没 人
　　　　　　zou231-din33-tsy31 hae51-hae44-ciae31 tshoh43-tsi523 ba0 m22-peh3 nyin223 ue523-
　　　　　　坐 定 仔 好 好 较④ 触 祭⑤罢，哚 不 人 会

　　　　　　跟 你 抢。
　　　　　　teh3 taeh43 ne231 tshian51 keh0
　　　　　　得 搭 倷 抢 个。

甲：Mum, the wing roots teast good. They are crispy, tender and delicious. The delicious smell from the kitchen makes my mouths water.

乙：You are like a greedy cat. Sit down and enjoy yourself.

---

① "佘"有两层意思：a. 炸。此义同"场景对话7"中"倷哀个鸡根佘得好得来"。b. 漂浮。例：好好较游，勠像个佘汤浮尸实梗。（好好较游，不要像浮起来的尸体一样。）

② "馋痨胚"虽然指责某人贪吃，像个馋鬼一样，但不含恶意。

③ "笃笃转齐齐转"是指在原地或较小的圈子里不停地打圈，一般是在心情焦虑的情况下。

④ "好好较"有两层意思：a. 好好地。词语同"场景对话7"中"坐定仔好好较胲济"。b. 大大地。例：好好较要多勒。（大大地要多呢。）

⑤ "触祭"是"吃"的意思，一般是长者对晚辈说的，同辈之间往往针对那些吃相不雅的人而言。

第八单元　邻里与家常

8. 甲： 普通话　有　　什　么　办　法　可　以　让　小　宝　宝

　　吴语音 aeh43-yeu231 sa523-keh3 chiae44-khe31 khou51-i23 nyian231 siae51-mae33-deu331

　　吴语文 阿　有　啥　个　窍　开　可　以　让　小　毛　头

　　　　　　不　闹？
　　　　　feh43 tsoh43 nyian44
　　　　　弗　作　孃？①

乙： 普通话　尿　片　要　勤　换，不　　能　湿　漉　漉　的。湿　了

　　吴语音 syu44-bu31 iae523 tou44-woe31 feh43-nen223 zae22- taeh3-taeh3-keh3 zae22-tsy33

　　吴语文 尿　布　要　多　换，弗　能　潮②答　答　个。潮　仔

　　　　　　不　舒　服　了　当　然　要　找　茬　闹　了。
　　　　feh43 seh43-i44-tsy31 taon44-zoe31 iae523 zaon22-chian33 tsoh43 tse44
　　　　　弗　适　意　仔　当　然　要　上　腔③作　哉。

甲： Can you share your experience to calm a baby?
乙： Change baby's diaper frequently. Don't wait the diaper too wet to change. The baby will feel very uncomfortable by using a wet diaper. That's why baby is crying.

9. 甲： 普通话　哪　里　来　的　一　股　焦　味？不　好，红　烧

　　吴语音 lo22-taeh3 le22-keh3 ih43-kou51 tsiae44-mae44-chi31 feh43 hae51 tse44 ghon22-sae44-

　　吴语文 哪　搭　来　个　一　股　焦　冒　气？弗　好　哉，红　烧

　　　　　　肉　粘　锅　了。可　惜　了。
　　　　nyioh3 teh43 ti51 tse44 tsoh43-nyih3 saeh43 tse44
　　　　　肉　得　底　哉。作　孽　煞　哉。

---

① 孃，语气词。

② 苏州话中从来不单用"湿"，一般用"潮"来表示"湿"的意思，或者把两个字合起来"潮湿"来表示。

③ "上腔"有两层意思：a. 找茬，挑衅。此义同"场景对话8"中"潮仔弗适意着当然要上腔作哉"。b. 犯老毛病。例：倷亦上腔哉。（你老毛病又犯了。）

乙：普通话 想 想 通 吧，不 就 是 一 锅 红 烧 肉 吗？
　　吴语音 phi44-phi31 khe44 ba0 feh43 zeu22-zy33 ih43-ghoh3 ghon22-sae33-nyioh3 meh0
　　吴语文 孬 孬 开 吧，弗 就 是 一 镬 红 烧 肉 末？

甲：I can smell a smell of burning. What's going on? Oh, no. The pork braised with sauce and sugar is burned. What a pity!

乙：Come on. It's not a big deal.

三　词语贴士

（一）居民基层组织

序号	英文	苏州话
1.	Street	ka44-dae31
	街道	街道
2.	Community	zo22-chiu33
	社区	社区
3.	Neighborhood Committee	ciu44-ue44-we31
	居委会	居委会
4.	Residents Team	ciu44-min33-siae44-tsou31
	居民小组	居民小组

（二）住宅小区

序号	英文	苏州话
1.	Owner	nyih23-tsyu31
	业主	业主
2.	Property	veh23-nyih3
	物业	物业
3.	Neighbors' Center	lin22-li33-tson44-sin31
	邻里中心	邻里中心
4.	Owners' Committee	nyih23-tsyu31 ue523-yoe33-we31
	业主委员会	业主委员会

(三）街坊、里弄

序号	英文	苏州话
1.	Residence community 住宅小区	zyu22-zah3-siae44-chiu31 住宅小区
2.	Residents' compound 居民大院	ciu44-min33-da22-yoe33 居民大院
3.	Lane 小路	lon22-daon33 弄堂
4.	Corridor 院内走道	be22-lon33 备弄
5.	Neighbor 邻居	lin22-ciu33,shian44-lin31 邻居、乡邻
6.	The building or door opposite 对门	te44-men31 对门

（四）邻里关系

序号	英文	苏州话
1.	Harmonious 和睦	ghou22-moh3 和睦
2.	Intimate 亲密	nyih23-loh3 热络
3.	Unfamiliar 生疏	san44-sou31 生疏
4.	Indifferent 冷漠	lan22-moh3 冷漠
5.	Turn against someone 交恶	ciae44-oh3 交恶

（五）家常事务

序号	英文	苏州话
1.	Living expense 家用	khe44 hou51-tshaon31 开伙仓
2.	Housework 持家	zyu22-ka33，tsou44-nyin33-ka31 持家,做人家
3.	Child care 育儿	yan231 siae51-kuoe23 养小倌
4.	Supporting the elderly people 养老	yan231 lae231 养老

序号	英文	苏州话
5.	House purchase	ma231 vaon223
	买房	买房
6.	Auto purchase	ma231 tsho44
	购车	买车
7.	Consumption	siae44-fi31
	消费	消费

（六）家常关系

序号	英文	苏州话
1.	Relationship between husband and wife	fu44-tshi31 kue44-yi31
	夫妻关系	夫妻关系
2.	Relationship between mother-in-law and daughter-in-law	bu22-sih3 kue44-yi31
	婆媳关系	婆媳关系
3.	Blood ties	shiueh43-tshin23 kue44-yi31
	血亲关系	血亲关系
4.	Relativeness	tshin44-cioe31 kue44-yi31
	亲戚关系	亲眷关系

（七）家庭理财

序号	英文	苏州话
1.	Saving	zyu22-shioh3，zen22 don22-die33
	储蓄	储蓄, 存铜钿
2.	Insurance	deu22-pae33
	投保	投保
3.	Stock	tshae51 kou51
	炒股	炒股
4.	Gold Futures	tshae51 waon22-cin33
	炒黄金	炒黄金
5.	Investment	deu22-tsy33
	投资	投资

（八）家居生活

序号	英文	苏州话
1.	Living Environment	ciu44-zyu31 gue22-cin33
	居住环境	居住环境
2.	Architecture structure	ciu44-seh3 cih43-keu523
	居室结构	居室结构
3.	Daily activity	zeh23-zan31 chi523-ciu33
	日常起居	日常起居
4.	Daily life	zeh23-zan31 sen44-weh3
	日常生活	日常生活

（九）起居有常

序号	英文	苏州话
1.	Wash your face with cold water	lan231-mie31
	冷面	冷面
2.	Brush your tooth with warm water	uen44-tshyu31
	温齿	温齿
3.	Soak your feet in hot water	nyih23-tsoh3，ou51-ciah43
	热足	热足，捂脚
4.	Get enough sleep	khuen44-kae31 khuen44-tsoh3
	睡眠充足	睏觉睏足
5.	Strike a balance between your work and rest	lae22-yih3 seh43-dou231
	劳逸适度	劳逸适度
6.	At least five portions of fruit and vegetables each day	me44-nyih3 ng223 sou44-kou31
	每天5蔬果	每日5蔬果
7.	Exercise 30 minutes each day	me44-nyih3 yuin22-don33 se44-seh3-fen31
	每天运动30分钟	每日运动30分钟

（十）饮食有度

序号	英文	苏州话
1.	Have your diet at a regular time and quantity	din22-zyu33 din231-lian31
	定时定量	定时定量

续表

序号	英文	苏州话
2.	Prepare your food not too hot or too cold	ghoe22-nyih3 seh43-nyi223
	寒热适宜	寒热适宜
3.	Keep a balanced diet	taeh43-phe523 gheh23-li31
	搭配合理	搭配合理
4.	Take more lite dishes	tshin44-de31 we231 tsyu51
	清淡为主	清淡为主

四 对话中的特色词汇

序号	英文	苏州话
1.	There is a long way to go	ih43-lih3 mi231 toh43 tsoh43, mi231-chi31 gha223 m22-peh3-leh3
	刚刚起步，根本不成气候	一粒米笃粥，米气也呒不嘞
2.	Work	tsou44-san44-weh31
	干活	做生活
3.	Careful	po51-si31
	细心	把细
4.	Recently	ke44-tshian31
	这一阵	该饨
5.	Add up	lou44-lou44-kuaeh3-kuaeh3
	合起来	啰啰刮刮
6.	Total	goh23-loh3-se44-men31
	总共	橱落山门
7.	Move house	poe44 zan223
	搬家	搬场
8.	Feud	tshih43-syu44-ioe44-ka31
	几世仇人	七世冤家
9.	In a mess	loh23-loh3-loe31
	一片狼藉	络络乱
10.	Drip	tih43-lih43-toh43-loh3
	滴里搭拉	滴沥笃落
11.	Sleepy	ih43-tsah3 kah43-ia44-mie33-khon31
	一脸没睡醒	一只隔夜面孔
12.	Move the position	thon51 we22-tsy33
	移位	捅位子

续表

序号	英文	苏州话
13.	Unarranged 没着落	fen44 zah3 kaon44 齼着矼
14.	Garrulous 说话啰唆	gheu231-tsyu44-naeh3-teh3 厚嘴呐得
15.	Inquisitive 管闲事	mo22-jie33-jie31 马健健
16.	Bright red 大红	shiueh43-phan33-da33-ghon31 血嘭大红
17.	Bad person 为人最坏	lou22-kueh3-tin44-chieu31 露骨顶丘
18.	Dislike and avoid 嫌弃	yie22-pi33 嫌比
19.	Fry 炸	then51 佘
20.	Crisp 颜色焦黄	tshah43-laeh3-tsiae44-waon31 赤辣焦黄
21.	Greedy cat 馋鬼	ze22-lae33-phe31 馋痨胚
22.	Hang out 不停转悠	toh43-toh43-tsoe31 zi22-zi33-tsoe31 笃笃转齐齐转
23.	well 好好地	hae51-hae44-ciae31 好好较
24.	Eat 吃	tshoh43-tsi523 触祭
25.	Make one's mouth water 口水直流	ze22-thou44-syu31 taeh43-taeh43-ti31 垂吐水答答渧
26.	Wet 湿漉漉	zae22-taeh3-taeh3 潮答答
27.	Picky 找茬	zaon22-chian33 上腔
28.	Burning smell 焦味	tsiae44-mae33-chi31 焦冒气
29.	Burnt 粘锅	teh43-ti51 得底
30.	Get it through 想想通	phi44-phi44-khe31 狓狓开

五、巩固练习

1 甲：你干嘛不停地转悠？我看得心里乱七八糟了。
乙：我是担心你，你不要故意找茬，是小偷偷了你的钱，你找我的茬说不通的。
甲：差不多两千块呢，一个月的家用呀，你说我要不要心疼？
乙：钱要紧还是人要紧，你看你一脸没睡醒，昨天一夜没睡好，犯得着吗？快点把这事想想通。

2 甲：喂，说得这么响，叫你陪我出去逛逛，你不见得没听见吧，不要装傻了。
乙：你吃饱了饭没事做，我忙死呢，你别来烦我。
甲：你去不去？不然，我让你不得安宁。
乙：你这把年纪了，别这样不正经，我还有很多事情要做呢。

六、参考答案

1

甲：普通话　你　干　嘛　不　停　地　转悠？　　我　看　得　心　里
吴语音　ne231 sa51-thi23 toh43-toh3-tsoe31 zi22-zi33-tsoe31 khoe44-teh3-ngou31 sin44-li31
吴语文　倷　啥　体　笃　笃　转，齐齐　转？　看　得　我　心　里

　　　　乱　七　八　糟　了。
　　　　mae22-tsa44-tshih43-tsa31 tse44
　　　　毛　爪　七　爪　哉。

乙：普通话　我　是　担　心　你，你　不　要　故　意　找　茬，是　小　偷
吴语音　ngou231-zy31 te44-sin44-ne31 ne231 fiae523 zin22- heu44-sy31 zy231 zeh23-kueh3-
吴语文　我　是　担　心　倷，倷　勿　寻　吼　思，是　贼　骨

　　　　偷　了　你　的　钱，　　你　找　我　的　茬
　　　　deu31 uaeh43-theh43 ne231-tsah3 pae44 keh0 ne231 zaon231 ngou231-keh3 chian44-
　　　　头　挖　脱　倷　只　包　个，倷　上　我　个　腔

说　不　通　的。
zy31 seh43-feh3-thon44-keh3
是　说　弗　通　个。

甲：普通话 差　不　多　两　千　块　呢，一　个　月　的
吴语音 mae22-mae33-ciae31 lian231-tshie44-khue44-teh3-le31 ih43-keh43 ghae22-deu33-keh3
吴语文 毛　毛　较　两　千　块　得来，一　个　号　头　个

家　用　呀，你　说　我　要　不　要　心　疼？
hou51-tshaon31 don22-die33-ia31 ne231 kaon51 ngou231 aeh43 iae523 nyioh23-thon44-keh3
伙　仓　铜　钿　呀，倷　讲　我　阿　要　肉　痛　个？

乙：普通话 钱　要紧还是人　要紧，你　看　你一　脸
吴语音 don22-die33 iae44-cin31 we22-zy33 nyin223 iae44-cin31 ne231 khoe523-ne31 ih43-tsah43
吴语文 铜　钿　要紧还是人　要紧，倷　看　倷　一　只

没　睡　醒，昨　天　一　夜　没　睡
kah43-ia44- mie33-khon31 zoh23-nyih3-tsy44-taeh3 ih43-ia44-thie31 fen44 khuen44 hae51-
隔　夜　面　孔，昨　日　仔　搭　一　夜　天　朆　瞓

好，犯　得　着　吗？快　点　把 这事想想通。
tseh3-ue31 aeh43 ve22-teh3-zah3-keh3-a31 ghae22-sae44-tie31 no223 li44 phi44-phi44-khe31
好则唲，阿　犯　得　着　个啊？豪　惗　点　拿　俚　狉　狉　开。

甲: Why are you hanging around all the time? You make me annoyed.

乙: I'm worrying about you. Don't be so picky. You are upset because the thief stole your purse. But don't blame me for it.

甲: Nearly 2000 RMB. It costs me a month's living expense. I'm really heart broken.

乙: Your health is more important than money. You look so tired. You must have stayed up late yesterday. It isn't worth it. Try and stay positive.

2

甲：普通话 喂，说　得 这么　响，叫　你　陪　我　出　去　逛　逛，
吴语音 ue51 he51-teh3 e44-zaon31 shian51 ciae523 ne231 be22-ngou33 tsheh43-chi523 daon22-daon33-
吴语文 喂，喊　得　哀状　响，叫　倷　陪　我　出　去　荡　荡

甲：普通话 你 不 见 得 没 听 见 吧，不要 装 傻 了。
吴语音 keh3 ne231 feh43- cie44-teh3 fen44-thin44-cie31 ue0 fiae523 ka51-tsyu44-ka44-nge31 tse44
吴语文 个，倷 弗 见 得 朆 听 见 㗎，覅 假 痴 假 呆 哉。

乙：普通话 你 吃 饱 了 饭 没 事 做，
吴语音 ne231-leh3 chih43 pae51-tsy33 daon22-khon33 sae44-ci44-ve31 m22-peh3 zy22-thi33
吴语文 倷 勒 吃 饱 仔 荡 空 烧 鸡 饭 朆 不 事 体

我 忙 死 呢，你 别 来 烦 我。
tsou523 ngou231 maon22-saeh3-leh3-he31 ne231 fiae523 le223 ve22-ngou33 ne0
做，我 忙 煞 勒 嗨，倷 覅 来 烦 我 呢。

甲：普通话 你 去不去？不然，我 让 你 不 得 安 宁。
吴语音 ne231 aeh43 chi523 feh43-zoe223 ngou231 siae523-teh3 ne231 loh23-kaon44-syu44-wen31
吴语文 倷 阿 去？弗 然，我 缫 得 倷 六 缸 水 浑。

乙：普通话 你 这 把 年 纪 了，别 这 样 不 正 经，
吴语音 ne231 gha223 ke44-po31 nyie22-ci33 tse44 fiae523 zeh23-kan31 feh43-zeh3-diae31
吴语文 倷 也 该 把 年 纪 哉，覅 实 梗 弗 入 调，

我 还 有 很 多 事 情 要 做 呢。
ngou231 we22-yeu33 feh43- sae31 zy22-thi33 iae523 tsou523 le0
我 还 有 弗 少 事 体 要 做 来。

甲：Hey, go shopping with me. Don't pretend that you didn't hear me.
乙：I'm not like you. I'm busy. Don't bother me.
甲：You have to. Or you will live without peace.
乙：Come on, you're no longer a child. Behave yourself. I have dozens of things to do now.

第九单元 升学与就业

一 情景引入

甲：普通话 陈 煌，你 高 考 考 得 不 错，祝 贺 你！
　　吴语音 zen22-waon33 ne231 kae44-khae31 khae51-teh3 lin22- keh3 tsoh43-ghou33-ne31
　　吴语文 陈 煌，侬 高 考 考 得 灵 个，祝 贺 侬！

乙：普通话 魏老师，我的成绩蛮尴尬的，
吴语音 we22-lae44-sy31 ngou231-keh3 zen231-tsih3 le22- teh3-keh3 ke44-li31 feh43 ke44-ka31
吴语文 魏老师，我个成绩来得个尴里弗尴尬①，

虽然比一本线高出几十分，但是要
se44-zoe31 pi51 ih3-pen44-sie31 kae44-tsheh4-tsy31 ci51-seh3-fen31 pih43-kou523 iae523
虽然比一本线高出仔几十分，不过要

指定读我喜欢的学校喜欢的专业，
tie51-shi31 doh23 ngou231 huoe44-shi44-keh3 ghoh23-daon31 huoe44-shi44- keh3 tsoe44-nyih3
点戏读我欢喜个学堂欢喜个专业，

还是挺困难的。老师，你说怎么办？
we22-zy33 me44 khuen523-ne33- keh3 lae44-sy31 ne231 kaon51 naeh23-han31 be231
还是蛮困难个。老师俫讲哪哼办？

甲：普通话 既然你与我商量，我就直截了当说
吴语音 ci44-zoe33-ne31 taeh43 ngou231 sian44 san43 ngou231 zeu223 zeh23-bah3-zeh3-kaon31
吴语文 既然俫搭我相商，我就直白直②讲

了，鱼与熊掌不能兼得，你可以问问
tse0 ng223 iu51 yon22-tsan33 peh43-nen223 cie44-teh3 ne231 khou51-i23 men231-men31
哉，鱼与熊掌不能兼得，俫可以问问

自己：学校的名气与专业的兴趣，
zy22-ka33 ghoh23-daon33- keh3 min22-chi33 taeh43 tsoe44-nyih3-keh3 shi523-tshi31
自家：学堂个名气搭专业个兴趣，

更加看重哪个？如果图的是响亮
ken51-ka33 khoe44-teh3-zon31 lo22-keh3 cia51-sy23 thoe44 phan44-phan44-shian44-
更加看得重哪个？假使贪碰碰响③

---

① "尴里弗尴尬"的尴尬是因为不上不下、不进不出引起的。
② "直白直"有两层含义：a. 直截了当。此义同"情景引入"中"我就直白直讲哉"。b. 笔直。
例：俫转个弯，直白直走到底就到哉。（你转个弯，笔直走到底就到了。）
③ "碰碰响"在表达非常响亮意思的同时，还带有响得光明磊落的意味在里面。

的 学 校 名 气, 那 么 选 个 相 对 冷 门 点
keh3 ghoh23-daon31 min22-chi33 geh23-meh3 sie51-tsah3 sian44-te31 lan22-men33-tie44-
个 学 堂 名 气, 箇 末 选 只 相 对 冷 门 点

的 专 业; 如 果 图 自 己 喜 欢 的 专 业, 那 么
keh3 tsoe44-nyih3 cia51-sy23 thoe44 zy22-ka33 huoe44-shi44-keh3 tsoe44-nyih3 geh23-meh3
个 专 业; 假 使 贪 自 家 欢 喜 个 专 业, 箇 末

选 个 稍 微 实 力 弱 一 点 的 一 本 学 校。
sie51-tsah3 sae51-we31 ngoe231-tshoe44-tie44-keh3 ih3-pen51 ghoh23-daon31
选 只 少 为 软 串① 点 个 一 本 学 堂。

乙: 普通话 本 来 心 里 杂 七 杂 八, 听 老 师 一 讲,
吴语音 pen51-le23 sin44-li31 zah23-keh3- lon33-ton31 keh0 thin44 lae44-sy31 ih43 kaon51 meh0
吴语文 本 来 心 里 杂 个 咙 咚② 个, 听 老 师 一 讲 末,

现 在 填 志 愿 能 把 握 得 了 了。谢 谢 老 师!
yie22-ze33 die223 tsyu523-nyioe23 chih43-teh3-tsen31 tse44 zia22-zia33 lae44-sy31
现 在 填 志 愿 吃 得 准 哉。谢 谢 老 师!

甲: Chen Huang, I heard you did a good job in the College Entrance Examination. Congratulations to you!

乙: Thank you, Ms Wei. But it turns out to be an embrassing situation to me. Although my total score has passed the enrollment marks for the key universities, it is still hard to say whether I can enter the exact school with the major I like. How can I make it?

甲: I'm happy you can talk this over me. Let me be straight about this. Well, it's like the old saying: you can't have your cake and eat it too. You can make a comparision. A well-known university and your favorite major, which is more important to you? If you want to enter a well-known university, you can choose a less popular major to make sure your

---

① "软串"有两层含义：a. 弱。此义同"情景引入"中"箇末选个少为软串点个本一学堂"。b. 软。例：倷拣软串点个柿子先吃。(你软点的柿子先吃。)

② "杂个咙咚"多指因物品杂乱、摆放无序而造成的杂七杂八的现象，这里是拿来借用形容人的混乱心理。

admission. If your favorite major is top priority, you can apply for a less competitive university.

乙: I was confused before I came here. After talking to you, I am confident that I can handle this very well. Thank you very much, Ms. Wei!

二 场景对话

1. 甲: 普通话 小鬼, 马上要中考了, 还一门
   吴语音 siae51-ciu44-deu31 man22-zaon33 iae523 tson44-khae31 tse44 we223 ih43-men33-
   吴语文 小鬼头, 马上要中考哉, 还一门

   心思想玩 游戏, 假如 中考考
   sin44-sy31 sian523 beh23-sian31 yeu22-shi33 cia51-sy44-dae31 tson44-khae31 khae51-
   心思想孛相游戏, 假使道中考考

   得很差劲, 看我怎么收拾你。
   teh3 wa22-wa33-tsa44-tsa31 meh0 khoe523 ngou231 naeh23-han31 seu44-tsoh3 ne231
   得坏坏喳喳①末, 看我哪哼收作②倷。

   乙: 普通话 好在我 扛得住, 抗击打能力比较强。
   吴语音 we22-hae33 ngou231 ghaon22-teh3-lae31 khaon523 cih43-tan51 nen22-lih3 pi51-ciae23 jian223
   吴语文 还好我 行得牢, 抗击打能力比较强。

   甲: Hey, secondary school entrance exam is around the corner. You still have your heart on computer games. If you mess it up, I will teach you a lesson.

   乙: Thanks to my thick skin. I'm not afraind.

---

① "坏坏喳喳" 泛指局面、情况、事情很糟糕。
② "收作" 有三层意思: a. 收拾。此义同"场景对话1"中"看我哪哼收作倷"。b. 修理。例: 藤交御个扶手坏脱哉, 有空收作收作。(藤椅的扶手坏了, 有空收拾收拾。) c. 整理。例: 台上乱得来, 快点收作。(桌子上乱得很, 赶快整理。)

2. 甲：普通话 总 算 一 夜　　没 白 排 队，我 孙 子 花 朵
　　　吴语音 tson44-soe31 ih43-ia44-thie31 fen44 bah23-ba33-de31 nyi231 sen44-tsy31 ho44-tou31
　　　吴语文 总 算 一 夜 天 齆 白 排 队，伲 孙 子 花 朵

　　　　　　 幼 儿 园 报 名　　录 取 了。
　　　　　　 ieu523-r33-yoe31 pae523 min223 lae223 tse44
　　　　　　 幼 儿 园 报 名 牢①哉。

   乙：普通话 小 孩 读 书 的 基 石 一 定 要 打 好，不
　　　吴语音 siae51-noe23 doh23-syu44-keh3 zah23-ciah3 ih43- din231 iae523 tan51 hae51 feh43-
　　　吴语文 小 囡 读 书 个 石 脚 一 定 要 打 好，弗

　　　　　　 可 以 输 在　　 起 跑 线 上。
　　　　　　 khou51-i23 syu44-leh3-tsy44-keh3 chi523-bae33-sie44-laon31 ue0
　　　　　　 可 以 输 勒 仔 个 起 跑 线 浪 哕。

   甲：I queued for a whole day to get my grandson to be admintted in the Blossom Kindergarden.

   乙：Kindergarden is always considered as the foundation in children's education. A good beginning is half done.

3. 甲：普通话 张 爷 爷，今 天 星 期 天，　 你 怎 么 还 带
　　　吴语音 tsan44-aeh3-tia31 cin44-tsae31 li22-pa33 nyih23 ue0 ne231 naeh23-han31 we223 ta523-
　　　吴语文 张 阿 爹，今 朝 礼 拜 日 哕，侬 哪 哼 还 带

　　　　　　 孙 子 去　　读 书 呀？
　　　　　　 tsy23 sen44- tsy31 chi523 doh23 syu44 cia0
　　　　　　 仔 孙 子 去 读 书 嘎？

---

① "牢"有四层意思：a. 录取。此义同"场景对话2"中"伲孙子花朵幼儿园报名牢哉"。b. 进入。例：俚前三名末，稳牢个哕。（他前三名么，稳进入的呀。）c. 结实、耐用。例：该种布料阿牢个？（这种布料耐用吗？）d. 放在动词后，相当于普通话里作动词补语的"住"。例：拿重要个知识点记记牢。（把重要的知识点记住。）

乙：普通话 别 去 说 它， 那 小 子 学 校 里 老师
吴语音 fiae523 chi523 seh43 li44 tse0 geh23 siae51-tsheh3-lae31 ghoh23-daon33-li31 lae44-sy31
吴语文 覅 去 说 俚 哉，箇 小 赤 佬 学 堂 里 老师

　　　　　　上 的 内 容 消 化 不 了， 一 直 受 责 备， 只
　　　　　　kae523-keh3 ne22- yon33 chih43 feh43 kuan44 ih43-cin523 chih43 ba22-deu33 tseh43-
　　　　　　教 个 内 容 吃 弗 光， 一 劲 吃 牌头①，只

　　　　　　好 在 双 休 日 去 补课。
　　　　　　hae51 leh23 saon44-shieu44-nyih3 chi523 pu51-khou31 tse44
　　　　　　好 勒 双 休 日 去 补课 哉。

甲：Hi, Mr. Zhang. Today is Sunday. Why do you take your grandson to school on weekend?

乙：Well, my grandson has some difficulties in study. So we go to classes on weekends to catch up with his studies.

4. 甲：普通话 我们 班 级 这 次 数 学 考 试 排 在 年 级 最
　　　 吴语音 nyi231 pe44-cih3 e44-thaon31 sou51-yoh3 kha51-syu31 ba22-leh3 nyie22-cih3 ah43-
　　　 吴语文 伲 班 级 哀 趟 数 学 考 试 排 勒 年 级 阿

　　　　　　后 一 名， 数 学 老 师 的 脸 铁 板 着， 你
　　　　　　meh43 ih43-min31 sou51-yoh3 lae44-sy44-tsah3 mie22-khon33 thih43-thih43-pe31 n22-
　　　　　　末 一 名， 数 学 老 师 只 面 孔 铁 铁 板②，尔

　　　　　　―――――――――

① "吃牌头"，就是遭受到领导或家人的数落、责备、批评。"牌头"有两种说法：其一，牌头原是古代当官的出来时举在前面的回避等牌子，后引申为"有一定名望、一定实力的人"。其二，源自地方上实行的保甲制：十户为一牌，十牌为一甲，十甲为一保。这十户之头就谓之"牌头"，哪户人家有事，肯定先去找"牌头"解决，慢慢延伸出来，成了"照牌头"——借光、依赖、靠得住、有把握的意思。"照牌头"变化延伸出来还可有："掮牌头"，就是打他人的旗号为自己办事或牟利。"隑牌头"，即表示靠山的意思，自认为靠了个过硬的牌头，就会一帆风顺，办事就不会有麻烦。

② "铁铁板"就是铁板的意思，但通过叠词，来加强语气。

们 两 个 人 还 不 乖 巧 一 些?
toh3 lian22-ka44-deu31 we223 feh43 kua44-tie44-leh3
笃 两 家 头 还 弗 乖 点 勒?

乙：普通话 就 是 呀, 已 经 高 三 了, 也 不 懂 得 察 颜
吴语音 zeu22-zy33 ue0 i44-cin31 kae44-se31 tse44 gha223 feh43 shiae51-teh3 gaeh23-gaeh3
吴语文 就 是 唲, 已 经 高 三 哉, 也 弗 晓 得 轧 轧

观 色, 见 机 行 事。
miae22-deu33 khoe523-khoe31 se44-seh3
苗 头, 看 看 三 色。

甲：The average point in maths of our class is at the bottom of the same grade. The maths teacher has been keeping a stony face. You need to be well behaved.

乙：Yeah, you have been in the Senior Grade Three. It would be tactful for you to read people's face and act according to circumstances.

5. 甲：普通话 李斌, 好 睡 了, 我 一 觉 都 醒 过 来 了。
   吴语音 li22-pin33 hae51 khuen523 tse44 ngou231 ih43-hueh43 gha223 sin51-kou44-le31 te44
   吴语文 李斌, 好 睏 哉, 我 一 吻 也 醒 过 来 哉。

   考 研 也 用 不 着 过 分 拼 命 的。
   khae51-nyie23 gha223 yon22-feh43-zah3 theh43 yie223 phin44 min231 keh0
   考 研 也 用 弗 着 忒 嫌 拼 命 个。

乙：普通话 是 的, 我 看 完 这 道 题 目 马 上 睡。
   吴语音 me44-tsen31 ngou231 khoe523 hae51 ke44-men31 di22- moh3 mo44-zaon31 khuen523
   吴语文 蛮 准, 我 看 好 该 门 题 目 马 上 睏。

   不 拼 命 不 行 呀, 考 不 上 多 丢 脸 呀。
   feh43 phin44-min231 feh43 le22-se33 ia44 khae51 feh43 lae223 aeh43 iae523 the44-tsae44-syu31 cia0
   弗 拼 命 弗 来 三 呀, 考 弗 牢 阿 要 坍 招 势①嘎。

---

① 苏州话"坍招势"、"坍台"都是"丢脸"的意思。

甲: Li Bin, it is too late. I have already had a sleep. You don't have to push yourself too far for National Entrance Test for MA/MS Candidates.

乙: Ok, I'll go to bed when I finish this question. I have to go to great lengths to make a good preparation, otherwise it will be a shame if I fail the exam.

6. 甲: 普通话 你 这 阵子 一 直 在 外 面 奔波，工 作 有没 有
   吴语音 ne231 ke44-tshian31 ih43-zeh3 leh23 nga22-deu33 deu231 ue0 kon44-tsoh3 aeh43 yeu231
   吴语文 倷 该 歇 一 直 勒 外 头 趑① 喴，工 作 阿 有

   结 果？
   min22-daon33-leh3 cia0
   名 堂② 勒 嘎？

   乙: 普通话 基 本 上 有 着 落 了。
   吴语音 ci44-pen44-laon31 yeu231 zah23-loh3 tse44
   吴语文 基 本 浪 有 着 落 哉。

   甲: I heard that you are busy hunting for job. Any good news?
   乙: Almost done.

7. 甲: 普通话 你 刚 刚 大 学 毕 业， 还 是 先 去 就 业，
   吴语音 ne231 kaon44-tsen31 da22-ghoh3 pih43-nyih43 we22-zy33 sie44-chi31 zeu22-nyih3
   吴语文 倷 刚 正 大 学 毕 业， 还 是 先 去 就 业，

---

① "趑"有三层意思: a. 奔波。此义同"场景对话6"中"倷哀馀一直勒外头趑喴"。b. 挣扎。例: 我打个是海盗结，倷亦趑亦紧。(我打的是海盗结，你越挣扎越紧。) c. (办事) 急躁，不稳重; 忙乱无条理。例: 俚做事体蛮趑个。(他做事情很不稳重。)

② "名堂"也可说成"名堂经"，有三层含义: a. 结果，成就。此义同"场景对话6"中"工作阿有名堂勒嘎"。b. 花样，名目。例: 倷勒搞点啥名堂? (你在搞啥花样?) c. 道理，内容。例: 说仔半半日日，也觉说出啥个名堂? (说了半天，也没说出什么内容。)

创　业　的　事　　　过　两　年　再　说，我们　家
tshaon523 nyih3 keh3 zy22-thi33 kou523 lian231-nyie31 tse44 kaon51 ba0 nyi231 oh43-
创　业　个　事　体　过　两　年　再　讲　罢，倷　屋

现　在　要　还　房　子　贷　款，平　常　用　账
li33-shian31 yie22-ze33 iae523 we223 vaon22-tsy33 de22-kuoe33 bin231-zan31 yon22 tsan33
里　向　现　在　要　还　房　子　贷　款，平　常　用　账

也　很　紧，　　凑　不　出　开　公　司　的　钱。
gha223 cih43-cih43-pan33-pan31 tsheu523-feh3-tsheh3 khe44 kon44-sy44-keh3 don22-die33
也　急　急　绷　绷①，凑　弗　出　开　公　司　个　铜　钿。

乙：普通话　我　听　你　们　的。我　也　跟　我　同　学　讲
　　吴语音 ngou231 thin44 n22-toh3-keh3 ngou231 gha223 taeh43 nyi231 don22-ghoh3 kaon51
　　吴语文　我　听　尔　笃　个。我　也　搭　倷　同　学　讲

那　笔　资　金　太　大，　　我　大　学　四　年　打
geh23-pin43 tsy44-cin31 theh43 dou231 tshe0 ngou231 da22-ghoh3 sy523-nyie33 tan51
箇　笔　资　金　忒　大　哉，我　大　学　四　年　打

工　的　收　入　帮　它　比　相　差　太　多。
kon44-keh3 seu44-zeh3 taeh43 li44 pi51 zah23-zeh3-yoe33-pan31
工　个　收　入　搭　俚　比　着　实　悬　迸。

甲：You have just graduated from university. It is better to find a job. I think it is not the right time to start business. My family has housing loan to pay. We are short of money these days. I don't think we can afford the initial fund.

乙：I agree with you. About the initial fund, I have talked over it with my classmate. But it is such a large amount of money, which is far beyond the sums of my 4 years salaries from the part time job in the university.

---

① "急急绷绷"也写作"急绷绷"、"紧绷绷"，既可以指东西、物品被捆扎得很紧，也可以指皮肤紧致、肌肉结实，还可以指手头不宽裕。

8. 甲：普通话 哦呦，人才交流市场里面 的人是挤
   吴语音 oh43-ioh3 nyin22-ze33 ciae44-leu31 zy22-zan33- li33-shian33-keh3 nyin22-zy33 thaeh43-
   吴语文 喔唷，人 才 交 流 市 场 里 向 个 人 是 塌

   得 满满的。
   thaeh43-phu44- phu31
   塌 潽 潽①。

   乙：普通话 是 的，老老实实排队， 一 天 最多
      吴语音 zy22-keh3 ia0 lae22-tan44-lae33-zeh3 ba22-de33 meh0 ih43-nyih3-thie31 tse523-tou23
      吴语文 是 个呀，老 打 老 实 排 队 末，一 日 天 最 多

   投 出 去 两份 简历。
   deu22-tsheh3-chi31 lian231-ven31 cie51-lih3
   投 出 去 两 份 简 历。

   甲：Ah, it is so crowded in the talent market.
   乙：Yeah, you have to wait in the line for a whole day to send no more than two resumes.

9. 甲：普通话 我班 的宗闻予在 公司实习了
      吴语音 nyi231 pe44-cih3-keh3 tson44-ven33-yu31 leh23- he31 kon44-sy31 zeh23-zih3- tsy31
      吴语文 倷班级个 宗 闻 予 勒 嗨 公司 实习仔

   一个月 就做领班了，手下 还
   ih43-keh43 gae22-deu33 zeu231 tsou523 lin22-pe33 tse44 seu51-gho33-deu31 we22-
   一个号头 就做领班哉，手下头还

   有几个本科生 呢。
   yeu33 ci51-keh3 pen51-khou44-san31 laeh43-li0
   有几个本科 生 拉里。

   乙：普通话 真的，好 为我们大专生争气 呀，
      吴语音 tsen44-keh3 ciae44-kue31 taeh43 nyi231 da22-tsoe44- san31 tsan44 chi523 tseh43-ue0
      吴语文 真个 交关 搭 倷大专生争气则啘,

---
① "塌塌潽潽"形容满得都快要溢出来了。

我 都 感 觉 脸 上 贴 金 了。
ngou231 i44-cin31 koh43-zah43 mie22-khon44-laon33-shian31 fi44 cin44 tse44
我 已 经 觉 着 面 孔 浪 向 飞 金 哉。

甲：Zong Wenyu, my classmate, gets the position of supervisor after one month's internship. He also leads several college graduators.

乙：Really! his success is a great encouragement for college students. I'm so proud of him.

词语贴士

（一）升学考试

序号	英文	苏州话
1.	Secondary School Entrance Exam	tson44-khae31
	中考	中考
2.	College Entrance Exam	kae44-khae31
	高考	高考
3.	National Entrance Test for MA/MS Candidates	khae51-nyie44
	考研	考研

（二）常见升学辅导班

序号	英文	苏州话
1.	Writing	tsoh43-ven223
	作文	作文
2.	English	in44-nyiu31
	英语	英语
3.	Mathematics	sou523-yoh3
	数学	数学
4.	Art	me51-zeh3
	美术	美术
5.	Vocality	sen44-yoh3
	声乐	声乐

（三）辅导形式

序号	英文	苏州话
1.	Tutorial Class	pu51 khou523
	补课	补课
2.	Tutor	cia44-ciae31
	家教	家教
3.	Tutorship	fu51-dae31
	辅导	辅导
4.	Homework Checking	mi22-phi33
	面批	面批

（四）升学数据

序号	英文	苏州话
1.	Students admission index	sen44-ghoh3 tsyu51-piae23
	升学指标	升学指标
2.	Students admission rate	sen44-ghoh3-lih3
	升学率	升学率
3.	Passing rate of students admission	daeh23-piae44-lih3
	达标率	达标率
4.	Excellent rate of students admission	ieu44-seu44-lih3
	优秀率	优秀率

（五）升学烦恼

序号	英文	苏州话
1.	Prssures from entrance exam	sen44-ghoh3-ah3-lih3
	升学压力	升学压力
2.	Intensive training of exercises	di22-he44-tsoe44-zeh3
	题海战术	题海战术
3.	Entrance exam	sen44-ghoh3 khae51-syu31
	升学考试	升学考试
4.	Education donation	tse523-zou33-fi31
	赞助费	赞助费

（六）就业理念

序号	英文	苏州话
1.	diligent 吃苦耐劳	chih43 khou51 ne231 lae223 吃苦耐劳
2.	Earn one's own living 自食其力	zy22-zeh3-ji33-lih3 自食其力
3.	Adapt to circumstance 适应环境	seh43-in523 gue22-cin33 适应环境
4.	Self evaluation 客观评价自我	khah43-kuoe44 bin22-ka33 zy22-ngou33 客观评价自我
5.	honest 实事求是	zeh23-zy33-jieu33-zy31 实事求是
6.	Two-way choice 双向选择	saon44-shian44-sie44-zeh3 双向选择
7.	Employers enjoy the rights to recruit required talents 企业自主用工	chi51-nyih3 zy22-tsyu33 yon22-kon33 企业自主用工
8.	Citizen enjoy the rights to select jobs for themselves 公民自主择业	kon44-min31 zy22-tsyu33 zeh3-nyih3 公民自主择业
9.	The government department offer services on employment 社会提供服务	zo22-ue33 di22-kon33 voh23-vu31 社会提供服务

（七）就业途径

序号	英文	苏州话
1.	Work for the school after graduation 留校工作	leu22-yae33 kon44-tsoh3 留校工作
2.	Inherit 自然继承	zy22-zoe33-ci51-zen31 自然继承
3.	Job hunting 市场就业	zy22-zan33 zeu22-nyih3 市场就业
4.	Be Recommended to a job by family members 亲友介绍	tshin44-yeu31 cia523-zae31 亲友介绍
5.	Select jobs for oneself 自主择业	zy22-tsyu33 zeh23-nyih3 自主择业

续表

序号	英文	苏州话
6.	Start one's own business	zy22-tsyu33 tshaon523-nyih3
	自主创业	自主创业
7.	directional in-house training	din22-shian33 ue51-be33
	定向委培	定向委培

（八）就业信息渠道

序号	英文	苏州话
1.	Mess media	zoe22-pu33 me22-cia33
	传播媒介	传播媒介
2.	Government department	tsen523-fu44-bu22-men33
	政府部门	政府部门
3.	Agent	tson44-ka44-ci44-keu31
	中介机构	中介机构
4.	Human relation	nyin22-tsi44-kue44-yi31
	人际关系	人际关系
5.	School	ghoh23-daon31
	学校	学堂

（九）就业实现

序号	英文	苏州话
1.	Application letter	jieu22-tseh3-sin31
	求职信	求职信
2.	Resume	li22-lih3-piae31
	履历表	履历表
3.	Apply for…	in523-phin31
	应聘	应聘
4.	Interview	mie231-syu31
	面试	面试
5.	Written Examination	pih43-syu523
	笔试	笔试
6.	Physical Examination	thi51-cie31
	体检	体检
7.	Salary	sin44-tsy31
	薪资	薪资
8.	Welfare	foh43-li231
	福利	福利

(十) 常见职业和分类

序号	英文	苏州话
1.	Teacher 教师	ciae51-sy23 教师
2.	Doctor 医生	i44-san31 医生
3.	Nurse 护士	ghou22-zy33 护士
4.	Policeman 警察	cin51-tshaeh3 警察
5.	Lawyer 律师	lih23-sy31 律师
6.	Writor 作家	tsoh43-cia23 作家
7.	Scientist 科学家	khou44-yoh3-cia31 科学家
8.	Civil Servant 公务员	kon44-vu33-yoe31 公务员
9.	Worker 工人	kon44-nyin31 工人
10.	Farmer 农民	non22-min33 农民
11.	Soldier 军人	ciuin44-nyin31 军人
12.	Waiter/Wasitress 服务员	voh23-vu33-yoe31 服务员
13.	Technician 专业技术人员	tsoe44-nyih3 ji22-zeh3-zen33-yoe31 专业技术人员
14.	Artist 艺术工作者	nyi22-zeh3-kon44-tsoh3-tse31 艺术工作者

四 对话中的特色词汇

序号	英文	苏州话
1.	embarrassing 尴尬	ke44-li31 feh43 ke44-ka31 尴里弗尴尬

续表

序号	英文	苏州话
2.	Be straight	zeh23-bah3-zeh3
	直截了当	直白直
3.	Well known	phan44-phan44-shian31
	响亮	碰碰响
4.	Less competitive	ngoe231-tshoe44-tie31
	弱一点	软串点
5.	confuesd	zah23-keh3-lon44-ton31
	杂七杂八	杂个咙咚
6.	Mess up sth.	wa22-wa33-tsa44-tsa31
	很差劲	坏坏喳喳
7.	Teach sb. A lesson	seu44-tsoh3
	收拾	收作
8.	Thanks to…	hae51-teh3
	好在	好得
9.	Be admitted by a school	lae223, loh23-tshi31
	录取	牢，录取
10.	Foundation	zah23-ciah3
	基石	石脚
11.	Cannot understand	chih43 feh43 kuaon44
	消化不了	吃弗光
12.	Be blamed	chih43 ba22-deu33
	受责备	吃牌头
13.	A stony face	thih43-thih43-pe31
	铁板	铁铁板
14.	Well behaved	tsah43-kua31
	乖巧	着乖
15.	Read people's face and act according to circumatances.	gaeh23 miae22-deu33, khoe44-se44-seh3
	察颜观色，见机行事	轧苗头，看三色
16.	Too/very	theh43-yie223
	过分，太	忒嫌
17.	Ashamed	the44-tsae44-syu31
	丢脸	坍招势
18.	Be busy with…	deu223
	奔波	赿
19.	End in	min22-daon33
	结果	名堂

续表

序号	英文	苏州话
20.	Short of	cih43-cih3-pan44-pan31
	很紧	急急绷绷
21.	Far beyond	yoe22-pan33
	相差太多	悬迸
22.	Be crowded with	thaeh43-thaeh43-phu44-phu31
	很满	塌塌潽潽
23.	honest	lae22-tan44-lae33-zeh3
	老老实实	老打老实
24.	Be proud of	fi44 cin44
	贴金	飞金

五 巩固练习

1 甲：你怎么凑热闹学起德语来了？前几天不是还在啃日语吗？

乙：我觉得德语比日语更有用，所以暂时把日语放一下。

甲：你还是先把英语四级过了再说吧，像你这样三天打鱼，两天晒网，什么也学不好。

乙：知道了，你告诉我好几遍了。

2 甲：嗬！你打字这么熟练！

乙：我苦练了一个月呢，你看我手指都有点僵了。

甲：你当初叫我一起练的，我没听，现在有些后悔了。

乙：后悔也用不着，现在抓紧还来得及。

六 参考答案

1

甲：普通话 你 怎 么 凑 热闹 学 起 德语 来 了？

吴语音 ne231 naeh23-han31 gaeh23 nae22-man33 ghoh23-chi31 teh43-nyiu31 le223 tse0

吴语文 倷 哪 哼 轧 闹猛 学 起 德语 来 哉？

前 几 天 不 是 还 在 啃 日 语 吗?
zie22-ci44-nyih3 feh43-zy231 we22-leh3 khen51 zeh23-nyiu31 leh23-meh3
前 几 日 弗 是 还 勒 啃 日 语 勒 末?

乙: 普通话 我 觉 得 德 语 比 日 语 更 有 用,
吴语音 ngou231 koh43-zah3 teh43-nyiu31 pi51 zeh23-nyiu31 ken51-ka23 yeu231 yon22-zan33
吴语文 我 觉 着 德 语 比 日 语 更 加 有 用 场,

所以暂时 把 日 语 放 一 下。
sou51-i23 ze22-zyu33-sin31 no223 zeh23-nyiu31 faon523-tsy23 ih43 faon523
所 以 暂 时 性 拿 日 语 放仔 一 放。

甲: 普通话 你 还 是 先 把 英 文 四 级 过 了 再 说 吧,
吴语音 ne231 we22-zy33 sie44 no223 in44-nyiu31 sy523- cih3 khou523-tsy23 tse44-seh3 ba0
吴语文 倷 还 是 先 拿 英 语 四 级 过 仔 再 说 吧,

像 你 这 样 三 天 打 鱼, 两 天 晒 网,
zian231-ne31 zeh23-kan23 keu51-deu33-laon31 tsa44-tsa31 mae22- deu33-laon31
像 倷 实 梗 狗 头 浪 抓 抓, 猫 头 浪

什 么 也 学 不 好。
la51-la31 sa523-meh3-zy31 ghaeh23 ghoh23- feh43-lie33-chie31 ke0
拉 拉, 啥 物 事 也 学 弗 连 牵 个。

乙: 普通话 知 道 了, 你 告 诉 我 好 几 遍 了。
吴语音 shiae51-teh3 tse44 ne231 kue44-tsae44-kou44-ngou31 hae51-ci44-da31 tse44
吴语文 晓 得 哉, 倷 关 照 过 我 好 几 埭 哉。

甲: How come you study German? Weren't you crazy about Japanese a few days ago?
乙: I think German is more useful than Japanese. So I decide to put Japanese aside.
甲: Well, it is better for you to pass CET-4 in the university. If you always work by fits and starts,you will gain nothing.
乙: Thank you for your advice.

2

甲：普通话 嘀！你 打 字 这 么 熟 练！
　　　吴语音 hoh43 ne231 tan51-zy31 lae22-ciu33 teh43-laeh3
　　　吴语文 嚯！俫 打 字 老 鬼 得 啦！

乙：普通话 我 苦 练 了 一 个 月　　呢，你 看 我
　　　吴语音 ngou231 khou51-lie33-tsy31 kou44-po31 ghae22-deu33 tse0 ne231 khoe523 ngou231
　　　吴语文 我 苦 练 仔 个 把 号 头 哉，俫 看 我

　　　　　　手 指　　都 有 点 僵　　　了。
　　　　　　seu51-tsih3-deu31 ghaeh23 yeu231- tie31 ciae44-ha44-ha31 tse0
　　　　　　手 节 头 也 有 点 僵 哈 哈 哉。

甲：普通话 你 当 初 叫 我 一 起 练 的，我 没 听，
　　　吴语音 ne231 taon44-tshou31 he51 ngou231 ih43-dae223 lie231-keh3 ngou231 fen44 thin44
　　　吴语文 俫 当 初 喊 我 一 淘 练 个，我 朆 听，

　　　　　　现 在　　有 些 后 悔 了。
　　　　　　yie22-ze33-zy31 yeu231-tie31 ae44-lae31 tse4
　　　　　　现 在 是 有 点 懊 劳 哉。

乙：普通话 后 悔 也 用 不 着，现 在 抓 紧　　还 来
　　　吴语音 ae44-lae31 ghaeh23 yon22-feh3-zah3-keh0 yie22-ze33 tsa44-cin44-tie31 we223 le22-
　　　吴语文 懊 劳 也 用 弗 着 个，现 在 抓 紧 点 还 来

　　　　　　得 及。
　　　　　　teh3-jih3-keh3-leh3
　　　　　　得 及 个 勒。

甲：Ah, you are a good hand at typing.

乙：Yeah, I practice it for a whole month. Look at my rigid fingers!

甲：I am ashamed that I didn't listen to you when you asked me to practice typing together. Oh, don't worry.

乙：Practise makes perfect.

第十单元

交友与聚会

一 情景引入

甲：普通话 老李,今天什么样子! 有气无力,
吴语音 lae22-li33 cin44-tae31 sa523-keh3 then44-deu33- syu31-cia0 yeu231-chi31 vu22-lih3
吴语文 老李,今朝啥个吞头势①嗄!有气无力、

---

① "吞头势"在苏州话中与"腔调"同义,均为"样子"的意思,但略带贬义。

第十单元 交友与聚会

灰 头 土 脸 的，与 平 时 大 不 一 样 呢。
hue44-mae33-loh3- thoh3-keh3 taeh43 bin231-zan31 dou22-the44-yoe33- pan44-leh3-he31
灰 毛 落 拓 个，搭 平 常 大 推 悬 迸 勒 嗨。

乙：普通话 别 提 啦， 昨 天 参 加 了 一 个 同 学 会，
　　吴语音 fiae523-chi31 seh43 li44 tse44 zoh23-nyih3 tshoe44- ka44-tsy44-keh3 don22-ghoh3-we31
　　吴语文 覅 去 说 俚 哉，昨 日 参 加 仔 个 同 学 会，

不 少 在 大 学 里 不 如 我 的 同学 现 在
feh43- sae51 leh23-he31 da22-ghoh3-li31 feh43-zyu231 ngou231-keh3 nyin223 yie22-ze33
弗 少 勒 嗨 大 学 里 弗 如 我 个 人 现 在

一 个 个 都 发 达 了，我 的 境 况 与 他 们
ih43-keh3- keh3 ze223 faeh43-daeh3 tse44 ngou21-keh3 cin523- huaon23 taeh43 li44-toh3
一 个 个 侪 发 达 哉，我 个 境 况 搭 俚 笃

比 差 距 太 远， 赤 脚 跑 赶 不 上
pi51-zy31 yoe22-khon33- poh43-tsah3-ciah3 tshah43-tsy51 ciah43 ghaeh23 koe51- feh3-zaon31
比 是 悬 空 八 只 脚①赤 仔 脚 也 赶 弗 上

呀。所 以 郁 闷 得 昏 头 昏 脑。
ue0 sou51-i23 ueh43-seh3-teh3- leh3 huen44-deu33-loh3-tshon31 tse44
唲。所 以 殟 塞 得 勒 昏 头 六 冲 哉。

甲：普通话 怪 不 得 换 了 个 人 似 的， 怎 说 闻 到
　　吴语音 bie22-ka44-leh3 woe231-tsy44-keh3 nyin223 tseh43- ue0 nyioe44-seh3 men22-zah3-tsy31
　　吴语文 便 加 勒 换 仔 个 人 则 唲，原 说 闻 着 仔

你 身 上 有 一 股 酸 酸 的 味 道 原 来 是 在
ne231 sen44-laon44- shian31 ih43-kou51 soe44-phaon44-chi31 nyioe22-le33-zy31 laeh23-toh3
侬 身 浪 向 一 股 酸 胖 气②，原 来 是 拉 笃③

---

① "悬空八只脚"与"悬迸"意思相近，都是指差距太大，距离太远。
② "酸胖气"原指食物将馊时的酸气味，这里引申为心里吃醋时的一种酸溜溜的滋味。
③ "拉笃"与前文的"勒"、"勒嗨"、"勒浪"意思一样，都表示"在"的意思，但"拉笃"的口语味道更浓。

吃 醋。各 人 头 上 一 片 福，你 的 日 子
chih43 tshou523 koh43-nyin223 deu22-laon33 ih43-pe523 foh43 ne231-keh3 nyih23-ciah3
吃 醋。各 人 头 浪 一 片 福，倷 个 日 脚

说 不 上 很 滋 润， 也 绝 对 不 是
seh43-feh3-zaon31 pae51-pae31-tsyu44-tsyu31 meh0 ghaeh23 zih23-te31 feh43-zy231
说 弗 上 饱 饱 支 支 末，也 绝 对 弗 是

口 袋 里 没 钱， 干 嘛 要 去 与 别 人
de22-de33- li31 pih43-taeh43-taeh43-keh3 sa523-thi23 iae523 chi523 taeh43 beh23-nyin33-ka31
袋 袋 里 瘪 搭 搭①个，啥 体 要 去 搭 别 人 家

攀 比 呢，弄 得 自 己 不 开 心， 犯
toh haeh43-pi51 nae0 lon44-teh3 zy22-ka33 chi44-chi44-nae33-nae33-keh3 aeh43
笃 瞎 比 呢，弄 得 自 家 气 气 恼 恼 个，阿

得 着 吗?
ve22-teh3-zah3-keh3 cia0
犯 得 着 个 嘎?

乙：普通话 我 也 想 把 它 想 想 开，的 确 不 是 一 下 子
吴语音 ngou231 ghaeh23-sian31 no223 li44 phi523-phi31 khe44 tae44-zy31 feh43-zy231 ih43-ci44-deu31
吴语文 我 也 想 拿 俚 㹅 㹅 开，倒 是 弗 是 一 记 头

就 能 瞥 得 开 的，最 近 一 阵 总 归 不
zeu22- nen33 phi523-teh3 khe44-keh3 ke44-zan33-syu44-li31 tson51-kue23 feh43
就 能 㹅 得 开 个，该 场 势 里 总 归 弗

会 快 乐 了。
kha44-weh3-laeh3-li31
快 活 拉 里。

---

① "袋袋里瘪搭搭"指口袋里缺东西充填，所以表面凹陷，借此说明没钱或钱很少。"瘪搭搭"也可写作"瘪塌塌"，还有两层含义：a. 形容身体非常单薄。例：倷多吃点，整个人立出来瘪搭搭个，简直勒吓人。（你多吃点，整个人站出来那么单薄，简直吓人。）b. 形容萎靡不振的样子。例：衣裳着得再好，样子瘪搭搭也弗受人欢迎个。（衣服穿得再好，精神面貌不好也不受人欢迎的。）

甲：普通话 还是 与 我们 情况差不多 的 人 多 呆 在
　　吴语音 we22-zy33 taeh43-nyi231 ban22-tshih3-ban33- poh3-keh3 nyin223 tou44 ten44-ten44-leh3
　　吴语文 还 是 搭 伲 碰 七 碰 八 个 人 多 登 登 勒

　　　　　一 起 好。
　　　　　ih43-dae223 hae51
　　　　　一 淘 好。

甲：Hi, Li. Look at you! So depressed! Has anything been bothering you?

乙：Don't mention it. I went to a class reunion party yesterday. Many classmates, who used to be average in class, have My conditiion is far behind them, developed very well now. It would be impossible for me to compete with them. I feel so frustrated.

甲：No wonder you look so upset. You are jealous now. I can get it To be honest, people have different ideas about what happiness means. Actually, your life is comfortable. And there isn't any life pressure on you.So don't be jealous. It is unnecessary to let this bother your life.

乙：I really want to pass this. But it is not so easy. I need some time to heal my myself.

甲：Take it easy,our conditions are similar. You can spend more time with me. I will help you to go through this.

二 场景对话

1. 甲：普通话 你 这衣服 也 太 新潮 了， 看 看, 这边
　　　 吴语音 ne231-keh3 i44-zaon31 gha223 theh43 sin44-zae31 tseh43-ba0 khoe523 nyian0 ke44-mie33
　　　 吴语文 倷 个 衣裳 也 忒 新潮 则罢， 看 孃, 该 面

　　　　　　一 个 洞， 那 边 又 挂 了 个 什 么 东 西，
　　　　　　ih43-tsah3 don231 ue44-mie33-meh3 yih23 ko523-tsy44-tsah3 sa523-keh3 lae22-ciu44-se44
　　　　　　一 只 洞， 弯 面 末 亦 挂 仔 个 啥 个 老鬼三①

① "老鬼三"有三层含义：a. 泛指各种东西、事物。此义同"场景对话1"中"弯面亦挂仔个啥个老鬼三"。b. 在特定语境中指代某种不便言明、需要婉约的事物。例：哀两日身上正好来老鬼三，弗好去游泳哉。（这两天身上正好来例假，不能去游泳了。）c. 人，带有贬义色彩。例：箇个老鬼三弗好当俚人看待个。（这个老赤佬不好当他人看待的。）

如此 打扮 太 不 像 样 了。你 别 忘
zeh23-kan23 tan51-pe31 theh43 feh43 zian231 chian44 tse44 ne231 fiae523 maon22-ci44--
实 梗 打 扮 忒 弗 像 腔 哉。倷 覅 忘 记

了 你 今 天 是 去 相 亲 呀。
theh3 ne231 cin44-tsae31 zy231 chi523 sian44-tshin44- keh3-ia0
脱 倷 今 朝 是 去 相 亲 个 呀。

乙：普通话 我 特意要以本色出现。我们出发吧。
吴语音 ngou231-meh3 dih23-we31 iae523 i51 pen51-seh3 tsheh43- yie231 ue0 nyi231 don231 sen44 ba0
吴语文 我 末 特 为 要 以 本 色 出 现 哦。伲 动 身 吧。

甲：What is this dressing? Wow, this is a hole. And that is a kind of decoration hanging there. How come you dress up so strange? Don't forget you are going to have a blind date today.

乙：I dress up in this way for this special day. Now, I am leaving for the date.

2. 甲：普通话 张 华，不 要 睡 了，你 跟 我 一 起 去 买
   吴语音 tsan44-gho31 fiae523 khuen44-kae31 tse44 ne231 ken44 ngou231 ih43-dae231 chi523 ma231
   吴语文 张 华，覅 睏 觉 哉，倷 跟 我 一 淘 去 买

   班级团拜会的礼品。
   pe44-cih3 doe22- pa44-we33-keh3 li22-phin33 ba0
   班 级 团 拜 会 个 礼 品 吧。

乙：普通话 好 不 容 易 盼 来 个 双 休 日 可 以 睡
   吴语音 hae51-feh3 yon22-yi33 ten51-zah3-tsy44-keh3 saon44-shieu44-nyih3 khou51-i23 khuen523-
   吴语文 好 弗 容 易 等 着 仔 个 双 休 日 可 以 睏

   个 懒 觉，你 却 把 我 吵 醒。
   keh3 e44- kae44 tse44 ne231 phie44-phie31 iae523 no22-ngou33 lon44 sin51
   个 晏 觉 哉，倷 偏 偏 要 拿 我 弄 醒。

第十单元　交友与聚会

甲：普通话 已 经 十　　 点　　 了，你 还　 睡，也 太 懒 了 吧。
　　吴语音 zeh23-tie31 ghaeh32 khae44-kou31 tse44 ne231 we22-leh3 khue523 le231-teh3 tsheh43 tshi44
　　吴语文 十 点 也　 敲 过　 哉, 侬　还 勒　睏, 懒 得 出 蛆。

乙：普通话 还 说, 要不要 我 陪 你 去 买 东 西 了? 弄 得 我
　　吴语音 we22-seh3 aeh43-iae44-ngou31 be22-ne33 chi523 ma231 meh23-zy31 le0 lon44-teh3-ngou31
　　吴语文 还 说, 阿 要 我 陪 侬 去 买 物 事 唻? 弄 得 我

　　　　　　 生 气 了　　　　 我 可 继 续 睡 觉 喽。
　　　　 kuan44-hou44-tsy44-chi44-le31 ngou231-zy31 iae523 ci523-zoh3 khuen523-keh3 oh0
　　　　　　 光 火 仔 起 来 我 是 要 继 续 睏 个 喔。

甲：Zhang Hua, wake up! We have to buy the presents for the Class New Year Celebration.

乙：I work for a whole week and finally can sleep late on weekend. But you are driving me crazy by waking me up so early.

甲：It's already 10:00am. You are sleeping late. How lazy you are.

乙：Hold it! Do you still want to me to go shopping with you? If you screw me up, I will go back to sleep now.

3. 甲：普通话 请 问　　 参 加 苏 州 评 弹 收 藏 鉴 赏
　　吴语音 tshin51 men231-ih3-san31 tshoe44-ka31 sou44-tseu31 bin22-de33 seu44-zaon31 cie523-saon33-
　　吴语文 请 问 一 声 参 加 苏 州 评 弹 收 藏 鉴 赏

　　　学 会 有 什 么　　 要 求?　　 我 很 想
　　　yoh3-we31 aeh43-yeu231 sa523- keh3 iae44-jieu33-keh3-aeh0 ngou231 lae231-zy31 sian51-
　　　学 会 啊 有 啥 个　 要 求 个 啊? 我 老 是 想

　　　　　 交 一 些 爱 好 评 弹 的 朋 友。
　　　iae31 gaeh23- tie31 e523-hae23 bin22-de33-keh3 dae22-boe33
　　　　　 要 轧 点 爱 好 评 弹 个 淘 伴。

乙：普通话 有 一 定 的 藏 品 和 欣 赏 水 平 就 可 以 了。
　　吴语音 yeu231 ih43-din33-keh3 zaon22-phin33 taeh43 shin51- saon23 syu51-bin23 zeu231 khou51-i23 tse44
　　吴语文 有 一 定 个 藏 品 搭 欣 赏 水 平 就 可 以 哉。

甲：Excuse me, may I know your requirement to apply for Suzhou Pintan Opera Appreciation Association? It is my pleasure to make friends with the same interests.

乙：If you are a fan of Pintan Opera and have some collections, you are welcomed to join the association.

4. 甲：普通话 我 穿 这 身 衣 服 漂 亮 吗？晚 上 我 要
　　吴语音 ngou231 tsah43 e44-sen44-i44-zaon31 aeh43 ten44- yan31 ia44-li31-shian31 ngou231 iae523
　　吴语文 我 着 哀身衣裳 阿 登 样？夜 里 向 我 要

　　　　　　参 加 迎 新 晚 会 呢。
　　　　　　tshoe44-ka31 nyin22 sin44 ue523-we31 keh43 oh0
　　　　　　参 加 迎 新 晚 会 个 喔。

乙：普通话 着 实 漂 亮， 这 下 你 可 以 大 出 风 头 了。
　　吴语音 zah23-zeh3 piae44-tsyu44-keh3 ke44-ci31 ne231 khou51-i23 dou22-tsheh3 fon44-deu33-tseh3-ue0
　　吴语文 着 实 标 致 个， 该 记 倷 可 以 大 出 风 头 则 哇。

甲：The dress looks perfect on me. I am going to wear this to New Year Celebration tonight.

乙：You look beautiful. I believe you will be the center tonight.

5. 甲：普通话 古 人 云， 近 朱 者 赤， 近 墨 者 黑， 你 与
　　吴语音 lae231-gho31 kaon51 jin231 tsyu44 tse51 tsheh43 jin231 meh23 tse51 heh43 ne231 taeh43
　　吴语文 老 话 讲， 近 朱 者 赤， 近 墨 者 黑， 倷 搭

第十单元 交友与聚会

　　不 向 上 的 人 交 往，对 自 己 不 利。
　　feh43 zih23-zaon33- keh3 nyin223 gaeh23-dae31 te523 zy22-ka33 feh43- lin223 keh0
　　弗 习 上 个 人 <u>轧 淘</u>①，对 自 家 弗 灵 个。

乙：普通话 放 心，　　　　我 　不 是 <u>傻 瓜</u>。他 们 都 很
　　吴语音 faon44-sin44-meh3 hae51 tse44 ngou231 yih23 feh43-zy231 yan22-boe33 li44-toh3 ze223 me44
　　吴语文 放 心 末 好 哉，我 亦 弗 是 <u>洋 盘</u>②。俚 笃 侪 蛮

　　　　　要 好 的，只 是 业 余 生 活 比 较 丰 富 罢 了。
　　　　　iae523 hae51-keh3 tseh43-zy231 nyih23-yu31 sen44-weh3 pi51-ciae31 fen44-fu31 ba22-tse33
　　　　　要 好 个，只 是 业 余 生 活 比 较 丰 富 罢 哉。

甲：As the old saying goes, "one takes the behavior of one's company". You are always hanging out with the bad ones, It will do no good to you.

乙：Relax, I know my friends. They are good people. The only problem is they have too many entertainments.

6. 甲：普通话 老 王，<u>待 会 儿</u> 吃 年 夜 饭 要 互 相 敬 酒 的，
　　　吴语音 lae22-waon33 ten51-theh3-shih3 chih43 nyie22-ia44- ve31 iae523 ngou22-sian33 cin523 tseu51 keh43-a0
　　　吴语文 老 王，<u>等 脱 歇</u> 吃 年 夜 饭 要 互 相 敬 酒 个 啊，

　　　　　我 是 一 点 　也 不 能 喝 的，<u>怎 么 办</u>?
　　　　　ngou231- zy31 ih43-tie33-tie31 gha223 feh43 ne223 chih43 keh43-ia0 naeh23-han31 be231 cia0
　　　　　我 是 一 点 点 也 弗 能 吃 个 呀，<u>哪 哼 办 嗄</u>?

乙：普通话 我们 两 个 是 　　甲 级 关 系，我 　<u>不 会</u> 袖 手
　　吴语音 nyi231 lian22-ka44-deu33-zy31 ciaeh43-cih3 kue44-yi31 ngou231 feh43-ue44-teh3 khoe44-
　　吴语文 倪 两 家 头 是 甲 级 关 系，我 弗 会 得 看

---

① "轧淘"就是"交朋友"。这里的"淘"是"群"、"众"的意思，一群有共同特征的人，就是"淘"，所以有"倷兄弟淘里"、"倷姐妹淘里"的说法。因此一群好人，就是"好淘"，一群坏人，就是"坏淘"。交往良师益友，就是"轧好淘"，结交狐群狗党，则是"轧坏淘"。

② "洋盘"有两层意思：a. 傻瓜。此义同"场景对话5"中"放心，我弗是洋盘。"b. 外行。例：倷搭我一样是洋盘，就勿硬冲内行哉。（你与我一样是外行，就别硬充内行了。）

旁观的。
lan33-phu44 keh3
冷　铺①个。

甲：Hi, Mr. Wang. As usual, people will propose toasts at the year-end dinner party. Drinking is my weakness. What should I do?

乙：We are buddies, right? I will cover for you. Take it easy.

7. 甲：普通话 我　是 俱乐部 新来的　22　号，别 看 我
　　　吴语音 noug231-zy31 jiu22-loh3-bu31 sin44-le33-keh3 nyie22-nyi33-ghae31 fiae523 khoe523-ngou31
　　　吴语文 我　是 俱乐部 新来个　2 2　号，覅 看 我

　　　　　　外貌 五大三粗，但　　　做　事　却
　　　　　　nga22-mae33 ng22- heh3-len44-ten31 de22-pih3-kou31 tsou523-chi31 zy22-thi33 le223 tae44-
　　　　　　外　貌　五黑愣登②,但不过　做起事体来倒

　　　　　　仔细耐心，　　希望大家接纳我。
　　　　　　zy31 si44-mo44-si44- yan33-keh3-oh0 shi44-vaon31 da22-ka33 tsih43-naeh43 ngou231
　　　　　　是 细模细样 个喔, 希望 大家 接 纳 我。

　乙：普通话 我们 俱乐部 成员　之间 很团结的，许多
　　　吴语音 nyi231 jiu22-loh3-bu31 zen22-yoe33-tsyu44- cie31 doe22-cih3-saeh3-keh3-a0 me44-hae44-
　　　吴语文 伲 俱乐部 成员　之间 团结煞个啊, 蛮好

---

① "看冷铺"，就是有能力帮忙，可是非但冷眼看着，漠不关心，袖手旁观，而且还有幸灾乐祸的意味在里面。

② "五黑愣登"与"细模细样"在形容人的外貌上构成一对反义词。只是"细模细样"除了形容外貌长得小巧细致以外，还有"仔细耐心做事"的意思。

第十单元 交友与聚会

```
              人   说  话   还   很      诙 谐,  你 在 这
tie31 nyin223 kaon51 ghe22-gho33 we223 le22-teh3-keh3 faeh43-shiueh3 le0 ne231 leh3 e44-
              点   人  讲  闲  话   还   来 得 个 发 噱①   来, 侬 勒 哀

              里  肯  定  会  很   快  乐 的。
taeh3 khen51-din31 ue523 me44 kha44-weh3 keh0
              搭  肯  定  会  蛮   快  活 个。
```

甲：Hello, everyone! I am new in this club, No.22. Although I'm big and strong, But I always treat my job with patience and diligence. I think we will get along well with each other.

乙：We are like a big family in the club. People here are humorous. You will enjoy your time here.

8. 甲：普通话 这 是 毕 业 聚 会,   同 学 们   要 各 奔 东
```
吴语音 e44-keh3-zy31 pih43-nyih43 zi231-we31 don22- ghoh3-dae33-li31 iae523 koh43-pen44 ton44
吴语文 哀 个 是 毕 业 聚 会, 同   学 淘  里 要 各 奔 东

       西 了, 本   来  心 里 就 不 好 受,    所 以 更 加
si44 tse44 nyioe22-pen33 sin44-li31 zeu31 feh43 seh43-i44-leh3-he31 Sou51-i23 ka44-nyi31
       西 哉, 原   本  心 里 就 弗 适 意 勒 海, 所 以 加 二

       应 该 突 出 喜 庆 的 主 题, 你 不 要 坚 持 把
in44-taon31 deh23-tsheh3 shi51-chin31-keh3 tsyu51-di23 ne231 fiae523 ngan22-cin33 no223
       应 当 突 出 喜 庆 个 主 题, 侬 覅 硬 劲② 拿
```

---

① "发噱"有三层意思：a. 诙谐幽默。此义同"场景对话7"中"蛮好点人讲闲话还蛮发噱个"。b. 可笑。例：看俚个样子，真个发噱个。（看他的样子，真的可笑呀。） c. 滑稽（带有责备的意味）。例：侬阿要发噱！我亦弗是领导，我哪哼晓得事体个来龙去脉呢？（你真滑稽！我又不是领导，我怎么知道事情的来龙去脉。）

② "硬劲"作"坚持"解时带有"固执、执拗，不听劝告，一定要（做某事）"的意味。

这 个 悲 切 的 内 容 放 进 来 了，弄 得 大 家 都
ke44-keh3 pe44-tshih3-keh3 ne22-yon33 pa51-tsin44-le31 tse0 lon44-teh3 da22-ka33 ze223
该 个 悲 切 个 内 容 摆 进 来 哉，弄 得 大 家 侪

伤 感。
saon44-koe31 aeh43-zy231
伤 感，阿 是？

乙：普通话 你 说 话 　要 负 责 任， 　不 要 硬
　　吴语音 ne231 kaon51 ghe22-gho33 nga22-tsy33 iae523 tsoh43 tsoh43 zi223 fiae523 ngan22-tsaon33
　　吴语文 倷 讲 闲 话 牙 子 要 作 作 齐，覅 硬 装

扣 帽 子，是 不 是 　到 时 同 学 们 　因 为
fu51-deu33-pin31 aeh43-zy231 tae523-zen33-kuaon31 don22-ghoh3-dae33-li31 in44-we31
斧 头 柄①，阿 是 到 辰 光 同 学 淘 里 因 为

离 别 不 舍 而 　　流 泪 　都 是 我 的
li22-bih3 feh43 so51-teh3-tsy44-meh3 leu223 nge231-li33-syu31 ze22-zy33 ngou231-keh3
离 别 弗 舍 得 仔 末 流 眼 泪 水 侪 是 我 个

罪 过。
ze231- kou31 a0
罪 过 啊？

甲：普通话 你 不 要 误 会， 　我 不 是 故 意
　　吴语音 ne231 fiae523 ngou22-ue33-aeh43 ngou231 feh43-zy231 ngae223 hae51-shi31
　　吴语文 倷 覅 误 会 啊，我 弗 是 熬 好 戏②

---

① "硬装斧头柄"除了"强加罪名，硬扣帽子"的意思外，还指"风马牛不相及的东西，硬要把它们放在一起"。

② "熬好戏"指"故意做不讨巧的事，故意说不中听的话"，但出现这种局面，当事人主要不是为本人考虑，恰恰是为大家着想。

第十单元　交友与聚会

说　这　不　中　听　的　话，我　是　生　怕　大　家　哭　作
kaon51 e44-tson31 ghe22-gho33-keh0 ngou231-zy31 tsan44-pho31 da22-ka33 khoh43-teh3
讲　哀　种　闲　话　个，我　是　张　怕　大　家　哭　得

一　团。
shi44-li33-hua44-la31 ia0
稀里　哗　啦　呀。

甲：After this graduation party, we will be apart from each other and start new lives. It makes me sad. I think we should focus on theme of "happiness". Your idea about graduation will make people depressed.

乙：Don't put a label on me. If classmates cannot bear to weep for seperating from each other, it is not my fault.

甲：Don't misunderstand me! I didn't mean to you. I just don't want the whole class to cry together at the party.

9. 甲：普通话 这　次　冷　餐　会　上　的　菜　是　中　看　不　中
吴语音　ke44-thaon31 lan22-tshoe44-we33-laon33-keh3 tshe523 zy231 tson44-khoe31 feh43 tson44-
吴语文　该　趟　冷　餐　会　浪　个　菜　是　中　看　弗　中

吃，叉　烧　　　倒　是　菜色深，味道浓，　可　是
chih3 tshah43-sae44-sae44-teh3 tae44-zy31 nyion22-yeu33-tshah3-tsian31 pih43-kou523
吃，叉　烧　烧　得　倒　是　浓　油　赤　酱，不　过

总　共　没　几　片，而　且　　　很　　薄。蔬　菜　看
gon231-tson51 m22-peh3 ci51-phie31 we22-kaon33 zih23-zih23 boh23 sou44-tshe31 khoe523-
共　总　呒　不　几　片，还　讲　绝　绝　薄。蔬　菜　看

上　去　碧　绿　碧　　　绿，但　吃　起　来　　淡
zaon33-chi31 pih43-loh3-san44 -tshin44-keh3 pih43-kou523 chih43-chi44-le31 de22-
上　去　碧　绿　生　青　个，不　过　吃　起　来　淡

而 无 味。
kua44-kua44-keh3 mi22-dae33 feh43 lin223
呱 呱 个，味 道 弗 灵。

乙：普通话 我 觉 得 还 可 以 的， 你 那 天 吃 得 不
吴语音 ngou231 koh43-zah3 we223 khou51-i33-keh3 ue0 ne231 geh23-nyih3 chih43-teh3 feh43-
吴语文 我 觉 着 还 可 以 个 啘, 倷 箇 日 吃 得 弗

是 挺 猴 急 的 吗。
zy231 me44 jih43-yin33-jih3-zaon33-keh3 meh0
是 蛮 急 形 急 状① 个 末。

甲：The food at the buffet looks good, but tastes terrible. The barbecued pork is delicious. The poor thing is that they are served in a few slices. The vegetables are green and fresh. But they are bland in teast.

乙：I think the buffet teasted good. You ate a lot that day, didn't you?

词语贴士

（一）朋友类型

序号	英文	苏州话
1.	Bosom friend /Close friend/ Intimate friend	tsyu44-ci31
	知己	知己
2.	Bosom friend /Close friend/ Intimate friend	tsyu523-yeu31
	挚友	挚友
3.	Friend who open out and tell the truth	tsen44-yeu31
	诤友	诤友
4.	Bosom friend /Close friend/ Intimate friend	mih23-yeu31
	密友	密友

---

① "急形急状"是指极想做某事都到了不顾颜面、身份的地步了。

续表

序号	英文	苏州话
5.	Good friend 好友	hae51-yeu31，siae51-ban33-yeu31 好友，小朋友
6.	New friend 新知	sin44-tsyu31 新知
7.	Old friend 老友	lae22-yeu33 老友
8.	Old acquaintance 旧交	jieu22-ciae33 旧交
9.	Bad friend 损友	sen51-yeu31 损友
10.	Fair-weather friend 酒肉朋友	tseu51-nyioh3-ban33-yeu31 酒肉朋友

(二) 朋友关系

序号	英文	苏州话
1.	Close 亲密	nyih23-loh3 热络
2.	Sincere 真挚	tsen44-tsyu31 真挚
3.	friendly 友好	yeu22-hae33 友好
4.	harmonious 和谐	ghou22-ya33 和谐
5.	indifferent 冷淡	lan231-de31 冷淡
6.	Turn against someone 交恶	ciae44-oh3 交恶
7.	Break up with someone 绝交	zih23-ciae31 绝交
8.	Compromise with someone 和解	ghou22-cia33 和解
9.	Reconciled 重修旧好	zon22-seu33-jieu22-hae33 重修旧好

（三）交友原则

序号	英文	苏州话
1.	Equal	bin22-ten33
	平等	平等
2.	Honesty	zen22-sin33
	诚信	诚信
3.	Tolerance	khuoe44-yon31
	宽容	宽容
4.	Mutual help	ngou22-zou33
	互助	互助
5.	Development	faeh43-tsoe51
	发展	发展

（四）交际用语

序号	英文	苏州话
1.	Glad to meet you.	yin231-we31
	幸会	幸会
2.	Go for a visit	pa44-faon31
	拜访	拜访
3.	Await ... respectively	kon44-gheu31
	恭候	恭候
4.	如果是指叫人不用再送出来的"请留步"，英文可以说：You don't have to bother to see me out. 如果是指叫别人等一下的"请留步"，英文是Wait a minute/second/moment, please	leu22-bu33
	留步	留步
5.	Received letter	we22-syu33
	惠书	惠书
6.	Bother ...	tan51-zae31, tan51-ciae33
	打扰	打扰,打搅
7.	Please ...	ve22-tshin33
	烦请	烦请
8.	Exeuse me.	tsia523 kuaon44
	借光	借光
9.	Would you mind to ...	pa523-thoh3
	拜托	拜托

续表

序号	英文	苏州话
10.	Would you please give me any advice on ...?	tshin51-ciae31
	请教	请教
11.	Please favour me with your instructions.	sy523-ciae31
	赐教	赐教
12.	Would you tell me ...	tshin51-men31
	请问	请问
13.	Great idea	kae44-cie31
	高见	高见
14.	Return	von231-we31
	奉还	奉还
15.	Forgive ...	pae44-ghoe31
	包涵	包涵
16.	Consume +(place)	kuaon44-kou31
	光顾	光顾
17.	Age	kae44-zeu31
	高寿	高寿
18.	Haven't ... for a long time	cieu51-we31
	久违	久违
19.	Looking forward to ...	cieu51-nyian31
	久仰	久仰
20.	Welcome to...	kuaon44-lin31
	光临	光临
21.	Excuse me	seh43-be223
	失陪	失陪
22.	Say goodbye	kae523-zy33
	告辞	告辞
23.	Take care	pae51-zon31
	保重	保重
24.	Would you kindly point out my inadequacies?	ia51-tsen31
	雅正	雅正

(五)社交原则

序号	英文	苏州话
1.	Punctuality	seu51-zyu23
	守时	守时

续表

序号	英文	苏州话
2.	Politeness	li231-mae31
	礼貌	礼貌
3.	Tact	teh43-thi51
	得体	得体
4.	Proporiety	yeu231 dou231
	有度	有度

（六）聚会类型

序号	英文	苏州话
1.	Business cocktail party	kon44-sy31 tseu51-we31
	公司酒会	公司酒会
2.	Classmates party	don22-ghoh3 zi231-we31
	同学聚会	同学聚会
3.	Family party	cia44-din31 pha44-te31
	家庭派对	家庭派对
4.	Friends party	ban22-yeu33 zi231-we31
	朋友聚会	朋友聚会
5.	Birthday party	san44-nyih3 pha44-te31
	生日派对	生日派对
6.	Mutual choice	saon44-shian31 sie51-zeh3
	双向选择	双向选择
7.	Buffet	lan22-tshoe44-we31
	冷餐会	冷餐会
8.	Ball	vu231-we31
	舞会	舞会
9.	New Year Celebration	doe22-pa44-we31
	团拜会	团拜会

（七）聚会礼仪禁忌

序号	英文	苏州话
1.	Inapproprite hair style	faeh43-yin223 theh43 sin44-zae31
	发型太新潮	发型忒新潮
2.	Disordered hair	deu22-faeh3 zyu22 loe22-tshae33
	头发如乱草	头发如乱草
3.	Thick make-up	ho523-tsaon44 theh43 khuo44-tsan31
	化妆太夸张	化妆忒夸张

续表

序号	英文	苏州话
4.	Inappropriate clothes 衣装太新潮	i44-tsaon31 theh43 sin44-zae31 衣装忒新潮
5.	Inappropriate dress-up 打扮太性感	tan51-pe31 theh43 sin523-koe33 打扮忒性感

（八）交际距离

序号	英文	苏州话
1.	Intimate space 亲密空间	tshin44-mih3 khon44-cie31 亲密空间
2.	Personal space 个人空间	kou44-nyin31 khon44-cie31 个人空间
3.	Social space 社交空间	zo22-ciae33 khon44-cie31 社交空间
4.	Public space 公众空间	kon44-tson31 khon44-cie31 公众空间

（九）交际"四有"

序号	英文	苏州话
1.	Tactful 有分寸	yeu231 fen44-tshen31 有分寸
2.	Polite 有礼节	yeu231 li22-tsih3 有礼节
3.	Good mannered 有教养	yeu231 ciae44-yan31 有教养
4.	Well educated 有学识	yeu231 yoh23-zeh3 有学识

（十）交际"四避"

序号	英文	苏州话
1.	Avoid inquiring privacy 避隐私	bi231 in51-sy23 避隐私
2.	Avoid superficial behaviors 避浅薄	bi231 tshie51-boh3 避浅薄
3.	Avoid bad manners 避粗鄙	bi231 tshou44-pe31 避粗鄙
4.	Avoid talking about taboos 避忌讳	bi231 ji231-we31 避忌讳

四 对话中的特色词汇

序号	英文	苏州话
1.	Appearance 样子	then44-deu33-syu31 吞头势
2.	Depressed 灰头土脸	hue44-mae44-loh3-thoh31 灰毛落拓
3.	Be distant from 差距太远	yoe22-khon44-poh3-tsah3-ciah3 悬空八只脚
4.	Frustrated and confused 昏头昏脑	huen44-deu33-loh3-tshon31 昏头六冲
5.	No wander 怪不得	bie22-ka44-leh3 便加勒
6.	And 怎说	nioe44-seh3 原说
7.	Jealous 酸味	soe44-phaon44-chi31 酸胖气
8.	In 在	laeh23-toh3 拉笃
9.	Comfortable living 滋润	pae51-tsyu44-tsyu31 饱支支
10.	Short of money 口袋里没钱	de22-de33-li31 pih43-taeh43-taeh3 袋袋里瘪搭搭
11.	Hang out with 呆在一起	ten44-leh3 ih43-dae231 登勒一淘
12.	Things 东西	lae22-ciu44-se31 老鬼三
13.	In an apprioprite way 像样	zian22-chian33 像腔
14.	Set off 出发	don22-sen33 动身
15.	Too lazy 太懒	le231-teh3 tsheh43 tshi44 懒得出蛆
16.	Angry 生气	kuan44-hou31 光火
17.	Partner 伙伴	dae22-boe33 淘伴

续表

序号	英文	苏州话
18.	Negtive attitude 不向上	feh43-zih3-zaon31 弗习上
19.	Make friends 交往	gaeh23-dae31 轧淘
20.	Fool 傻瓜	yan22-boe33 洋盘
21.	Wait a moment 待会儿	ten51-teh3-shih31 等脱歇
22.	Both of us 我们两个	nyi231 lian22-ka44-deu31 伲两家头
23.	Stand by 袖手旁观	khoe44-lan33-phu31 看冷铺
24.	Big and Strong 五大三粗	ng22-heh3-len33-ten31 五黑愣登
25.	Patient 仔细耐心	si51-mo33-si44-yan31 细模细样
26.	Humorous 诙谐	faeh43 shiueh43 发噱
27.	Here 这里	ke44-taeh43,e44-taeh3 该搭,哀搭
28.	Insist on 坚持	ngan22-cin33 硬劲
29.	Put a label on sb. 硬扣帽子	ngan22-tsaon44 fu51-deu33-pin31 硬装斧头柄
30.	Drop a clanger 故意说不中听的话	ngae223 hae51-shi31 kaon51 e44-tson31 ghe22-gho33 熬好戏讲哀种闲话
31.	Delicious 菜色深，味道浓	nyon22-yeu33-tshah3-tsian31 浓油赤酱
32.	Slice 很薄	zih23-zih3 boh23 绝绝薄
33.	Green 碧碧绿	pih43-loh3-san44-tshin31 碧绿生青
34.	Bland 淡	de22-kuaeh43-kuaeh43 淡呱呱
35.	Eager 猴急	jih43-yin33-jih3-zaon31 急形急状

五、巩固练习

1 甲：今天晚上系里有个大型舞会，我们两个一起去吧。
乙：口袋里没钱，不去。
甲：你傻得啦，学校里的舞会又不收门票的。
乙：你才是傻瓜呢。舞会结束，请舞伴吃个宵夜不要钱吗？

2 甲：你小子居然撒起谎来了，看我怎么收拾你。
乙：爸爸，是王兵叫我这么说的。这次你就原谅我吧。
甲：我叫你眼睛睁睁开，要交益友，你偏偏不听，专门结交损友。你真的要气死我才罢休。
乙：不是的，我知道错了。爸爸，你别生气了。

六、参考答案

甲：普通话 今 天 晚 上 系 里　　有 个 大 型 舞 会 我们
吴语音 cin44-tsae44-ia44-li31 yi22-li33-shian31 yeu231-keh3 da22-yin33-vu22-we33 nyi231
吴语文 今 朝 夜 里 系 里 向　有 个 大 型 舞 会 伲

　　　　　两 个　　一 起 去 吧。
　　　　lian22-ka44-deu31 ih43-dae231 chi523 ba0
　　　　　两 家 头 一 淘 去 吧。

乙：普通话 口 袋 里 没 钱，　　不 去。
吴语音 de22-de33-li31 pih43-taeh43-taeh3 feh43 chi523
吴语文 袋 袋 里 瘪 搭 搭，弗 去。

甲：普通话 你 傻 得 啦，学 校 里 的 舞 会 又 不 收
吴语音 ne231 gaon231-teh3-leh3 ghoh23-daon33-li33-keh3 vu22-we33 yih23 feh43-seu44
吴语文 倷 憨 得 勒，学 堂 里 个 舞 会 亦 弗 收

门　　票　　的。
men22-phiae44-keh3-la0
门　　票　　个　啦。

乙：普通话 你　才　是　傻　瓜　呢。舞会　结　束，　　请　舞　伴
吴语音 iae523-meh3 ne231 yan22-boe33 noh0　vu22-we33 cih43-soh3-tsy31 tshin51 vu22-boe33
吴语文 要　末　倷　洋　盘　喏。舞会　结　束　仔, 请　舞　伴

吃　个　夜　宵　不要　钱　　吗？
chih43-keh3 ia44- siae51 fiae523 tshae44-phiae31 keh43-aeh0
吃　个　夜　宵　覅　钞　票　个　阿？

甲：How come we go to the ball in the department?

乙：I don't think so. I'm bankrupt.

甲：Don't be silly! The ball won't cost you any money for ticket.

乙：Come on! A date after the ball will cost you more.

2

甲：普通话 你　小　子　　　居　然　撒　起　　　谎　来　了,
吴语音 ne231-tsah3 siae51-tsheh3-lae31 ciu44-zoe31 seh43- chi44-tsy31 huaon51 le22-tseh3-a0
吴语文 倷　只　小　赤　佬　居　然　说　起　仔　谎　来　则啊,

看　我　怎么　收拾　你。
khoe523 ngou231 naeh23-han31 seu44-tsoh3 ne231
看　我　哪哼　收作　倷。

乙：普通话 爸爸, 是　王　兵　叫　我　这么　说　的。这次
吴语音 tia44-tia31 zy231 waon22-pin33 ciae523 ngou231 zeh23- kan31 kaon51-keh3 ke44-thaon31
吴语文 爹爹, 是　王　兵　叫　我　实梗　讲　个。该趟

你　就　原　谅　我　吧。
ne231 zeu231 nyoe231- lian31 ngou231 tseh43-ue0
倷　就　原　谅　我　则婉。

甲：普通话 我 叫 你 眼 睛 睁 睁 开，要 交 益 友，
　　吴语音 ngou231 ciae523 ne231 nge22-ou44-tsyu31 tan44-tsan31 khe44 iae523 gaeh23-hae44-dae31
　　吴语文 我 叫 倷 眼 乌 珠 睁 睁 开，要 轧 好 淘，

　　　　　你 偏 偏 不 听，专 门 结 交 损 友。你
　　　　　ne231 phie44-phie31 feh43 thin44 tsoe44-men31 gaeh23 wa22-dae33 ne231 aeh43-zy231
　　　　　倷 偏 偏 弗 听，专 门 轧 坏 淘。倷 阿 是

　　　　　真 的 要 气 死 我 才 罢 休。
　　　　　zeh23-deu31 iae523 chi523-saeh3-theh3 ngou231 tse44 shih43-koh3-teh3-le31
　　　　　实 头 要 气 煞 脱 我 再 歇 搁 得 来。

乙：普通话 不 是 的，我 知 道 错 了。爸爸，你 别 生
　　吴语音 feh43-zy33-keh3 ngou231 shiae51-teh3 tsho44 tse44 tia44-tia31 ne231 fiae52 kuaon44-
　　吴语文 弗 是 个，我 晓 得 错 哉。爹爹，倷 覅 光

　　气 了。
　　hou31 tseh43-ue0
　　火 则 啘。

甲：I can't believe you are lying. I will teach you a lesson.
乙：Come on, Dad. Wang Bin asked me to tell it. Can you forgive me this time?
甲：I told you to be careful when you are making friends. A good friend will teach, but you always make the bad ones. You are driving me crazy.
乙：I know I'm wrong. Don't be so disappointed at me, Dad.

参考文献

[1] 吴语协会网（http://wu-chinese.com/）

[2] 苏州闲话网（http://www.suzhouhua.org/）

[3] 汪平.苏州方言语言研究[M].武汉：华中理工大学出版社，1996.

[4] 叶祥苓.苏州方言志[M].南京：江苏教育出版社，1988.

[5] 李荣，叶祥苓.苏州方言词典[M].南京：江苏教育出版社，1993.

[6] 游汝杰，杨剑桥.吴语声调的实验研究[M].上海：复旦大学出版社，2001.

[7] 吴连生，骆伟里.吴方言词典[M].上海：汉语大辞典出版社，1995.

[8] 沈行望.实用苏州话[M].南昌：江西人民出版社，2009.